EXTERNALISM IN THE PHILOSOPHY OF MIND

For Robyn

Externalism in the Philsophy of Mind

STEVE EDWARDS
Faculty of Health Studies
Buckinghamshire College

Avebury

Aldershot · Brookfield USA · Hong Kong · Singapore · Sydney

Published by
Avebury
Ashgate Publishing Company
Gower House
Croft Road
Aldershot
Hants GU11 3HR

Ashgate Publishing Company
Old Post Road
Brookfield
Vermont 05036
USA

British Library Cataloguing in Publication Data

Edwards, Steven D.
 Externalism in the Philsophy of Mind. -
 (Avebury Series in Philosophy)
 I. Title   II. Series
 128.2
 ISBN 1 85628 946 X

Library of Congress Cataloging-in-Publication Data

Edwards, Steven D., 1957–
 Externalism in the philosophy of mind / Steven D. Edwards.
     p. cm -- (Avebury series in philosophy)
 Includes bibliographical references.
 ISBN 1-85628-946-X : $63.95 (U.S.)
 1. Philosophy of mind.   I. Title   II. Series
 BD418.3.E38   1994
 128.2--dc20   94-25510
                                                        CIP

Printed in Great Britain by Ipswich Book Co. Ltd., Ipswich, Suffolk

Contents

Preface

The view that the mind is ontologically independent of the body is one which goes back at least as far as Plato (see, e.g. *Phaedo*); more famously, perhaps, it is stated in the work of Descartes (see e.g. *Meditations II*). Philosophers since Descartes have been increasingly reluctant to accept the alleged ontological independence between psychological and physical states. Progress in the physical sciences has apparently demonstrated the close links between psychological states and neurophysiological states to the extent that it is now generally held that the mind is ontologically dependent upon the body.[1]

However, just as proponents of the traditional view of the mind-body relationship held the natures of psychological states to be independent of the nature of the physical and social environments of the subjects of those states, so too, it seems, do many modern philosophers. For example, a philosopher who wishes to concede the ontological dependence of the mind upon the body may hold that the mind is identical with the brain - that types of psychological states are identical with types of neurophysiological states (e.g. Place, 1956; Armstrong, 1968). Such a philosopher is then logically bound to hold that the environment beyond the body of the subject bears no constitutive relevance to the individuation conditions of the psychological states of the subject (providing it is held that neurophysiological states are not themselves individuation-dependent upon features beyond the body of the subject).

Externalism is a thesis according to which at least some psychological states are individuation-dependent upon certain aspects of the physical and social environments of their subjects.[2] Hence externalism is radically at odds both with a traditional view of the mind-body relationship, since according to that mental states are ontologically independent of the physical and social environments of the subject; and with a more modern view of the mind-body relationship, since according to that the physical and social environments of subjects are not considered constitutively relevant to the identities of mental states of subjects.[3]

One of the questions which externalism forces consideration of, then, is this: How are psychological states individuated? But the term "psychological state" is itself one which needs clarification before the question can properly be answered. One way to begin to clarify the question is to point out that the externalist claim is directed at the posits which are recruited in the explanation of human behaviour - what Fodor describes as "commonsense belief/desire psychology" (1987, p.x) - i.e. the terms in which (human) behaviour is explained in our day to day interactions with one another. This enterprise involves positing explanatory types - e.g. beliefs that p and desires that q - in order to explain the behaviour of human subjects.

Hence, the externalist question then becomes: How are the states recruited by commonsense belief/desire psychology in the explanation of human behaviour individuated?

Thought experiments devised by Putnam (1975) and Burge (1979a) have been taken to indicate that the way of individuating psychological states in accord with the commonsense scheme for explaining human behaviour conflicts radically with plausible views concerning the nature of the relationship between psychological states and neurophysiological states. Crudely, the experiments seem to show that identity in the neurophysiological state types instanced by a subject is neither a necessary nor a sufficient condition of identity of psychological state types - if the latter are individuated by the commonsense individuative scheme.[4]

The difficulty can be resolved, according to some theorists (e.g. Fodor, 1987), by arguing that the states recruited by commonsense belief/desire psychology are divisible into two components: an inner component which is not individuation-dependent upon features of the environment of the subject, and another component which is so dependent; the genuine, so to speak, psychological state is held to be that which is not individuation-dependent upon features of the environment of the subject. Such theorists can, thus, be seen to preserve a category of psychological states the individuation conditions of which are independent of the nature of the environment of their subjects. Proponents of the thesis that there are such states are describable as internalists. The motivations for internalism are discussed in chapters one and two below.

This essay involves a defence of a type externalist theory of psychological states, specifically, one which is constrained by a token physicalist theory of mind; the truth of that theory of the relation between psychological and physical events is taken for granted (it is defended in detail in Macdonald, 1989).[5]

One other point. It is presumed in what follows that there are other human subjects (this is plainly taken to be the case in commonsense belief/desire psychology).

The essay is divided into three parts. In the first, the motivations for internalism and externalism respectively are described and evaluated. It is concluded that externalism is the more plausible thesis. In the second part of the essay, a substantial problem for externalism is discussed; this is the problem of reconciling externalism with certain intuitively correct views concerning the nature of a subject's epistemic authority with respect to the contents of his own psychological states. It is argued that the reconciliation can be effected. Part three focuses solely on specific kinds of psychological states (thoughts). Externalist accounts of demonstrative thoughts and thoughts which concern natural kinds are set out and defended.

Finally, I would like to take this opportunity to acknowledge a debt of gratitude to Dr.Cynthia Macdonald for her help and influence during the course of the preparation of the material in this book.

Notes

1. For a survey of the main options, see e.g. Macdonald,1989; and Churchland, 1989.
2. The claim that certain psychological states are individuation-dependent upon certain features of the environments of their subjects may be understood as follows: Canonical descriptions of such states (descriptions of the states in terms of their individuation conditions) necessarily make reference to features beyond the bodies of the subjects of such states.
3. The term "constitutively relevant" is employed here to indicate individuation-dependence.
4. This consequence arises since the thought experiments suggest that subjects may be physical duplicates yet psychologically distinct - in the sense that they think different thoughts (see ch.1 below for the details of the experiments).
5. More notes on terminology: By "token physicalism" I mean the thesis that "every event is a physical event" (Macdonald, 1989,p.96); a token physicalist theory of mind holds that token mental events are identical with token physical events. With

respect to the term "type externalism", as will be seen (ch.3), type externalism is a thesis which claims that externalism is true for at least some of the types of psychological states recruited in explanations of action. Such states are standardly ascribed by the use of expressions which have the logical form "S F's that p" where "S" is a variable for the actor, "F" is a variable for an attitude-type (e.g. believes, desires, fears, hopes etc.) and "that p" is a variable for a type of content-clause (e.g. water is wet). Attention in this essay centres on the third argument-place in this schema. I will use the term "that-clause" to refer to specifications of the contents of attitude-types. So in the expression "S believes that water is wet", the that-clause which features is "that water is wet".

Part I
INTERNALISM AND EXTERNALISM

1 Motivations for internalism

1. Internalism and two thought experiments

According to Burge (1988a, p.64), there are three main motivations for internalism: ontological, explanatory, and epistemic. Before discussing each of these motivations separately, the defining feature of internalism with respect to psychological states (both types and tokens) needs to be identified.

Burge defines internalism as follows,

> According to [internalism] about the mind, the mental natures of all a person's or animal's mental states (and events) are such that there is no necessary or deep individuative relation between the individual's being in states of those kinds and the nature of the individual's physical or social environments (Burge, 1986a, pp.3-4; also, Burge, 1988a, pp.63-64).[1]

Hence it can be seen that internalism involves a conception of mental states in accordance with which their natures are held to be independent of the nature of the physical and social environment inhabited by the subjects of those states.

A more precise way to characterise the nature of the independence of psychological states from the environments of their subjects may be to state the following:

According to internalism, the individuation conditions of psychological states do not violate what will be termed here The Solipsism Claim. This is the claim that descriptions of psychological states in terms of their individuation conditions do not make reference to objects, events, states of affairs or properties beyond the confines of the body of the subject of

3

the states (cf. Putnam, 1975, p.136).[2]

Two kinds of thought experiments have featured prominently in the debate concerning internalism and both have been thought to threaten the proposed independence of certain types of psychological states from the environments of their subjects. The first is Putnam's so-called Twin Earth thought experiment (Putnam, 1975). In this we are asked to imagine the existence of a planet, Twin Earth, which is "exactly like" (Putnam, 1975, p.139) Earth apart from the fact that no water is present on Twin Earth; what is found there instead is a liquid which looks, tastes and behaves as water (call it water*) but it has the chemical composition XYZ and not H2O.

Putnam employs the Twin Earth idiom to argue, plausibly, that the meanings of natural kind terms are determined by the actual extension of those terms, and, hence, that "meanings are not in the head" (1975, p.139).[3]

One of the points which can be drawn from the experiment is that two subjects "who are molecule for molecule identical" (Putnam, 1975, p.144), S on Earth and S* on Twin Earth, can instantiate tokens of the same physical state types but tokens of distinct psychological state types, e.g. when they respectively desire water/water* (cf. Pettit and McDowell, 1986, p.2). The conclusion follows if it is allowed, not unreasonably, that that-clauses employed in commonsense explanations of action to characterise the beliefs, desires, fears, hopes, and so on of the subjects S and S*, serve to individuate the contents of their respective psychological states.[4]

A series of thought experiments devised by Burge (e.g. Burge, 1979a) have been thought to deliver a similar conclusion; but whereas in the Putnam Twin Earth case attention is focused on the physical environments of the subjects, in Burge's experiments the physical environment of the subject is (allegedly) held constant whilst the social environment of the subject differs.

Burge asks us to consider the case of a subject S who believes he has arthritis in his thigh - a false belief since arthritis occurs only in joints. S is otherwise a normal speaker of English and has true beliefs concerning arthritis, e.g. that the elderly are more prone to it than the young and so on. Burge suggests, plausibly, that commonsense attributions of beliefs would ascribe to S a belief about arthritis when he says "I have arthritis in my thigh"; that is, although S incompletely understands the meaning of the term 'arthritis' commonsense attributions of beliefs involve ascribing beliefs about arthritis to him.

In Burge's example the subject's belief is false but it is still a belief about arthritis. The assumption being here that the meaning of the term (in this case "arthritis") is determined by the extension it has for the members of the subject's linguistic community (1979a, p.79); and further, that the individuation conditions of S's psychological states when he entertains beliefs about (e.g.) arthritis are similarly so determined (i.e. by the extension the term "arthritis" has for members of S's linguistic community (ibid.)).

Burge then constructs a counterfactual situation in which S's physical states from birth to the present, described in nonintentional language, remain as they are in the actual case but in which there is a difference in the linguistic community or social environment. In the counterfactual situation the term "arthritis" refers, in the counterfactual linguistic community to which S belongs, to a disease which can occur in both muscles and joints.

By Burge's intuitions it would be wrong to ascribe to S, in the counterfactual situation, a belief about arthritis. For Burge, the meaning of the term "arthritis" is fixed by S's actual linguistic community; minimally, it may be unclear exactly how it would be correct to characterise S's belief in the counterfactual situation, but it is plausible to hold that it is at least different in content from S's belief in the actual situation. The main point is that S's physical states remain fixed in both actual and counterfactual situations whilst his psychological states appear to differ. Burge constructs examples which invite similar conclusions for terms such as "sofa" and "contract" (1979a). And, in later papers (e.g. 1982a, 1982b, 1989) Burge exploits the counterfactual idiom again to argue that at least some psychological states are individuation-dependent upon features of the physical environments of their subjects.

Burge's thought experiments may be taken to threaten the claimed independence of psychological states from the environments of their subjects in roughly the same way in which Putnam's experiment may be believed to threaten that claim.

It should be repeated that the thought experiments presume that ascriptions of mental content can be specified adequately by the employment of that-clauses; in these, general terms and singular referring expressions occur obliquely - i.e. in ways which do not permit the substitution of co-referring terms or expressions.

Internalists, in seeking to preserve the view that mental states are not individuation-dependent on the environments of their subjects, have responded in a number of ways. One of the most plausible is to bifurcate total content into two components: one of which respects the demands of The Solipsism Claim (p.3 above) (narrow content) and the other which does not (broad content); the further proposal is then advanced that it is narrow states which are the genuinely explanatory states (this is a strategy

5

developed by Fodor (e.g., 1987), and McGinn (1982a), and will be discussed below).[5]

It has been noted briefly, then, how internalism may be motivated by explanatory considerations, and these receive much more attention below; but, as indicated by Burge (1988a, p.64), motivations for internalism come from two other perspectives: ontological and epistemic. Let us turn now to consider the first of these: ontological motivations for internalism.[6]

2. Ontological motivations for internalism

Cartesian dualism

As noted earlier, internalism is a thesis which denies that there is a relationship of individuation-dependence between the psychological states (types and tokens) of subjects and their physical and social environments. Descartes's view was, of course, that the mind (or, more accurately the soul) is ontologically independent of the body. Hence, he writes

> I [am] a substance whose whole essence or nature is to be conscious and whose being requires no place and depends on no material thing (*Discourse on Method*, IV, p.32)

Roughly, this conclusion appeared compelling to Descartes on the grounds that the existence of certain of his psychological states - e.g. his doubts about his own existence - were self-refuting, but doubts about the existence of entities other than himself, qua thinking thing, did appear to be possible (see, e.g. *Discourse on Method*, IV, p.32; *Meditations* II; and Williams, 1978, ch.4))

As may be anticipated, Descartes proposal of a general ontological independence between the psychological and the physical is apparently conceived by him to apply also to particular psychological states - to particular, token thoughts. Thus, when Descartes envisages the possibility that he is being deceived by "an evil spirit" (*Meditations* I, p.65), he cannot be confident that his thoughts concerning himself and his environment are true, but he can be confident that he at least knows the contents of these thoughts - he knows what it is that he is doubting (see, e.g. Meditations ibid.)

Hence, it is evident that the ontological proposal that the mind is independent of the body motivates internalism; a theorist who holds such a view of the mind-body relationship must be committed to internalism

6

given Burge's characterisation of that thesis quoted above (p.14).

It is also evident that the Putnam-Burge thought experiments threaten internalism motivated in this way. This is due to the fact that if the details of the experiments are accepted, the individuation conditions of at least some psychological states are not independent of the environments of their subjects. So the experiments threaten the independence of the psychological from the physical which is an essential feature of the Cartesian position.

With respect to The Solipsism Claim, according to this, descriptions of psychological states in terms of their individuation conditions do not make reference to objects, events, states of affairs or properties beyond the confines of the body of the subject of the states (p.3 above). It might be thought that the Cartesian position violates this and so fails to qualify as a version of internalism. For example, suppose a Cartesian, S, doubts that Cantona lives in England. The doubt apparently has a referential component - one which refers to Cantona. If the individuation conditions of S's doubt include the name "Cantona" in referential position it appears that the doubt violates The Solipsism Claim (p.3 above) with the result that Cartesian Dualism does not entail internalism with respect to psychological states.

However, the Cartesian can simply deny that "Cantona" really is a referential component of the doubt - perhaps by insisting that expressions which are employed as names in ordinary language are really descriptions (viz. Russell (1956), see ch.3 for elaboration of this strategy).

In the Cartesian position, then, internalism with respect to psychological states is motivated by the view that mental states in general are essentially distinct from physical states. Therefore no mental state can be individuation-dependent upon a physical state of affairs - within or beyond the body. But ontological views other than Cartesian Dualism also seem to motivate internalism.

Type-type mind-brain identity theory[7]

As noted, the Cartesian position holds there to be no ontological dependence between mental and physical states. But according to a more recent thesis, type-type mind brain identity theory, mental state types are identical with physical state types - specifically, types of neurological states (see, e.g. Place, 1956; Smart, 1959). Hence, on this account, there is a clear ontological dependence between psychological and physical states.

The move away from Cartesian Dualism in the philosophy of mind was partly due to the incompatibility of non-spatial mind substance with scientific explanations (cf. Place op.cit.; Smart op.cit.): nonspatial mind-substance cannot be incorporated into physical theory. But overwhelming evidence from psychopathology points to an intimate connection between mental states and brain states. Evidently, damage to certain parts of the nervous system results in impairment of certain areas of cognitive function (see, e.g., Wilson, 1979, pp.56-57 and references therein).

Type-type identity theory, then, is motivated at least partly by a desire to explain human action within the constraints of explanation in the natural sciences - something which is ruled out in the Cartesian position. This could be achieved by identifying psychological state types and tokens (e.g. a psychological state of type P - say, a desire that p) with neurological state types and tokens (e.g. a neurological state of type N). The latter types of states are then to be subsumed under physical laws (see esp. Smart, 1959, p.53).

Such a view of the relationship between psychological and neurological state types motivates internalism in the following way. It appears to entail that two subjects who instance the same types of neurological states must also instance the same types of psychological states. So if it is accepted that, say, the Twins in Putnam's Twin Earth case are exactly alike from the neurological perspective, they must also instance tokens of the same types of psychological states.

In fact, according to type-type mind brain identity theory, since psychological state types are identical with neurological state types, the question of what psychological state a subject is undergoing at a time t is, in principle, resolvable by examination of the subject's neurological states at t (cf. Armstrong, 1973, p.35). Hence, it is plain that the environment of the subject bears no constitutive relevance to the identity of the psychological states of the subject, and type-type mind brain identity theory clearly motivates internalism with respect to the psychological states (types and tokens) of subjects.

The Putnam-Burge thought experiments bring evident conflict with type-type mind brain identity theory since according to these, subjects instance tokens of the same neurological types but distinct psychological types - provided the latter are individuated in accord with commonsense belief/desire psychology.[8]

Having, now, indicated how two kinds of views of the relationship between mental and physical states serve to motivate internalism, I propose to move on to a third ontological motivation; this stems from the view that psychological states supervene upon within-the-body physical states. Since the relevant within-the-body states are commonly taken to be brain states (i.e. neurological states) the term 'mind-brain

8

supervenience' will be employed to refer to such views (cf. e.g. Fodor,1987, p.30). (See next note.)

Mind-brain supervenience

Difficulties in the development of type-type mind brain identity theory (see below, ch.2 sec.1) led some theorists (e.g. Fodor, 1987) to hold a weaker view of the relationship between psychological state types and physical state types; namely, the view that psychological state types supervene upon brain state types - mind-brain supervenience. In Fodor's formulation of the supervenience relation it is held to be a dependence relation between types of mental and physical states such that,

> States of type X supervene on states of type Y iff there is no difference among X states without a corresponding difference among Y states (Fodor, 1987, p.30).[9]

When taken to apply solely to the relationship between types of psychological states and neurological states the supervenience relation entails that if two subjects instance the same neurological state types, then they cannot differ with respect to the psychological state types they respectively instance.

Empirical evidence which suggests that the nature of the links between psychological states and neurological states is particularly intimate leads one easily to the view that the natures of psychological states are determined by neurological states; the latter appearing to serve as an ontological anchor for the former in the way that, say, the molecular composition of water (or tables) serves as an ontological anchor for the liquidity of water (or the solidity of tables).

Mind-brain supervenience is enthusiastically endorsed by Fodor, he goes so far as to say that

> [Any] scientifically useful notion of psychological state ought to respect supervenience; mind/brain supervenience...is, after all, the best idea that anyone has had so far about how mental causation is possible (1987, p.30; see also Stich, 1978, and 1983, pp.164-165).

Also, as Fodor claims, mind-brain supervenience appears congenial to scientific explanation of psychological states since it holds that they are anchored in states which are explicable within the language of physical theory.

It should be said that the relevant physical states here, for Fodor, are

9

neurological states and not physical states beyond the body of the subject. The presumption is that this view of the relationship between neurological states and psychological states leads to the most plausible way of conceiving of mental causation.

For example, Fodor claims that if it is allowed that the Twins in Putnam's Twin Earth thought experiment instance distinct types of psychological states, then "[The] intelligibility of mental causation goes..." (ibid., p.42). The worry here is this. It seems plausible to hold that certain psychological states are caused by states of affairs beyond the body of the subject. So S's belief that he is now perceiving a pool of water may be said to be causally related to the pool of water he presently perceives: the psychological state (S's belief) is the effect, and the pool of water is its cause. The causal relation is such that there is a logical independency between causes and effects - as Hume (1739) famously pointed out. But this logical independency seems threatened if it is held that certain psychological states (types and tokens)   are individuation-dependent upon certain features of the environment of the subject (an externalist claim). Any proposed relationship of individuation-dependence between, say, S's belief that he is currently perceiving water and the presence of the water seems to conflict with the logical independence which appears to obtain between causes and their effects.

So not only does Fodor find internalistic individuation of the psychological states of the Twins well-motivated, he finds externalistic individuation of the psychological states of the Twins badly motivated since it conflicts with mind-brain supervenience; and, Fodor's strong implication is that externalistic individuation of psychological states entails a scientifically unbridgable gap between mental and physical states (see e.g. 1987, p.44).

Mind-brain supervenience motivates internalism since according to that thesis it should turn out that the subjects in the Putnam-Burge thought experiments instance tokens of the same types of psychological states. This is due to the fact that the subjects are conceived to instance the same types of neurological states,and, hence, by mind-brain supervenience, should thereby instance the same types of psychological states.

But the Putnam-Burge thought experiments threaten mind-brain supervenience. This is due to the fact that although the subjects in the experiments are conceived to instance the same types of neurological states, they are supposed to instance distinct psychological state types as the latter are individuated in commonsense belief/desire psychology.

Having, now, offered three ontological motivations for internalism (the view that there is no essential relationship between mental and physical states; the view that mental and neurological states are type identical; and the view that mental states supervene upon neurological states), we turn to look at explanatory motivations for internalism.

2. Explanatory motivations for internalism

It was noted in the introduction to this essay that the internalism/externalism debate concerns the individuation conditions of psychological states. It was noted further that psychological states are referred to in explanations of action couched in the language of commonsense belief/desire psychology. The discussion of mind-brain supervenience above indicated that psychological states do not respect mind-brain supervenience as they are individuated in the commonsense scheme. This has led some commentators to posit a range of psychological states, narrow states, which do respect mind-brain supervenience (e.g. Fodor, 1987; McGinn, 1982a). When considered in relation to the Putnam-Burge thought experiments, it turns out that the narrow psychological states of the Twins have individuation conditions which are of the same type on both Earth and Twin Earth and are states for which internalism is true and externalism false. Fodor (e.g. 1987), finds narrow states well-motivated due to mind-brain supervenience and what he terms "Methodological individualism...the doctrine that psychological states are individuated with respect to their causal powers" (ibid., p.44).

Another commentator, Brian Loar, has argued that narrow states can be motivated on grounds other than those recruited by Fodor (Loar, 1988a; Bilgrami, 1988).

In this section we will look at these two ways of motivating narrow states, the first is set out by Fodor (e.g. in his "Individualism and Supervenience", in Fodor, 1987) and the second is set out by Loar (e.g. in Loar, 1988a).

As we have seen above, Fodor finds internalism well-motivated due to his adherence to mind-brain supervenience. But he also finds internalism well-motivated due to what he describes as a "Methodological point" the point that

> Categorisation in science is characteristically taxonomy by
> causal powers. Identity of causal powers is identity of causal
> consequences across nomologically possible contexts (1987, p.44).

Roughly, the view is that not all of the properties of particulars are

11

relevant to their typing in scientific taxonomies; only the causal powers of particulars are relevant to the question of their identities.

Fodor claims that individuation in science is individuation by causal powers. But the psychological states of the Twins in the Twin Earth case appear to differ by the criterion of individuation employed by the commonsense scheme. Fodor claims that individuation by causal powers has the consequence that the psychological states of the Twins turn out to be tokens of the same type and that, therefore, mind-brain supervenience is upheld.

Fodor proposes that causal powers should be assessed across contexts and not just within them (1987, pp.35-38). The suggestion is that the causal powers of an entity cannot be determined by evaluating its behaviour in just one setting; determining the causal powers of an entity requires testing or projecting how that entity would behave in more than one context. If this is done in the case of the psychological states of the Twins, Fodor argues, they turn out to instance the same types of psychological states since their states have the same causal powers.

For example, if S* is, unbeknownst to him, transported to Earth, the psychological states which, say, would motivate him to utter "Bring water" result in his being brought water; similarly when S is transported to Twin Earth, he is brought water*.

Although this might seem simply to indicate that the psychological states of the Twins have distinct causal powers (i.e. since their effects differ, one results in water being brought and the other results in water* being brought) and, therefore, ought to be regarded as being of distinct types, Fodor rejects such an inference (ibid.). For him, such a difference in the causal powers of the states of the Twins is not one which would count in a scientific taxonomy. This is due to the supposition that, if S, counterfactually, had asked to be brought water on Twin Earth, then he would have been brought water*; similarly, if S*, counterfactually, requests water* on Earth, he will be brought water.[10] Hence, Fodor puts forward a case for classifying the psychological states of the Twins as type-identical due to their having the same causal powers were the Twins, counterfactually, in the same contexts. The difficulty now is to characterise the psychological states of the subjects: that is, how can narrow states be described?

Fodor points out what goes wrong if content is construed as a function from "thoughts to truth conditions" (1987, p.47). For example,

(1) C(thoughts) → truth conditions

in which the argument values are thoughts and the function values are truth conditions.

When the Twin Earth case is considered the thoughts of the Twins turn out to have different truth conditions since S entertains a thought about water and S* entertains a thought about water*. Fodor finds this consequence objectionable due methodological individualism and to mind-brain supervenience. Fodor modifies (1) so that the argument values are composed of both thoughts and what he calls contexts, in this case, the relevant planets (Fodor, 1987, p.47). Thus we now have,

(2) C(thoughts, contexts) $\rightarrow$ truth conditions

By schema (2) the contents of the intentional states of the Twins turn out to be of the same type. This is the case since, for example, if S travelled to Twin Earth his thoughts would, by Fodor's reasoning, share the same truth conditions as those of S* in that context; the same would apply in reverse for S* should he ever visit Earth.[11]

When psychological states are individuated in the way proposed by Fodor they respect the constraints of both mind-brain supervenience and methodological individualism.

Fodor says little in Fodor (1987) with respect to the question of characterising further narrow states in order to individuate distinct types of such states; that is, how are we to characterise the "thought" component of the functional expression C described above? In an earlier paper (Fodor, 1981, p.111) he is a little more forthcoming.

Narrow states can be further characterised, Fodor indicates, by specifying narrow content in the language of first order quantification theory (ibid.). So in the case of Putnam's Twins it turns out that the Twins instantiate tokens of the same type of narrow content since, when they desire water/water*, they are each in states which can be characterised thus: For any x, if x is thirst-quenching, clear, and can be used for washing in, then I desire x.[12] If this gloss is accepted, then it would appear that further grip can be got upon the suggestion that the Twins are in the same type of narrow psychological state and that such states can be individuated along the lines just given.[13]

Fodor's position, then, can be seen to be internalistic in that it respects the Solipsism Claim for narrow contents (see p.3 above). These latter may be construed as states which remain of the same type throughout the kinds of differences envisaged in the Putnam-Burge thought experiments. It is these narrow states which would be referred to in legitimate explanations of human action.[14]

With specific reference to demonstrative thoughts, it should be said that Fodor's line has the implication that if Putnam's Twins were to entertain demonstrative thoughts rather than natural kind thoughts then these too turn out not to be individuation-dependent upon contextual factors. The psychological states of the Twins would be of the same type due to their having the same causal powers as evinced in the behaviour of the Twins, and hence, they would instance the same type of narrow psychological state.

Support for such a position may be gleaned from the following example. Suppose S and S* respectively perceive type-identical vases. Each Twin simultaneously utters the words "That's nice", and they each walk towards their respective vase, and pick it up to admire it.

From the third person perspective it seems that their psychological states are of the same type due to the fact that the Twins appear to behave in the same type of way: they each move towards their vase, and they each utter the same type of sentence. So, considered from the third person perspective, it appears that there is a strong motivation to hold that the psychological states of the Twins are type-identical in such cases. Loosely following McCulloch, such motivations may be described as motivations from third person symmetry (McCulloch, 1989, p.209).

As seen, then, Fodor's proposal of narrow content is motivated by mind-brain supervenience and methodological individualism. But another commentator Loar (e.g. 1988) finds narrow states well-motivated on other grounds, but grounds which also stem from explanatory considerations. It is to Loar's account that we now turn.

Loar and narrow content

As I understand Loar, his proposal is that that-clauses are insufficiently fine-grained to serve as individuators of psychological contents (e.g., 1988a, p.102). Clearly, his proposal could be supported by the provision of examples in which a subject's psychological states are of the same type when specified by the employment of a that-clause, but for which there are grounds to doubt that the that-clause captures the contents of the subject's psychological state. Loar attempts to provide such an example (Loar, 1988a, pp.102-103).

Loar (recruiting an example of Kripke's (1979)) introduces us to Pierre, a native Frenchman. Whilst being brought up in in France, Pierre learns of a place which he calls "Londres". Further, Pierre comes to believe that the place he calls "Londres" is pretty. This belief is ascribed to him by his fellow Frenchman by employment of the that-clause "Londres est jolie". Pierre, as it happens, is also a great fan of Oscar Wilde and forms the intention, whilst in France, to visit Oscar Wilde's house should he ever happen to be in London. The example continues with Pierre finding

14

himself in London but being unaware that London and the place he calls "Londres" are the same place. Further, Pierre even forms the belief that London is pretty. The fact that Pierre does not go to visit Oscar Wilde's house, let it be agreed, serves as evidence in support of the conclusion that Pierre has failed to realise that Londres is London.

It is suggested by this example that that-clauses are insufficient to individuate psychological content since the characterisations of Pierre's psychological states as

(i) Pierre believes that Londres est jolie,

and (ii) Pierre believes that London is pretty

seem to ascribe to Pierre tokens of the same belief type; that is assuming, reasonably enough, that the French sentence "Londres est jolie" can be translated "London is pretty".

Loar concludes that there are in fact two distinct states here and that this is evidenced by the fact that the states ascribed by the two that-clauses "Londres est jolie" and "London is pretty" have distinct conceptual roles in the cognitive life of Pierre. They have distinct conceptual roles since they have different inferential links with other psychological states instantiated by Pierre (Loar, 1988,p.103). This latter point is indicated by the fact that the "Londres est jolie" belief is closely connected with an intention to visit Oscar Wilde's house whereas the "London is pretty" belief is not so connected.

So Loar's example at least shows some motivation for positing some kind of content which is not captured in that-clauses and which can be individuated in some other way - perhaps by their conceptual roles. Further, these narrow states do appear to have intimate links with action and so, it seems, should take their place in psychological explanations of action.

It should be said that Loar does not offer any sustained positive account of how content might be individuated (in Loar, 1988a, or 1988b; but see Loar, 1981) but he does state that he takes psychological states to be "individuated (somehow) in terms of conceptual roles" (1988b, p.134). So it may be worth briefly outlining how such a pattern of individuation might look.

Descriptions of narrow states appear to respect the Solipsism Claim (p.3 above) due to the fact that the individuation conditions of such states are allegedly given by instantiations of stimulus types, formulae types, and bodily movement types. All these types are characterised in nonintentional language. Stimulus types are individuated in the language

15

of neurophysiology (e.g. sensory receptors of type F are stimulated at t). Formulae types are envisaged as being formulae couched in first-order quantification theory (cf. our description of narrow content in the account of Fodor's view above). And bodily movement types are individuated nonintentionally (e.g. the subject's arm moves n degrees at t). So when a stimulus type of type A is tokened by a subject, and a formulae type of type B is tokened, then a bodily movement of type C occurs (cf. Loar, 1981; Field, 1978; and Forbes, 1987). Concerning the formulae types, an example provided by Schiffer might help to see further what is being claimed. Schiffer invents a character HM who has a transparent head. In this head there is a "belief box" and a "desire box" (Schiffer, 1981, p.212). In each of these boxes there are formulae couched in quantificational language; let it be supposed that when a formulae type is tokened it lights up. Given a sensory stimulus of type A it might be noticed that the predicate "Bx" is tokened in HM's belief-box and that "Gx" is tokened in his desire-box. It might be noticed, further, that when this formulae type is tokened (Bx ∧ Gx) then bodily movement of type C occurs. In such way generalisations concerning the explanation of HM's behaviour might be constructed (e.g. whenever A, and Bx and Gx, then C). These generalisations might be recruited in explanation of HM's behaviour and be the kind of narrow states which would be referred to in psychological explanations of behaviour.

To return specifically to Loar (1988a). In that paper, Loar begins by motivating the claim that that-clauses are insufficiently fine-grained to serve as individuators of psychological states; the Pierre example is deployed to this end. Further, the example apparently supports a view according to which psychological states can be individuated by their conceptual roles; specifications of latter satisfy The Solipsism Claim and so are individuated in accord with internalism. Applied to the Twin Earth case, it could be argued, similarly, that the psychological states of the Twins, when they respectively desire water/water*, are in fact type identical since they instance the same types of conceptual role. Individuating the psychological states of the Twins in such a way conflicts with the pattern of individuation endorsed by externalism with respect to those states.

Hence, Loar's attempt to provide explanatory motivations for individuating psychological states internalistically is motivated by the Pierre case and can be generalised to apply to Twin Earth cases also.[15]

Something has been said, then, about just how so-called narrow content might be motivated, might have a role to play in explanation of action, and might be characterised. Let us move, now, to consider epistemic motivations for internalism.

4. Epistemic motivations for internalism

In our earlier discussion of Cartesian Dualism, it was noted that, according to that thesis, it is of the essence of psychological states that they are not existence-dependent upon any physical states. Hence, Descartes considered the possibility that his beliefs about the world are widely mistaken and that "[There] is no earth, no sky, no extended objects, no shape, no size, no place" (*Meditations* I (pp.63-64)).

The point here is that, from the first person perspective, Descartes considers that his beliefs about the nature of the world in which he lives could be wholly false, yet, despite this, he can be sure that he knows what it is that he is doubting. So, for example, he might doubt that water exists, but be sure that his doubt really is a doubt about the existence of water.

The tenability of the project of Cartesian doubt is one which philosophers have taken seriously (see, e.g. Russell, 1912, ch.1). The main difficulty has been to establish the existence of the world beyond the thinking subject. But if externalism is true (construed roughly, for now, as the denial of internalism), then it appears that some psychological states are both existence-dependent and individuation-dependent upon features of the environment of the subject. This conflicts with the Cartesian intuition that it is of the essence of mental states that they are not existence-dependent upon any physical states, nor, it would seem to follow, are they individuation-dependent on any physical states.[16]

A further feature of the Cartesian view is that when subjects entertain psychological states, they are in a position of epistemic privilege which gives them a position of authority when it comes to determining the identity of such states. This feature of the Cartesian conception of psychological states is also apparently threatened by an externalist conception of such states. For example, according to the externalist view, the individuation conditions of some psychological states are determined by the nature of the environment of the subject (recall, e.g. the Putnam-Burge thought experiments).

Clearly, the subject is not in a position of epistemic privilege when it comes to determining the nature of his surroundings. But if the individuation conditions of certain psychological states are determined by features of the environment of the subject, the position of authority afforded to the subject with respect to determining what it is that he is thinking, appears to come under threat.

Commentators unsympathetic to externalism (e.g. Georgalis, 1990, p.108) point out that it conflicts with certain key aspects of the Cartesian view of the first person perspective on thought. It is suggested further that in so far as internalism is compatible with the relevant features of the Cartesian conception of first person thinking then this constitutes a strong motivation in favour of internalism (e.g. Georgalis, op.cit.; Blackburn, 1984, pp.302-345; and Searle, 1983, p.230). Additionally, in so far as externalism brings about a conflict with important aspects of the Cartesian conception, then this constitutes a considerable obstacle to the acceptance of externalism. Externalist responses to this charge will be considered later (in part II), but, for now, it may be useful to have a clearer picture of the Cartesian conception so that it is clear just which areas of it are supposed to conflict with externalism, and which aspects of it motivate internalism.

Cartesian conceptions of first-person thinking

In Descartes' own position on first person thinking, when a subject introspects upon a mental item, all the properties of that item are revealed to the subject. In Russell's phrase, the Cartesian position makes "...subjective things most certain" (1912, p.8). The subject is able to determine whether, for example, the introspected item is an idea of gold or fool's gold, or water or water*. Subjects' judgements with respect to these mental items are held to be infallible; and subjects are regarded as omniscient with respect to the contents of their intentional states (see, e.g. *Meditations* III, p.78).

A weaker but still Cartesian conception of first person thinking is one in which subjects' epistemic capabilities concerning their own intentional states are still distinctive but are less extensive than that supposed in the view just described. The work of Freud has sufficiently influenced Western thought to the extent that modern intuitions concerning first person thinking tend to allow that subjects are neither omniscient nor infallible with respect to the contents of their thoughts (e.g. unconscious thoughts, beliefs, fears and so on). Further, the purported fallibility extends even to cases where subjects give voice to occurrent thoughts. Examples of this phenomenon may be considered to occur in technical or abstract discussions in which the utterer is unclear about the meaning of a technical term and about what he himself means by it. Nonetheless, the conception of first person thinking under discussion is sufficiently similar to that ventured by Descartes that it is appropriate to label it "Cartesian".

It is possible to identify five main features of this Cartesian conception of first person thinking. These will now be outlined.

(a) The view that subjects have access to an inner realm of psychological states - an inner realm of thoughts, ideas or concepts.

These items are located "within" the mind or the mental realm; the mind being considered to be located in the head.

There is clearly some difficulty in attaching location to non-spatial entities; this is more a description of a problem with the Cartesian view rather than a feature of it. So this difficulty with the Cartesian conception will not be pursued. The main point to note is that subjects are alleged to have private access via the faculty of introspection to a realm of items which are located, so to speak, in the mind of the subject; the mind being located (again, so to speak) in the head.[17]

(b) The second aspect of the Cartesian view is the view that the natures of the mental items referred to in (a) are independent of the environment of their subjects.

(c) This is the claim that the first-person perspective makes available a perspective on the states posited in (a) which differs in kind from that available from the third-person perspective. It is in this sense that subjects are said to have a distinctive epistemic access to their mental states - a privileged access; a form of access which brings with it an epistemic advantage for the subject. This privileged access can be claimed to generate an asymmetry between first- and third-person perspectives on psychological states (cf. Davidson, 1984b). This asymmetry is partially manifested in the fact that, at least with respect to occurrent intentional states, other subjects are often required to make inferences to the contents of those states whereas no such inference is normally required when the states are considered from the first-person perspective. So this third aspect of the Cartesian position asserts that subjects have a privileged access to the entities posited in (a).[18]

(d) The fourth element of the Cartesian position to be mentioned here is the claim that the first-person perspective on intentional states affords immediate, direct knowledge of the contents of those states (see, e.g. Alston, 1971, p.224). This differs from (c) in that (c) notes that access is privileged whereas (d) notes that the knowledge acquired from the privileged perspective is direct. The Cartesian conception of first-person thinking has it that when subjects do know the contents of their first-order occurrent states, then they do so directly. Directness here can be taken to indicate knowledge arrived at without conscious inference (cf. Heil, 1988a, p.239). By contrast, knowledge of the natures of the mental states of others is typically inferred from their actions (i.e. including their speech).

(e) This is the view that the subject is authoritative with respect to the contents of his own token intentional states - he knows authoritatively which types they are. This fifth feature of the Cartesian account of first-person thinking simply falls out of the previous four features

19

mentioned. If subjects have unfettered access to a realm of items the natures of which are open to view to them, in an epistemically privileged way, it would be anticipated that subjects would be authoritative when it comes to the question of knowledge of the natures of those items - where the items in question are conceived to be introspected, inner thoughts, ideas, or concepts.

Roughly, it can be said that features (a) and (b) of the Cartesian conception are ontological and that features (c), (d), and (e) are epistemic. As will be seen, externalists wish to preserve certain of the epistemic aspects of the Cartesian account but dispense with its ontological aspects. [19]

One further point. It should be clear that mere access to a realm of items is not sufficient for authority with respect to the natures of those items. For example, a security guard (or an insect) might have access to a room full of rare paintings without knowing anything about these paintings (i.e. the name of the artist, the nature of their subject matter etc.). This kind of access is distinct from a notion of access which does imply some epistemic privilege. It is clear that in the Cartesian conception as that has been described here, the nature of the access which subjects have to their intentional states is one which is supposed to secure an epistemic advantage for the subject. In the security guard example there is no epistemic privilege which accompanies the guard's physical access to the paintings; but in the Cartesian conception of mind such access is supposed to be accompanied by an epistemic advantage.[20]

In the epistemic aspect of the Cartesian account the prominent notions are those of privileged access, first person authority and direct knowledge. It should be pointed out that direct knowledge cannot, by itself, be regarded as a defining characteristic (i.e. a necessary and a sufficient condition) of first person thinking.

This follows since subjects can come to know what they believe by the use of evidence, e.g., their actions; so it is not necessary that one knows the contents of one's own intentional states directly. Nor is it sufficient that if p is known directly, then p is a proposition concerning one's own intentional states.

It is standardly claimed that subjects can have direct knowledge of empirical facts (e.g. that the table is brown, that the door is open and so on). The way directness features in first person thinking is in the sense that one's own intentional states are directly knowable rather than are directly known; that is, one's own intentional states are not necessarily directly known, but it is necessary that they could be (Heil, 1988a).

So, borrowing from Heil, it can be said that what is distinctive about one's own intentional states considered from the first person perspective is, both, their "direct knowability" (Heil, 1988a, p.242), together with the fact that they are essentially such for the subject but not for others. This reconciles the possibility that others as well as I can know directly the contents of my own intentional states (e.g. perhaps others can know directly that I am in pain) with the fact that the relevant intentional states are metaphysically dependent upon me (my token thought that I am cold is metaphysically dependent upon me), and are directly accessible to me.

Given acceptance of the suggestion that there does seem to be an epistemic advantage attached to first person thinking, a term which may be used to denote that epistemic advantage may be useful at this point. The term "privileged access" may be recruited to play such a role; that is, it denotes a form of access which is not just metaphysical in the way that the security guard's access to the paintings can be said to be metaphysical. So privileged access here indicates an access which brings with it an epistemic advantage for the subject. This epistemic advantage is such that the subject is (i) in a better position to know the natures of his intentional states than others and (ii) the relevant intentional states are essentially such that they are directly knowable by the subject. The conjunction of (i) and (ii) can then be said to constitute first person authority.

Note that none of what has been said so far suggests that the contents of intentional states cannot be determined from the third person perspective; all that is being claimed in the Cartesian conception is that when intentional states are considered from the first person perspective that perspective affords an epistemic advantage for the subject.

It should also be mentioned why it is that knowledge of one's own intentional states should be regarded as direct rather than as based on evidence. If it is taken to be the case that subjects do in fact know the contents of their own first-order occurrent intentional states, then it must be true that, for at least some of such knowledge, justification is not required. To see this, suppose that such knowledge does require justification. A second-order belief A, to the effect that I know that p requires a further justifying belief B. But this justifying belief B is not sufficient for me to know A due to the fact that I have to know that B is relevantly justifying. To know that B is relevantly justifying a further belief C is required, and so on (cf. Boghossian, 1989; Burge, 1988c, p.654). Hence, apparently, if subjects are to be accredited with any knowledge of the contents of their own intentional states,then some of that knowledge must be obtained directly.

In summary. For the Cartesian, first person thinking affords a perspective on a realm of items; the natures of those items are wholly independent of the nature of the subject's environment. The subject knows directly the natures of those items (knows their contents), is authoritative with respect to knowledge of the natures of those items, and has a privileged access to the items.

Given the description of the Cartesian conception just offered, we can now see further just how that conception provides epistemic motivations for internalism. Blackburn (1984, pp.310-328) discusses Putnam's Twin Earth thought experiment. In the discussion, Blackburn offers consideration of two kinds of thoughts which might occur on both Earth and Twin Earth: thoughts about natural kinds (as occurs in Putnam's discussion) and demonstrative thoughts. In addition to Earth and Twin Earth, Blackburn suggests a third context in which thoughts might take place; this may be described as The Empty World, it is a world in which the only inhabitant is the thinking subject (cf. the quote from Descartes (*Meditations* I, pp.63-64) offered earlier). Hence we have three proposed contexts in which a subject S might think a particular thought, Earth, Twin Earth, and The Empty World.

Consider, first, a subject who entertains a thought about a natural kind, e.g. water, in each of the three contexts.

In the first context, we are to envisage that a subject S, located on Earth, thinks about water. Secondly, suppose now that the same subject is, unknown to him, transported to Twin Earth and takes himself to be thinking about water when, really, his thought is about water*. Thirdly, consider that the subject, in fact, inhabits an Empty World and that although it seems to him that, say, on a particular occasion he is thinking about water, really this is not the case since nothing exists in this Empty World apart from the subject himself.

The Cartesian view, apparently endorsed by Blackburn, implies that although the subject is mistaken with respect to the liquid that his thoughts concern in the second and third contexts - Twin Earth and The Empty World - the subject can be confident that he knows what it is that he is thinking.

If that powerful intuition is accepted, this is entirely compatible with internalism since, recall, internalism denies that the environment of subjects has constitutive relevance to the identities of the psychological states of subjects.

Further, Blackburn's account appears to lend weight to the view that subjects know what they think authoritatively. If we were to ask the subject during his time on Twin Earth what it is that he thinks water* is, it seems that he would be the one in the best position to give an answer to that question.

Consider, now, that S has demonstrative thoughts in each of the three contexts just referred to (Earth, Twin Earth, and The Empty World).

Suppose, for example, that S, on Earth, thinks demonstratively of a vase just in front of him, e.g. "That's pretty". As before, suppose that S is then, unknown to him, transported to Twin Earth; there he thinks demonstratively about an apparently identical vase but one which is numerically distinct from that he thought of whilst on Earth. Again, as before, suppose that S is now in The Empty World and takes himself to be thinking demonstratively of a vase in front of him. In each of these cases it seems from the perspective of the subject both that there is no difference in the nature of his thoughts, and that he is in the best position to judge whether or not his thoughts differ in the three contexts. This is highly congenial to internalism and appears to constitute an obstacle to acceptance of externalism in so far as externalism conflicts with S's own intuitions with respect to the identities of his own psychological states.

Having considered each of the three kinds of motivations for internalism we now move on to consider some responses.

Notes to chapter one

1.　Burge employs the term "individualism" (e.g. in Burge, 1979a) to denote the thesis being described here as "internalism". The latter usage will be preferred in this essay to distinguish what Burge means by individualism (i.e. what I am calling internalism) from Fodor's understanding of "Methodological individualism" (1987, p.42) by which he means "[The] doctrine that psychological states are individuated with respect to their causal powers"(ibid.). Also, concerning Burge's characterisation of what we are calling internalism, it should be pointed out that McGinn draws a distinction between strong and weak versions of externalism. For McGinn (1989, p.7), strong externalism asserts that some psychological states are individuation-dependent upon features of the environment of the subject. Weak externalism asserts only that certain psychological states are individuation-dependent upon features beyond the bodies of their subjects - i.e. whether or not such features occur in the environments of the subjects. Thus, by Burge's definition, internalism denies only strong externalism and seems compatible with weak externalism as this is defined by McGinn. Our discussion will focus on the truth or other of strong externalism. There are two reasons for this. First, clearly, strong externalism implies weak externalism. And second, our main concerns are with natural kind thoughts and with demonstrative thoughts. With respect to natural kind thoughts, say thoughts about water, it seems possible that subjects could entertain thoughts

23

concerning water in a water-less environment if such subjects had the concepts of the constituents of water - hydrogen and oxygen and of, say, chemical composition. But that would not show that strong externalism with respect to thoughts concerning hydrogen and oxygen is thereby false (cf.McGinn, 1989, p.35). Also, with respect to demonstrative thoughts, as will be seen in part III of the essay, these seem to require a perceived object and so seem context-bound in a stronger way than is claimed by weak externalism.

2. The ambiguity of the term "psychological state" is deliberately exploited here. Crudely, in what follows, intentional states will be regarded as a sub-class of psychological states; a sub-class, the members of which, represent features of the world of the subject. In order not to beg the question against the internalist it has to be allowed that some psychological states which are referred to in explanations of action may be individuated in ways other than by employment of a that-clause (see discussion of narrow content below (section three)).

3. Support for Putnam's claim may be shown thus: It is a plausible constraint in the theory of meaning that if two declarative (nonindexical) expressions have the same meaning, then, necessarily, they have the same truth conditions. But clearly, the two expressions (i) "Water is wet", (ii) "Water* is wet" have distinct truth conditions; and, therefore, by the plausible constraint described, do not have the same meaning.

4. By "commonsense explanations of action" it is meant explanations which ascribe beliefs, desires etc. to subjects which are individuated by that-clauses. So the fact that S's belief that London is south of Manchester differs from his belief that Aberdeen is north of Manchester is indicated by the difference in the that-clauses employed to characterise what it is that S believes. Such explanations are described variously as "folk-psychological" explanations (see, e.g. Stich, 1983); or, explanations which recruit "the common-sense scheme" (Davidson, 1980, p.231); or explanations couched in the language of "commonsense belief/desire psychology" (Fodor, 1987, p.x).

5. A further strategy, which will not be considered in this essay, is to be an eliminativist with respect to the posits of commonsense belief/desire psychology (see, e.g. Churchland, 1979). For, arguments against the strategy, see, e.g., Macdonald and Pettit (1981, ch.2) and Rudder-Baker (1988).

6. It should be said that the division of motivations into ontological,

explanatory and epistemic is far from unassailable. E.g. Searle (1992, ch.1) draws attention to the temptation to tailor the ontology of psychological states according to epistemological considerations. Also, it can be pointed out that explanations of phenomena frequently involve ontological presuppositions (e.g. explanations in psychiatric medicine generally presume that psychological changes result from physical changes). Hopefully though, the reader will agree that the distinction is of some value and is worth pursuing.

7. Macdonald (1989, p.vi) points out that there are two distinct kinds of type-type identity theories, strong theories (e.g. Place, 1956) and causal-role theories (e.g. Armstrong, 1968). I do not discuss the latter kind of type-type identity theory since they closely approximate to versions of functionalism and it is not clear that this is in fact incompatible with externalism (see next note).

8. I have omitted to discuss other main positions on the relationship between mental and physical states, notably behaviourism (see, e.g. Skinner (1953)), and functionalism (see, e.g, Putnam (1960)). In brief, this is due, first, to the fact that behaviourism and functionalism (on some versions) each motivate internalism in much the same way as type-type mind brain identity theory (i.e. simply substitute "behavioural states" or "functional states" for "neurological states"); and second, it is not clear that functionalism is incompatible with externalism. A version of functionalism which is congenial to externalism has been proposed by Pettit and Jackson (1988). The reader will recall that the truth of a token physicalist theory of mind is being taken for granted here, though it does receive discussion below (ch.3,sec.3).

9. Of course there are a number of ways of construing the supervenience relation. For example, strong supervenience is commonly contrasted with weak supervenience (e.g. Davies, 1992). Roughly, in weak supervenience, property A weakly supervenes on property B if it is necessary and sufficient that objects identical in all A respects are identical in all B respects. Property A strongly supervenes on property B if it is both a necessary and a sufficient condition of an object's instancing property B that it also instances property A (see, e.g. Heil, 1992, p.68). Put another way, in strong supervenience, wherever property B is instanced, necessarily, property A is instanced. But in weak supervenience, property B may be instanced but there be no instances of property A. Evidently, strong and weak construals of the supervenience relation concern the modality of that relation - hence Davies refers to "modally weak supervenience" and

25

"modally strong supervenience" (1992). But the extension of the subvening properties also matters (i.e. which states count as "X states" ? (Fodor, 1987, p.30)). Two other ways of construing the supervenience relation are as local supervenience and nonlocal supervenience (cf. Fodor (ibid.)). According to the thesis of local supervenience mental properties supervene upon within-the-body physical properties of subjects. Mind-brain supervenience thus counts as a version of local supervenience except that mental properties are held to supervene more narrowly on neurophysiological properties. According to the thesis of nonlocal supervenience, mental properties are held to supervene upon physical properties both beyond and including those which occur within the bodies of subjects. Hence, at least four possible combinations of views open up: (i) strong local supervenience, (ii) strong nonlocal supervenience, (iii) weak local supervenience, and (iv) weak nonlocal supervenience. Fodor's definition is silent on the strong/weak distinction but explicit that he favours a version of local supervenience, mind-brain supervenience.

10. As put by Fodor, "If [S*'s] utterance...had occurred in [S's] context, it would have had the effects that [S's] utterance...did have; and if [S's] utterance...had occurred in [S*'s] context, it would have had the effects that [S*'s] utterance... did have. For [the utterances of S and S*] to have the same causal powers, both of those counterfactuals have to be true" (1987, p.35).

11. Hence, Fodor writes, "Two thought contents are identical only if they effect the same mapping of thoughts and contexts onto truth conditions" (1987, p.48).

12. E.g.: $((\forall x) (Tx \wedge Cx \wedge Wx) \rightarrow$ [Self s/s*] desire(s) x).

13. It is worth noting that the expression given in the last note does have truth conditions once a domain is specified for the quantified variables.

14. Also, it should be added that the descriptions of narrow states just offered do not violate the Solipsism Claim (p.3). This is due to the fact that referential expressions may be parsed as descriptions (e.g. the natural kind term "water" may be replaced by a series of descriptions).

15. Just to make things as clear as possible here. In the Pierre case, theorists who hold that psychological states are individuated by that-clauses (namely, externalists) appear committed to the view that Pierre's London-beliefs and his Londres-beliefs are of the same type. But Loar argues that they differ due to their distinct conceptual roles. In the Twin Earth case, for externalists, the

psychological states of the Twins are of distinct types. But Loar's claims indicate that they are of the same type due to their instancing the same types of conceptual roles.

16. On the distinction between existence-dependence and individuation-dependence. A particular, P, may be existence-dependent upon another particular, Q, but Q need not be referred to in the individuation conditions of P. E.g. consider a case in which P is a vase, and "Q" names the maker of the vase.

17. See, e.g., Descartes' *Meditations II*, p.73. Of course, such a conception of world-independent inner items is to be found among some of the British Empiricists - specifically Locke, Berkeley and Hume.

18. By "occurrent intentional states" it is meant states which have content specifiable in a that-clause, and which are currently undergone by subjects. Also, it should be said that some behaviourists (e.g. Skinner (1953) and Ryle (1949)) disagree with the claim concerning an asymmetry of access.

19. That is - Davidson apart (whose account will be examined below (part II)) - externalists seek to agree with proponents of the Cartesian conception that the first person perspective on intentional states differs in kind from the third person perspective; that the first person perspective on intentional states affords direct knowledge of the contents of those states; and that subjects are authoritative with respect to the contents of their first-order occurrent intentional states.

20. We might, with Macdonald (1991a), term access without epistemic advantage "metaphysical access" and access with epistemic advantage "epistemic access".

2 Responses to motivations for internalism

In this chapter, responses to both ontological and epistemic motivations for internalism are offered; it is concluded that the responses reveal severe difficulties for internalism when motivated in either of these two ways.

1. Responses to ontological motivations for internalism

Cartesian dualism

The difficulties inherent in the Cartesian account have been well-documented in the philosophical literature so little further comment will be added here (see, e.g. Campbell, 1980; Williams, 1978). The central difficulty with the theory is that which Descartes himself recognised; namely, the problem of accounting for interaction between non-spatial mind-substance and spatially located physical substance (see, e.g. his letter to Elisabeth, 21/5/1643, in Wilson, 1969, p.374).

It is evident that certain physical stimulii result in mental changes, e.g. a pinprick results in an experience of pain; and further it is plausible that certain mental events result in certain physical changes, e.g. the phenomenon of bio-feedback in which subjects learn to reduce their pulse rates.

Descartes proposed that "animal spirits" (*Passions of the Soul* pt.I, p.362 (in Wilson, 1969)) serve as a connecting medium between the two substances. But this proposal does not seem to advance matters. Descartes' ontological categories were exhaustive: for any any particular entity (other than God) that entity is composed of either extended physical substance, or non-extended mind-substance, or both. So if we construe the animal spirits as a variety of nonspatial substance, the problem of interaction with extended physical substance remains; conversely, if we construe animal spirits as a variety of physical substance, there is a problem accounting for their interaction with mind-substance.[1]

Type-type mind-brain identity theory

Although type-type identity theory avoids the central problem which besets Cartesian Dualism - since no claims for interaction between mental and physical substances are made - it too has well-documented problems (see, e.g. McGinn, 1982c; Macdonald, 1989, chs. 1, 2). The first objection stems from the possibility of variable realisation (Putnam, 1967; Macdonald, 1989, ch.1), and the second objection stems from Leibniz' principle of the indiscernibility of identicals.

A version of the objection from variable realisation runs as follows (for more thorough treatment see Macdonald ibid.). Type-type identity theory asserts a relationship of identity between types of mental state and types of neurological state (recall our earlier account of the theory). But for a particular psychological state of type M, held to be identical with neurological states of type N, it seems plausible that a human subject S could lack the relevant neurological types but still instance a psychological state of type M (this claim is associated in particular with Kripke, 1971). The presumption is, here, that the conditions for possession of types of psychological states are more closely related to behavioural data (e.g. including first person reports of introspective data) than they are to neurological data.

The presumption seems highly plausible. For example, suppose that M-states are pain states and that N-states are a particular type of neurological state. Suppose S lacks N-states but behaves as other humans do when in pain and himself claims to be experiencing pain. It is difficult to believe that it would be denied that S really is in pain here and that the neurological data would trump, so to speak, the behavioural data in combination with S's reports of the phenomenal aspects of his experience.

A second kind of objection to type-type identity theory stems from Leibniz' principle of the indiscernibility of identicals. Roughly, the principle that if two things are identical, then they share all properties. But at least some psychological states instance properties such as those expressed by "...is reasonable, or "...is coherent", and do so, it seems, essentially (i.e. they would not be the states they are unless they instance these properties). But it is problematic to hold that these properties could be essential to the identities of neurological states.[2]

29

We saw earlier that this thesis provides strong motivation for internalism. According to the thesis the individuation conditions of the psychological states instanced by a subject are determined by the individuation conditions of the neurological states instanced by that subject. The version of the supervenience thesis stated earlier says that

> States of type X supervene on states of type Y iff there is no difference among X states without a corresponding difference among Y states (Fodor, 1987, p.30; also see Davidson, 1980, p.214).

It is worth noting that nothing in this version of the thesis commits its proponent to the view that the relevant "states of type X" (ibid.) are neurological states.

It is, of course, possible that neurological states are themselves individuation-dependent upon features of the environment of the subject. This possibility is rejected outright by Fodor (1987, p.31) on the grounds that it will imply that sub-atomic particles which constitute the nervous system of the subject will also be individuation dependent upon aspects of the environments of subjects - an implication he hopes the reader will find "plain silly" (ibid.).

Suppose we agree with Fodor on this. The problem for the theorist who wishes to resist mind-brain supervenience is to motivate the view that the individuation conditions of at least some psychological states need not be taken to be determined by "local microstructure" (Fodor, 1987, p.44) - i.e. types of neurological states instanced by the subject. Of course, a theorist who rejects mind-brain supervenience need not deny that psychological states are existence-dependent upon neurological states; what needs to be denied is that psychological states are individuation-dependent upon neurological states.

Before going on to consider patterns of individuation in science which appear not to supervene on "local microstructure" (ibid.) it is worth making the following point. The commonsense scheme seems to license ascription of psychological states to subjects in a way which conflicts with mind-brain supervenience (i.e. if the intuitions concerning the Twin Earth case are accepted). This can reasonably be taken to count against mind-brain supervenience. So mind-brain supervenience does, at least, require motivating (cf. Burge,1986a, p.13).

Burge (1989) argues that there are precedents for the type of individuative schema which Fodor opposes: i.e. where the type identities of the "base" properties do not determine the type identities of the supervening properties. He provides examples of two sciences which individuate their posits in such a way that the individuation conditions of the types they employ do not appear to supervene upon the molecular composition of the posits. The provision of such examples provides motivation for opposing Fodor's view concerning the relationship between mental and neurological properties.

Of the examples Burge provides, one is taken from the physical sciences - specifically, geoscience - and one from the biological sciences. In both cases, the individuation of types is shown not to supervene on local microstructure.

Burge points out that the geological typing of "landmasses" (Burge, 1989, p.309) as plates does not supervene on the microstructure of those landmasses.[3] It is the fact that such landmasses move in relation to other landmasses which motivates their being typed as plates. Physically the same landmass could be typed other than as a plate if it were, say, a component of a plate and not a plate itself.

Also, it should be pointed out that the individuation of a landmass as a plate P rather than plate Q does not appear solely to depend upon the physical composition of the plate. Individual plates are identified by their relations to other plates as opposed to their specific physical constitution. So a plate P is identified by its relations to other plates - say, plates Q and R. The identity of P as P would not be affected, if counterfactually, it was composed of a different type of rock (e.g. granite rather than basalt).

This is enough to show that the geological type plate does not supervene on the physical properties of the components of the plates - whether these are described in the language of geology (e.g. so that the plates are conceived to be composed of distinct types of rock), or in the language of, say, particle physics. Also, the above considerations indicate that the identities of particular plates are not exhaustively determined by the physical types (e.g types of rock) which constitute them.

A second example, this time from biological science, is provided by Burge. He repeats the point that typing in the sciences need not respect local supervenience by observing that

> Something is a heart because its organic function is to pump blood in a circulatory system that extends beyond the surfaces of the heart (Burge, 1989, p.310).

The suggestion here is that it is the function and location of hearts in circulatory systems and not simply their physical structure, described in the language of particle physics, which determines their being typed as hearts.

Burge's point can be strengthened in the following way. The wall of the human heart is composed of three kinds of tissue (the pericardium, myocardium and the endocardium). Suppose, counterfactually, that the wall of the heart consisted of only two kinds of tissue - perhaps this may occur in the future due to some evolutionary factors. It seems clear that such a difference in the structure of the heart would not result in its being typed differently. This point indicates, again, that kind individuation in science need not respect supervenience on local microstructure.

Consider also the typing of lumps of matter as planets. Suppose, not unreasonably, that a planet P is individuated in part by its position in a system of other planets and its behaviour in that system. And suppose further that there are no oceans or seas on P. If, counterfactually, it is conceived that P does have, say, a large ocean on its surface, it seems clear that this would have no effect on the identity of P.

These points concerning patterns of individuation in geology, biology, and astronomy indicate that there are precedents in the sciences which support the view that type identity is not determined by local microstructure (to use Fodor's term).

The point seems true in at least some areas of the three sciences just mentioned but it also seems true for the social sciences and for large sections of cognitive psychology. The subject matter of the latter two disciplines includes the behaviour, the beliefs, the desires and so on of their subjects (see e.g., Eysenck and Keane, 1990, and Lukes' introduction to Durkheim, 1895). Further, the descriptions of behaviour employed in these disciplines unashamedly employ that-clauses in such a way that the psychological states of subjects are individuated in ways congenial to externalism (see, e.g., Macdonald and Pettit, 1981, ch.3). So there are precedents for the individuation of types of psychological states by that-clauses in the specifically human sciences. Given acceptance of at least the last point, consider the following remarks made by Burge,

> [The] kinds recognised by these sciences are individuated by reference to patterns in a normal environment that reaches beyond the surfaces of individuals typed by those kinds, [and so] the kinds are not in general supervenient on the constituents of those individuals (Burge, 1989, p.317).

With particular reference to disciplines such as cognitive psychology Burge can be taken as saying here that types of psychological states are individuated by reference to, e.g., the types of objects with which subjects interact and about which such subjects retain and convey information. In the light of this it should come as no surprise that the identity conditions of at least some types of psychological states fail to supervene on brain states.

Neural kinds are individuated with respect to a different set of concerns than those with respect to which intentional states are individuated. To make this latter claim is not to say that neural kinds are individuated in complete ignorance of environmental stimulii. Such kinds may be individuated by the way they react to a particular type of stimulus. But given the point that, e.g., different types of object can cause the same type of stimulus (e.g. water and hydrochloric acid can be indistinguishable to the eye, as can gold and iron pyrites) it seems clear that intentional types will be individuated more finely than neural types. Although it makes no difference to the individuation of a neural type whether it is stimulated in the appropriate way by water or hydrochloric acid, the fact that a subject buys a fake gold ring when he believes himself to be buying real one is a difference which matters when it comes to explaining his behaviour. The behaviour of the neural type is unaffected by the difference between, e.g., water and hydrochloric acid since this is not detectable from examination by sight only.

These last remarks suggest that mind-brain supervenience should, at least, not be taken as true without serious consideration. The arguments of Fodor are developed in the context of uncritical acceptance of mind-brain supervenience. The points taken from Burge and developed above can be taken to show at least that that thesis is not as well-motivated as Fodor seems to think.

One final point here: in our earlier discussion of mind-brain supervenience it was noted that Fodor finds views which conflict with that thesis badly motivated due to problems which stem from explaining mental causation. In the introduction to this essay it was pointed out that a version of token physicalist theory of mind is presumed to be true. The version is able to address Fodor's worries in this area as follows. Macdonald's version (and other versions) of token physicalism (Macdonald, 1989) is able to sustain causal links between physical and mental events since it is held that each mental event is identical with a physical event; the latter being subject to causal laws (more detail is provided later concerning Macdonald's token physicalism (ch.3)).

Let us turn, now, to consider responses to explanatory motivations for internalism - specifically, those advanced by Fodor (Loar's motivations are discussed later in chs.3 and 11).

2. Responses to explanatory motivations for internalism

These are simply responses to the explanatory considerations, described above, which Fodor was seen to recruit in support of internalism. There are four responses, all of which focus on what Fodor describes as his

> Methodological point: [the point that] categorization in science is characteristically taxonomy by causal powers. Identity of causal powers is identity of causal consequences across nomologically possible contexts (1987, p.44).

The first two responses centre on Fodor's claim that "Identity of causal powers is identity of causal consequences across nomologically possible contexts" (ibid.). It may be recalled that Fodor recruits this claim (call it The Context Claim) to support the view that the psychological states of the Twins are of the same type in the Twin Earth case. The claim is also recruited in criticism of externalist individuation of the psychological states of the Twins since according to externalism, the psychological states of the Twins are type distinct (i.e. when they respectively desire water/water* etc.). The second two responses are directed at Fodor's claim that "Categorization in science is characteristically taxonomy by causal powers" (ibid.). Again, this claim is recruited by Fodor to ground support for internalism and opposition to externalism.

The first response is this. Fodor was seen to argue that The Context Claim supports internalistic individuation of the psychological states of the Twins. But Burge points to the possibility of a "device" (1989, p.311) which is capable of determining the causal histories of individuals. So if we were to suppose that S is transported to Twin Earth and requests water, then he would be brought water (presuming there is some available) and not water*. This is due to the device determining the causal history of S and concluding that when S expresses a desire for water, he desires H2O and not water* (XYZ). Instead of positing a mysterious device, one could simply suppose that an experimental psychologist is responsible for S's journey and, knowing relevant aspects of the causal history of S, is aware that in expressing a desire for water, S desires water and not water*. The example indicates that even if The Context Claim is accepted the circumstances of a test in which the causal powers of the Twins differ can be described. (It has to be assumed that the experimental psychologist does not accompany S* on a similar planetary transfer.)

A second response to The Context Claim can be drawn from remarks made by Davies (1986, pp.270-271). This response consists in contesting

Fodor's claim that, in science, causal powers are to be assessed across contexts. Davies points out that the individuation conditions of the kind planet do not appear to require assessment of causal powers across nomologically possible contexts. For example, the amount of water a planet would displace if it fell into an ocean on a much larger planet would seem to constitute a causal power of the planet, but not one relevant to the typing of a piece of matter as a planet. An entity is typed as a planet if it behaves in a particular way (e.g. has a roughly elliptical orbit and so on) in a particular context in which environmental conditions remain more or less stable (cf. Davies, ibid.; also Fodor,1991, p.20).

Further, Burge (1989, p.312) suggests plausibly that scientists typically type entities with reference to how they function in their normal environments. Thus hearts are individuated by their function (their physiology) and by the type and structure of the tissues which compose them (their anatomy). Determination of the function of hearts consists in examination of their role in the circulatory systems of certain types of organisms. The fact that a heart may behave in a particular way when it is outside its normal environment does not seem to enter so centrally into the considerations which determine the individuation of the biological kind heart; parallel points can be made about other organs.

The relevant considerations in relation to the typing of kinds in the biological sciences appear to centre on behaviour in a normal context - by "normal" it is meant the context in which the type of entity is standardly located; structure and composition; and, as will be seen shortly, causal history.

These two responses to The Context Claim seem to me to have not inconsiderable weight. Let us move on now to the third and fourth responses to the explanatory motivations for internalism recruited by Fodor. These focus on Fodor's claim that "Categorization in science is characteristically taxonomy by causal powers" (1987, p.44).

The third response is this. There is ambiguity in the claim that individuation in science is individuation by causal powers. For example, is Fodor saying that all the causal powers of an entity are relevant to its categorisation? If so, such a view is almost certainly false. To use an example provided by Burge (1989, p.316), the fact that a heart will stain a hard surface red if dropped onto it from a sufficient height is surely not a causal power which enters into the individuation conditions of hearts. With imagination, similar examples can be constructed (see Burge ibid. for a range of them).

This latter consideration suggests that although Fodor may be right to say that causal powers are relevant to the individuation of entities (witness the importance of physiology to the typing of human organs), this is not the whole truth of the matter. It is a subset of an entity's causal powers which enter into its individuation conditions and not all its causal powers.

Since this is clearly the case, it is evident that certain criteria must be employed in the selection of factors deemed relevant to the individuation of types in the sciences. Our earlier points concerning the types planet and heart strongly suggest that it is the behaviour of entities in the contexts in which they are normally located which are important to categorisation in the sciences.

If this last point is accepted, it seems plausible to agree with Fodor that causal powers are relevant to taxonomising in science, but qualify this as follows. It is only a subset of the causal powers of types of entities which are relevant in scientific taxonomies; and the criteria of selection for members of these subsets appear to be determined by considerations relating to how the entities behave in their normal environments - i.e. in at least some sciences.[4]

The fourth and final response to Fodor to be discussed here involves a direct challenge to the claim that categorisation in science is solely categorisation by causal powers. It is plausible that other considerations such as causal histories are also relevant to questions of type individuation in scientific taxonomies.

The point may be made with the aid of a creation of Davidson's: The Swampman(!). We are to

> Suppose lightning strikes a dead tree in a swamp; I am standing nearby. My body is reduced to its elements, while entirely by coincidence (and out of different molecules) the tree is turned into my physical replica (1987, p.443).

The Swampman proceeds to behave exactly as Davidson would have done - appearing to recognise friends, writing perspicuous articles and so on.

Having introduced us to this creature, Davidson makes the claim that "[Subjects] who are in all relevant physical respects [identical] can differ in what they mean or think" (ibid., p.452). The implication is that Swampman and Davidson may be physically identical, but are not psychologically identical and that this is due to a difference in their causal histories.

For example, Davidson suggests that The Swampman cannot be said to recognise his (Davidson's) friends because that requires that The Swampman and the friends have met previously and, of course, they have not. So despite the fact that The Swampman can be said to be physically identical to Davidson (they both instantiate tokens of the same physical state types) they can be said to differ psychologically. (The point works better if it is supposed that Davidson survives the horrendous event he describes.)

The point of The Swampman example is to show that the causal histories of subjects, and of particulars in general, are at least relevant to the question of their type identity. But the example may be of further use for purposes here since the Swampman case might be taken to suggest biological as well as psychological differences between Davidson and The Swampman.

It seems correct to agree with Davidson that the psychological properties of The Swampman will differ from Davidson's due to their distinct causal histories; and, hence to conclude that causal histories are relevant to questions of type identity. Possibly, analogous points apply to biological properties too. It seems at least plausible that typing an entity as, say, a heart requires that the heart has a particular kind of causal history. For example, that it has a particular kind of biological origin - in the case of hearts, this would mean that they develop from the distinctive type of organic cells which form muscle tissue. Further, it could be suggested that this process of development is one which takes place within a specified timespan.

If this claim is correct, it will not be the case that Davidson and The Swampman are biologically identical (even if they are physically identical) since (presumably!) Davidson's heart, nervous tissue, skin etc. developed in the usual way in the womb but The Swampman's organs do not result from a gradual process of development.[5]

Davidson's example suggests that even though, say, he and Swampman have hearts which are molecularly identical and have the same causal powers, this may not be sufficient for the claim that Swampman's heart is a genuine heart (similarly for his other organs).

The heart example can be elaborated on further to cast more doubt on Fodor's claim that it is the causal powers of types of entity which determine their individuation conditions in scientific taxonomies. The current state of medical technology has advanced to the point where it is possible to manufacture artificial hearts. These perform all the functions of a genuine heart and so, by Fodor's criterion, they should be indistinguishable, for the purposes of science, from actual hearts. However, this is clearly not the case. Artificial hearts are distinguished from genuine hearts even though they have the same causal powers.[6]

At least part of the motivation for distinguishing artificial from genuine hearts stems from the suggestion that causal histories in addition to causal powers enter into criteria for individuating entities. The biological kind heart denotes entities which have causal histories which are significantly distinct from the causal histories of artificial hearts. Parallel points may be made with respect to other organs, e.g. the central nervous system. It is not simply the causal powers of the central nervous system which determine its type identity, it is its structure and composition. Fodor, it seems, can be charged with taking questions about typing in (e.g.) human biology to be exhausted by questions relating to physiology when it appears that such questions take into account the anatomy of the relevant organ in addition to its function.

3. Conclusion

Thus far, we have considered three kinds of motivations for internalism: ontological, explanatory, and epistemic.

Ontological motivations came in three varieties: Cartesian dualism, type-type mind-brain identity theory, and mind-brain supervenience. In response to these it was suggested that Cartesian dualism and type-type mind-brain identity theory are each open to such serious and well-documented objection that neither position can reasonably be taken as theoretical basis adequate to motivate internalism. Mind-brain supervenience, however, proved a more hardy thesis; nonetheless, responses were offered in the text to cast serious doubt on the general claim that kind membership is determined by local microstructure in at least some scientific taxonomies (those of geology, biology and astronomy).

Explanatory motivations derived from two theorists, Fodor and Loar. Loar's views have yet to be responded to so will not be commented upon here. Fodor's proposals were seen to stem from his claims (i) that categorisation in science is, exhaustively, categorisation by causal powers, and (ii) that identity of causal powers has to be assessed across nomologically possible contexts (cf. Fodor, 1987, p.44); the latter claim was termed The Context Claim.

Two objections to The Context Claim were offered. The first suggested that it may be compatible with externalism. The second objection pointed out that the causal powers of planets do not seem to be assessed across contexts, but rather within a particular context - specifically the context in which the entity is located; similar points were made concerning the typing of entities as hearts.

Two related objections were offered against claim (i). First it was pointed out that only a subclass of the causal powers of an entity are relevant to its typing; and, it is plausible that the criteria of selection for

38

membership of the subclass is determined by consideration of how the entity behaves in its normal environment. The final objection to Fodor's claim exploited Davidson's Swampman example which indicates the relevance of causal history to categorisation in science. Further,the possibility of distinguishing genuine from artificial hearts can be seen to cast further doubt on the plausibility of Fodor's claims.

In sum, then, it seems that considerable headway has been made against internalism motivated both by ontological and explanatory considerations.

However, no responses have yet been offered to epistemic motivations for internalism. As seen above, epistemic motivations for internalism stem from a conception of the mind reasonably characterised as Cartesian. The main features of that conception were seen, both, to be congenial to internalism and to conflict seriously with externalism. The brief account presented of natural kind and demonstrative thoughts in this context serve to illustrate the difficulties in reconciling externalism with key features of the Cartesian view. These difficulties are so severe as to warrant sustained treatment so I return to them in ch.5 below. For now, we turn to consider motivations for externalism.

Notes to chapter two

1. Williams goes so far as to suggest that the kind of interaction - between spatially located substance and nonspatially located substance - apparently required in the Cartesian account may be "inconceivable" (1978, p.288).

2. Crudely, due to Davidsonian reasons: e.g. that explanation of physical phenomena is subject to different constitutive constraints than is explanation of mental phenomena (see, e.g. Davidson, 1980, pp.221-223; Kim, 1985; McDowell, 1985; Lennon, 1990,p.118).

3. I understand that the correct technical term here is "tectonic plates" (Asimov, 1984, p.173).

4. A possible objection here may be this. Bats and whales are each classified as mammals even though they inhabit radically different environments. This does not constitute a counterexample to the proposal made in the last paragraph since they are classified together due to the facts that they "give birth to living babies (instead of laying eggs) and feed them on mother's milk" (Asimov, 1984, p.698). Also, of course, the term "mammal" is more general than the terms "bat" and "whale".

5.   It can be pointed out that, e.g., skin can be grown under
     artificially created conditions, and that embryos can survive outside
     a womb. But I do not think that these facts threaten the point being
     made: that causal histories are a factor in the individuation of at
     least some types of entities and that a plausible case can be
     mounted for the view that Swampman and Davidson are not
     biologically identical since Swampman does not have a heart, or a
     kidney etc.

6.   On the distinction between natural and artifact kinds, Wiggins
     writes, "Artifacts are collected up not by reference to a
     theoretically hypothesised inner constitution but under functional
     descriptions that have to be indifferent to specific constitution and
     particular mode of interaction with the environment" (1980,p.87).

3 Motivations for externalism

In this chapter, we consider logico-semantic motivations for externalism, and two kinds of explanatory motivations: one kind provided by Burge (e.g. 1988a) and the other by Macdonald (e.g. 1992).

1. Logico-semantic motivations for externalism

These stem from a particular interpretation of the works of both Frege (e.g. 1892) and Russell (e.g. 1956) which is canvassed by McDowell (e.g., 1986), Evans (1982) and McCulloch (e.g. 1989). For the purposes of exposition, the views of these three commentators can be assimilated. I will begin by setting out relevant aspects of the views of Frege, then do the same with respect to Russell, and, finally, describe how McDowell (etc.) combines these to form a thesis which is a version of externalism.

Evans describes a view according to which there are

> Thoughts which would not have been available to be thought...if the object [thought of] had not existed (1982, p.64; also, pp.71-73; see also McDowell,1986, e.g. p.142).

A view such as that described in the above quotation seems to amount to a version of externalism since, according to the view, certain psychological states are constitutively bound to aspects of the environment of the subjects of such states. Such a proposal is, of course, incompatible with internalism.

Evans and McDowell indicate that a position like that described in the quotes is derivable from an interpretation of the work of Frege according to which referring expressions cannot have sense unless they have reference. The main aspects of that interpretation are to be set out here.

Roughly speaking, the elements of Frege's proposals which have been thought to motivate externalism fall into two main categories: Frege's semantic theory and what might be described as his cognitive theory. As will be seen, the two aspects are interrelated. Consider his semantic theory first.

According to Frege, semantically significant units of a language have both a sense (sinn) and a reference (bedeutung); for Frege, such units include singular referring expressions, predicates, and sentences which express propositions

Crudely, the reference of a sentence is a truth value;its sense is what is expressed by the sentence - what can be described as a proposition or Thought.[1] The reference of a singular referring expression is the object it denotes. And, the sense of a singular referring expression is the mode of presentation of the object it denotes. (See Frege's "On Sense and Meaning" in Geach and Black, 1956.)

A central feature of the Fregean view, then, on this construal of it, is that sentences have meaning by virtue of having truth conditions (cf. Evans, 1982, p.8). Expressions composed of a singular term and a predicate have truth conditions by virtue of the singular term's having a referent, and the predicate expression having an extension.[2]

The theory is systematic (with qualifications to be made later) in that it respects what has come to be known as the Principle of Compositionality (Ramberg, 1989, p.35; LePore, 1986,p.9; Davidson, 1984, ch.2). This is roughly the principle that the semantic properties of a sentence are a function of the semantic properties of its semantically relevant component parts (also, see Evans, 1982, p.25 for this way of expressing the principle).[3]

The systematic nature of Frege's semantic theory can be indicated by recruiting the technical apparatus of first- and second-level functions which feature in Frege's account of generality. A first-level function can be conceived of as an abstract object denoted by a functor of the form "Fx" in which a property is ascribed to an object in the domain under consideration (e.g. the domain of first year philosophy students). First-level functions take objects as argument values and give truth values as function values. So for the functor "Fx" where "F" stands for "...is one-legged" the functor "Fx" will be true if there is a one-legged first year philosophy student.

Second-level functions are referred to by quantifier expressions, e.g. expressions of the form "everything is F" ($\forall$x Fx), or "something is F" ($\exists$x Fx). Second-level functions take first-level functions as argument values and give truth values as function values. So the function denoted by "∀x Fx", for the domain specified (in this case first year philosophy students), will give the value True if every first-level function presented to it also gives the value true (a most unlikely occurrence if "F" represents "...is one-legged"). The second-level function denoted by "∃x Fx" similarly gives the value true if at least one first year philosophy student is one-legged.[4] It should be made explicit that this approach relies on the plausibility of the notion of a singular referring expression (henceforth, the less cumbersome expression "singular term" will be employed), a device for referring to a specific object. It is supposed that each member of the domain of first year philosophy students either has a name (where these form a sub-class of the class of singular terms) or can be given a name. Suppose there are ten such students and that each is named by the first ten letters of the alphabet. The function denoted by "∀x Fx", in the example given, will take as argument values the functions denoted by "Fa", "Fb", "Fc"...and so on.[5]

A further perceived virtue of Frege's theory lies in its account of logical validity (McCulloch, 1989, p.6). The logical apparatus just described connects up with the notion of logical validity since arguments of the form "All As are Bs; S is an A; therefore S is a B can be recast in logical symbolism thus: (∀x) Fx → Gx; Fa; therefore Ga. If it assumed that all objects in the relevant domain presented to first-level functions give the value True if they are F and similarly if they are G if a is such an object - i.e. one which has the property F, it will be correct to ascribe to it property G. Validity connects up with truth since, of course, in a valid argument if the premisses are true, so is its conclusion.

Fregean semantic theory, as outlined so far, might reasonably be described as reference based or object-invoking (McCulloch, 1989, pp. 21-29; Evans, 1982, ch.1). The point behind such a description is to emphasise the role played in the theory by the relationship of reference which is supposed to hold between names and objects. This relationship secures the relationships between first- and second-level functions, objects, and truth values.

One way to express the nature of the supposed relationship is to say that semantic power is dependent upon reference (cf. McCulloch, 1989, ch.1; Evans, 1982, ch.1). That is to say, the power of a name to affect the semantic properties of a sentence depends upon that name's having a referent. Since the semantic properties of a sentence contribute to the question of the validity of an argument in which it features, it can be suggested that reference is at the root of semantic power and that validity is thus dependent upon reference in the way just outlined.

Why ought consideration of such a complex set of interrelations be taken seriously in the context of a discussion of the extent to which the natures of psychological states are dependent upon features of the environments of their subjects? Answering this question leads us to consideration of Frege's cognitive theory.

As noted above, Frege employs the term "Thought" to denote the sense of a sentence. This, roughly, is what is expressed by the sentence (Frege, 1892, p.62) and gives the content of a subject's psychological state when he entertains a particular belief, desire, or fear etc. Given acceptance of the claim that Frege's theory is reference-based, it seems to follow that for a subject to entertain a Thought (following Frege's usage) about an object O, it is necessary that O exists. Otherwise, no object is presented to the relevant function, or truth value determined; and, if it were an expression, it would have no meaning.

When presented in this way Frege's theory can be deployed to motivate to externalism. This is due to the fact that Thoughts appear to be existence-dependent upon the objects thought about, and, crucially, that Thoughts are individuation-dependent upon the object thought of - i.e. if it is allowed that the Thought is individuated by the referent of the singular term which would feature in a canonical description of it (a description of it in terms of its individuation conditions).[6]

Commonsense explanations of human action typically involve the ascription of patterns of reasoning to subjects. If it is agreed that commonsense explanations of action employ explananda such as S desired that A, and believed that by doing B he could bring it about that A, it can be seen that such explanations attempt to make actions intelligible by ascribing psychological states to subjects. If such states are construed as Fregean Thoughts, it turns out that commonsense explanations of action involve ascribing to subjects psychological states - Fregean Thoughts - which are individuation-dependent upon features of the environment of their subjects.

Further, the aspects of Fregean apparatus described above have been recruited by some theorists (e.g. Evans, 1982; McCulloch, 1989; McDowell, 1977, 1986, p.156) to explicate the notions of communication and understanding. Roughly, these theorists argue that a speaker S can be said to be attempting to communicate a Fregean Thought, construed as what is expressed by a declarative sentence, to a hearer H when S is speaking meaningfully; that is, S attempts to communicate a Thought which H grasps if S has successfully communicated with H.

Similarly with understanding: H has understood S when H has grasped the Thought which S intends him to grasp - the Thought he, S, intends to communicate. Also, the idea that expressions, written and verbal, can be employed to convey information is present in the Fregean apparatus as employed by the theorists just mentioned.

These, then, are the aspects of the work of Frege which may be recruited by theorists sympathetic to externalism: Fregean Thoughts are individuation-dependent upon objects thought of by subjects. To determine a truth value it is necessary that there be an object thought of which is presented to a first-level function. The relevant object is named by a singular term in a description of the individuation conditions of the Thought.

Justification for the emphasis on reference can be gleaned from the point that commonsense explanations of behaviour, at their most basic level, involve reference to objects, events and states of affairs with which such subjects regularly interact. In everyday commonsense explanations of behaviour it is the thoughts subjects have about, e.g., buses, food, babies, cups and so on which feature prominently. In explaining a subject's action such as his switching on a TV it appears to be obvious that the thoughts of the subject concern that TV.[7]

Russellian motivations for externalism

Now let us move on to discuss the relevant aspects of Russell's work; specifically, aspects of his logical atomism (Russell, e.g. 1956).

A problem not really addressed by the Fregean semantic theory, as this was described earlier, is the problem of empty names and descriptions. For expressions in which such empty singular terms occur no object is presented to a function and so no truth value is determined. Russell's theory of descriptions is designed to circumvent this difficulty. Further, it conforms to linguistic intuitions to the effect that empty names are meaningful and do have semantic power (i.e. they can feature in valid arguments). If S utters "The present king of France is bald" on Russell's analysis this utterance comes out false but on the Fregean account (at least as it is construed above - i.e. as being reference-based) it has no truth value and is not meaningful.[8]

One way to characterise the differing treatments of singular terms in Russell and Frege is to point to the different logical form of expressions in which they feature according to their respective theories. Russell treats expressions which are ordinarily construed as names as descriptions; he regards what we might term ordinary names as "truncated descriptions" (1956, p.243). Genuine names, what Russell calls logically proper names, cannot fail to refer. For Frege, expressions containing an ordinary name and a predicate (henceforth "atomic sentences") have the logical form "...F". But for Russell they have the logical form "$(\exists x ...x) \wedge (\forall y ...y$ $y=x) \wedge (...x)$". In Russell's treatment ordinary names play the role of predicates which objects in the relevant domain satisfy or not. Since no object in the domain of presently existing particulars satisfies the predicate "...is King of France" in Russell's theory the expression "The present King of France is bald" comes out false.

In Russell's theory, only those atomic sentences which contain a logically proper name will have the logical form ascribed to ordinary names by Frege.

Russell's theory is also describable as reference-based. But for Russell ordinary names are to be analysed in the way prescribed by the theory of descriptions. Logically proper names play the role of connecting up thought and reality; they purportedly name objects with which the subject is acquainted. In Russell's view subjects are only acquainted with themselves and their present sense data (1917, p.214). (Hence there is a tension in the suggestion that logically proper names connect thought and the external world.)

Further, when a subject entertains a thought which involves a logically proper name, these are such that if one thinks one is entertaining such a thought, then necessarily, this is the case. And, the identity of the thought entertained is determined by the identity of the object thought of (the object being an item of the subject's experience). Thus, suppose a subject entertains a thought concerning a sense datum, e.g. "This red patch", since it refers to an experience of the subject, the subject "cannot be in error" (Russell, 1956, p.130) first, that he is thinking, and (b) what it is that he is thinking (cf. Sainsbury, 1979, p.26).[9]

In his logical atomist theory Russell proposes that names are the basic units of meaning (e.g. Russell, 1956, p.197). Typically, an atomic or, singular proposition consists of a name and a predicate, e.g. Fa, where "F" names a property and "a" names an object. Such singular propositions are combined via the use of logical connectives to generate molecular propositions; these latter propositions derive their meaning from the singular propositions of which they are composed.

So the meaningfulness of sentences in natural language ultimately depends upon the relation between names and objects with which subjects are acquainted. It is in this sense that the theory can be described as reference-based. But as noted, the objects concerned are not tables, chairs and so on, but are a peculiar species of objects: sense data.

As it stands then, it is not obvious that Russell's semantic theory, as described here, is of any use to the externalist. According to the theory the meaningfulness of expressions and thoughts derives ultimately from the reference relation which is supposed to hold between logically proper names and sense data. Subjects' understanding of expressions depends, again ultimately, on acquaintance with the objects to which logically proper names refer.[10]

46

So it appears that, in Russell's theory, the intentional states of subjects do not depend in any way upon the world which the subject inhabits. The existence of the external world is not a necessary condition for a subject to undergo intentional states; all that is necessary, it seems, is that the subject be acquainted with his own sense data - hence the theory as outlined so far seems more congenial to internalism than to externalism.

However, as indicated at the start of this chapter, some theorists have focused their attention on the Russellian idea of a range of psychological states whose individuation and existence conditions require the existence of a range of objects; such thoughts are described by Evans as "Russellian" (Evans, 1982, p.71).

Further, it is supposed by some philosophers (Evans 1982; McDowell, 1986), in a departure from Russell, that the range of Russellian thoughts are not individuation-dependent upon sense data but on what it is more usual to call objects i.e. tables, chairs, persons and so on (cf. McDowell, 1986; Evans, 1982; Sainsbury, 1986, pp.220-221). There is some textual support for such an interpretation (see next note) but, as will be seen shortly, even if Russell is interpreted in such a way, the resulting position which we may label "Russell's Constituency Thesis" requires modification if it is to be useful to externalists.

Russell's constituency thesis

Although Russell's statements of his logical atomist theory indicate that the objects to which logically proper names correspond are sense data, there are passages in which he appears to say, concerning the relationship between thoughts and objects, that ordinary objects feature amongst the constituents of thoughts. E.g., Russell does say in a letter to Frege that "Mont Blanc itself is a component part of what is actually asserted in the proposition "Mont Blanc is more than 4,000 metres high"" (quoted in Salmon and Soames, 1988, p.57).[11]

In Russell's Constituency Thesis it is held that objects standardly regarded as distinct from thoughts feature as components of those thoughts (cf. Russell, quoted in Salmon and Soames, 1988, p.57). The thesis might appear to be congenial to externalism since it may be claimed to ensure the required constitutive relation between intentional states and aspects of the environment of the subject. If the object is a component of the psychological state the existence of the state depends upon the existence of the object, and the individuation conditions of the state are similarly dependent upon it.

By way of a test for establishing a criterion of what it is for a thought to be constitutively related to aspects of the world of its subject it may prove useful to reconsider the following three possible situations in which a subject S makes a judgement concerning an object O (cf. ch.1 above also): (a) in which S perceives O, (b) in which S perceives an object which appears identical to O but is numerically distinct from O, and (c) in which S has the illusion of seeing O - say, he's hallucinating - but in which there is no perceptual contact with O. (Cf. Blackburn, 1984, pp.312-313.)

It appears to be the case that Russell's Constituency Thesis ensures that S only has a thought concerning O in situation (a), in which he is actually perceiving O. In cases (b) and (c) O cannot be regarded as a constituent of S's psychological state since objects other than O are constituents of his thoughts. Russell's thesis thus seems to imply externalism. But as it stands the theory requires modification due to at least three weaknesses in it.

First, it is strongly counter-intuitive. It has the consequence that at least part of the thoughts of a subject are not located where the body of that subject is (cf. Macdonald, 1990). Consider the suggestion that the thought which S entertains about the man Bryan Robson includes as a constituent Robson himself. So a component of S's thought, Bryan Robson, occurs at a location distinct from the location at which S is situated.[12]

Second, the thesis entails a conception of the psychological which is insufficiently fine-grained (cf. McDowell, 1986, p.142). As noted in the earlier discussion of Fregean cognitive theory, explanations of action require reference to agents' conceptions of objects, states of affairs, objects, events and so on. For example, suppose S hears noises in the kitchen late at night. He suspects that there is a burglar in the house. He goes downstairs and strikes the burglar. But when S switches on the light he discovers that the person who he has struck is his wife: there is no burglar. S's action and his subsequent remorse can be explained by reporting that he conceived of his wife as an unwelcome intruder, he believed her to be a burglar.

In Russell's Constituency Thesis the object which is a constituent of S's thoughts when, say, he sees a shadowy figure creeping about his kitchen is, in our example, S's wife. Assuming S does not beat his wife and in the light of S's remorse it is problematic to explain S's action in Russell's Constituency Thesis since by that S believed that he was hitting his wife (see, e.g. Russell, 1956, p.245). Hence the charge may be made that the thesis is insufficiently fine-grained and has no role to play in explanations of action (McDowell makes this point (McDowell, 1986, p.142)).

Third, an internalist might recruit epistemic considerations to argue that throughout test cases (a), (b) and (c) there is a single type of psychological state instantiated by S in all three cases; perhaps narrow content may be recruited to play such a role (cf. Blackburn, 1984, ch.9).[13]

So it should be clear that Russell's own proposals either (i) do not lend themselves to externalist interpretation due to his view that the referents of logically proper names are sense data; or (ii) are not congenial to a plausible externalism due to problems with Russell's Constituency Thesis. But McDowell (and Evans) draws attention to the possibility of combining certain aspects of Russell's view with aspects of the Fregean account.

McDowell's construal of Russell-Frege

McDowell refers to

> [A] conception of object-dependent thought extended outside Russell's restriction and enriched with Fregean fineness of grain (McDowell, 1986, p.163).

The proposal appears to be to combine aspects of the views of Russell and Frege in order to arrive at a theory of content which is congenial to externalism. In Russell's semantic theory, as described above, it seems to be the case that the referential base for the theory lies in the relationship of acquaintance between subjects and sense data: logically proper names refer to the latter. McDowell suggests that the acquaintance relation should be "extracted" (1986,p.140) from such an epistemological setting so that it is envisaged to apply to what it is more usual to describe as objects - i.e. tables, chairs etc. This is what is meant by conceiving of a class of object-dependent thoughts which lie beyond "Russell's restriction" - i.e. they apply to objects other than sense data. If that is allowed, what are left are a range of thoughts which are both existence and individuation dependent upon the objects thought of.[14] Since such thoughts are "enriched with Fregean fineness of grain" (ibid.) they are not open to one of the major problems which was seen to beset Russell's Constituency Thesis (i.e. that concerning the necessity of a role for agent's conceptions in action explanation).

McDowell points to two problems which stem from the adoption of such a strategy, each of which relates to the nature of the acquaintance relation as this is apparently conceived of by Russell, and each of which can be overcome in his view.

The first problem concerns the objects of acquaintance. As we have seen, construing these as sense data is more congenial to internalism than to externalism. McDowell suggests that the acquaintance relation be considered to hold between subjects and objects as these are ordinarily conceived. Further, McDowell suggests that a distinction is made between the terms ""figure in" [and] "be a constituent of"" (1986, p.146). The latter expression suggests a position such as Russell's Constituency Thesis and which is objectionable on grounds given earlier. But the former expression, McDowell suggests, is "[A] natural way of insisting on object-dependence" (ibid.); that is to say, the latter expression claims individuation-dependence but not (literal) constitution.

A second problem identified by McDowell stems from certain epistemological properties of the acquaintance relation as this is conceived of by Russell. Russell held that subjects' knowledge of the objects of acquaintance is infallible. McDowell plausibly regards this as too strong when the acquaintance relation is taken outside of Russell's restriction: acceptance of Russell's view would entail that subjects could not make perceptual errors. So in McDowell's hands the acquaintance relation is weakened to accommodate the possibility of perceptual error (McDowell,1986, p.141). It may be pointed out that there is no necessary connection between acquaintance and infallibility. So there seems nothing objectionable in principle to McDowell's strategy here (see also Sainsbury, 1986, pp.220-221 for a similar claim).

We have seen, then, that both Frege and Russell put forward semantic theories which have implications for the individuation of psychological states. Frege's theory is construed as reference based by Evans (1982; also, McDowell 1986, and McCulloch, 1989), and object-dependent Fregean Thoughts lend themselves for recruitment in explanations of action due to Frege's sense/reference distinction: the distinction allows room for agent's conceptions of what is the case.

Russell's semantic theory is also reference-based, but the relata of the reference relation differ from those which obtain in Frege's theory. Further, sense does not feature in the Russellian account (in as much as logically proper names are deemed not to have sense by Russell (e.g. 1956, p.245)).

What has impressed McDowell (and Evans) are aspects of Russell's account of an acquaintance relation between subjects and the objects they think about. In Russell's hands, the acquaintance relation grounds the epistemological relationship between subjects and their own experiences: the items subjects are acquainted with are such that they are not possible in the absence of the relata of those thoughts.

McDowell and Evans seek to marry a reference-based interpretation of Fregean semantics with a Russellian acquaintance relation tailored in the way described above in order to meet the requirements of the position described in the quotes from McDowell (given above, 1986, p.163) and Evans (quoted at the start of this section). The outcome is a position in which certain thoughts are held to be object-dependent in a way congenial to externalism.

2. Explanatory motivations for externalism (I): perceptual content [15]

In this set of motivations we look at an argument provided by Burge (1986a; 1988a) to the effect that externalism is true for perceptual content. "Perceptual content" here has a similar import to "representational content"; that is to say, it concerns perceptual states where these have contents which purport to represent features of the environment of the subject (cf. Burge, 1986a, p.3).

Burge suggests that the thought experiments of the kind described above (ch.1) apply to what he terms "higher cognitive capacities" (1986a, p.26) - e.g. judging and reasoning. But the argument he presents for externalism with respect to perceptual content is intended to apply to a more basic level of cognitive capacities.

Of such a level, Evans writes "The informational states which a subject acquires through perception are non-conceptual, or non-conceptualised. Judgements based upon such states necessarily involve conceptualisation..." (1982, p.227). We will be looking at Evans' distinction between conceptual and nonconceptual states later in the essay (ch.9). But, for now, it may be noted that Burge's argument is centred on what Evans would term "nonconceptual states"; these are perceptual states. Burge's claim is that such states are individuated externalistically. (I am indebted to Davies (1991) here.) Those states which Evans describes as "conceptual states" (op.cit.) are those which figure in specifications of the outcomes of what Burge terms the "higher cognitive capacities" (1986a, p.26).

Specifications of perceptual states which are congenial to internalism do seem to be available. Such specifications may include references to patterns of light and retinal states caused by these (so-called "grey arrays" (cf. Burge, 1988a; Marr, 1982; Segal, 1989b)) as opposed to references to environmental features. It is towards specifications of states which arise from such retinal states to which the externalist argument is directed. A perceptual content can be said to be a psychological state which arises from a computation or series of computations performed on patterns of retinal stimulations by the visual system (see esp. Marr, op.cit.; Eysenck and Keane, 1990, ch.2). Burge's strategy is to argue that specifications of the individuation conditions of at least some perceptual states make essential reference to aspects of the environment of the subject. If true, this argument conflicts with internalism with respect to perceptual content since internalists would argue that the individuation conditions of such states need not make reference to features of the environment of the subject (cf. Blackburn, 1984, ch.9; Forbes, 1987; Searle, 1983, p.230).

With reference to the three test cases referred to earlier (i,e where there is actual perception of an object O; perception of a duplicate of O; and an illusion of perceiving O); the internalist position would be that a subject can undergo a perceptual state with the same type of perceptual content in each of the three cases - the genuine, the counterfeit, and the empty. Let us turn now to the details of Burge's argument.

Burge provides both a general argument for his position (1986a, pp.39-43; 1988a), and supports this with an account of a successful theory in cognitive psychology (Marr's theory of vision (Marr, 1982)). I provide Burge's general argument first and give an outline of Marr's theory in discussion of a response to Burge offered by Segal (1989b).

In his "Cartesian error and the objectivity of perception" (1988a) Burge constructs the following argument.

1. "Perceptual experience represents or is about objects...that are objective" (ibid. p.69).
2. "[We] have perceptual representations...that specify particular objective types of objects, properties, or relations as such" (ibid.).
3. "[Some] perceptual types that specify objective types of objects, properties, and relations as such do so partly because of relations that hold between the perceiver (or at least members of the perceiver's species) and instances of those objective types" (ibid. p.70).

The first premise says that there is always a possibility present of misperception. This is partly what objectivity consists in for Burge: the possibility of error.

The second premise claims that specifications of perceptual representations include references to external objects (and "properties and relations" (ibid.)). So a description of such a representation will include reference to, say, environmental features of a specified type. Descriptions of such types are contrasted with internalistic descriptions of such representations, e.g. "whatever normally causes this sort of perceptual representation" (Burge, ibid.). In the latter case the expression is said to refer to the experience of the perceiver and not, as in the former case, to the type of objective entity which normally causes the perceptual experience (ibid. pp.69-70).[16]

In the third premise Burge is claiming that at least some perceptual types are of the types they are due to the fact that subjects interact with actual instances of that particular type. (This comprises the main advance on premiss (ii).) So if, to take a relatively unproblematic example, a description of a subject's perceptual representation includes reference to the type cube, then this is because such a subject, or other members of his species, is actually perceptually related in some way to cubes.

By way of extending the argument, Burge asks us to suppose that a perceiving subject S "normally perceives" instances of a type of object O. In accordance with premise 1 there are occasional misperceptions; for example, S may mistake an instance of an object of type C for an O. Burge claims that premise 1 shows that the physical states of S can remain fixed - his retinal states will be of the same type since they will be stimulated by (caused by) the same type of light pattern - whether or not an instance of O or C is perceived; the fact of occasional error, misperception, indicates this. In misperceptions, S may have an experience as of perceiving an instance of O but this is not sufficient for S's actually perceiving an O.

Burge then conceives of a counterfactual situation in which S's physical states remain fixed, and in which Os do not occur in the environment inhabited by S and the members of S's species. In this counterfactual situation, as it is constructed by Burge, it is claimed that "the sort of proximal stimulations that are actually normally caused by instances of O are counterfactually normally caused by instances of C" (ibid. p.74). A "proximal stimulation" here, as I understand it, is what I described above as a "retinal state". It is a state which provides the brain with information from which a state which can be characterised in intentional language may be constructed.

Burge claims that premise 3 entitles him to conclude that, in the counterfactual situation, S "perceives a C as a C and not as an O" (ibid.). It appears that, in a particular perception of a C, the proximal stimulus, allegedly remains of the same type.[17] But the distal stimulus changes in the counterfactual situation. In that situation S is related to Cs and not to Os and, by premise 3, S cannot therefore be ascribed perceptual contents which include references to Os.

In short, then, Burge is arguing that at least some of the types employed to individuate perceptual contents are essentially related to features of the environment of their subjects. This claim is at odds with internalism with respect to such states since for the internalist they can be individuated without essential reference to parts of the environment of their subjects.

As stated so far the argument begs for an example; fortunately Burge obliges. In his example we are to construe Cs as thin cracks and Os as thin shadows. In one case, call it case one, both Os and Cs occur in S's environment, but the environment contains mostly Os and few Cs. Occasionally S mistakes a C for an O. Next, consider a counterfactual situation, case two, in which "there are no visible Os" (ibid. p.75). Burge concludes, by premiss 3, that

> In such a counterfactual situation, [S] would normally be visually representing Cs - relevantly small cracks - as Cs. [S] would never be visually representing, or misrepresenting, anything as an O....Counterfactually, [S's] intentional perceptual states are different: [S] sees Cs as Cs (ibid. p.76).

According to Burge, attributions of perceptual types to subjects make essential reference to the types of objects which subjects regularly and systematically interact with. In the light of this, despite the fact that the subject S instances the same physical state types (where these are individuated without reference to S's environment) in both the actual and counterfactual cases, the representational content of S's perceptual states is claimed to differ. The types of proximal stimulation experienced by S in both cases are the same but the "intentional perceptual states are different" (ibid.). What makes for the difference is that in case one S interacts largely with Os and not Cs; but in case two S largely interacts with Cs and not Os.

Burge's expression "intentional perceptual states" can be interpreted as a state which represents a feature (or features) of the environment of the subject. So, in the first case, an ascriber of perceptual content to S would employ the expression "S is perceiving an O" (or something with this general import), and this expression might feature in an explanation of some act performed by S. In the second case, such an ascription of perceptual content would employ the expression "S is perceiving a C" (again, or some similar phrase).

It should be fairly clear that what Burge has done is, in effect, to mount an argument for externalism with respect to perceptual content which is of the same form as the Twin Earth/Arthritis cases discussed earlier (chs. 1,2). In this Os/Cs example, the nonintentionally individuated physical states of the subject are kept constant, the physical environment is changed and the claim is made that perceptual content differs in actual and counterfactual cases (or, the argument could employ the Earth/Twin Earth device instead of the counterfactual case). It was pointed out above that Burge's argument centres on nonconceptual states as these are understood by Evans (1982, e.g. p.227).

The argument for externalism we turn to now focuses on what Evans terms "conceptual" states (ibid.). These are states of what may be termed the higher cognitive faculties; e.g. that faculty which engages in chains of reasoning (see Evans, ibid.).

3. Explanatory motivations for externalism (II)

Macdonald presents the case for an explanatorily motivated externalism in Macdonald (1990) and Macdonald (1992). In the first paper she outlines a theory of the relationship between mental and physical events - a token physicalist theory - which constitutes an ontological foundation for her version of externalism (the theory is set out in detail in her (1989)). I will describe that briefly first, and then give her arguments for externalism as these are presented in her 1992 paper.

Macdonald's token physicalism

Macdonald distinguishes four theses: (i) internalism, (ii) externalism, (iii) type externalism combined with token internalism, and (iv) type internalism combined with token externalism. She describes theses (iii) and (iv) as versions of, "weak externalism" (1990,p.388). (The term "type externalism" will be used here to describe Macdonald's position in preference to "weak externalism" to avoid confusion with weak externalism as this is understood by McGinn (1989).)[18]

For Macdonald, internalism is true for intentional state tokens but not for intentional state types. Internalism is true for a class of states if and only if descriptions of such states in terms of their individuation conditions do not violate the Solipsism Claim (p.3 above); so in Macdonald's view, the Solipsism Claim is true for intentional state tokens and false for intentional state types. According to her, descriptions of the individuation conditions of intentional state tokens are given by their physicalistic descriptions (see, e.g. 1990, p.401; 1989, p.216).

As far as I can determine, her position stems from the following commitments. (1) First, she endorses token physicalism, the doctrine that "every event is a physical event" (1989, p.96). (2) With respect to the relationship between token mental events and token physical events, she holds that token mental events are identical with token physical events. And she endorses a property exemplification theory of events (Macdonald, 1989; Kim, 1976) in which events are construed as exemplifications of properties at times in objects. She rejects token externalism on the grounds that (3) "[It] cannot be of the essence of any physical event that it be an exemplification of an intentional property"

55

(1990, p.402); and token externalism seems to conflict with this view.

Her token event identity theory is distinct from type-type identity theory since it rejects the view that there is a relationship of identity, or some other reductive relation, which obtains between psychological and physical properties. As we saw earlier (ch.1) type-type identity theorists assert a stronger relationship between mental and neurological types. On such a conception of the relationship between the mental and the neurological, instantiation of a particular neurological property type would be necessary and sufficient for instantiation of a particular intentional type. In Macdonald's version of token identity theory the relationship between mental and physical properties is less strong.

Further, in Macdonald's version of token identity theory a version of nonlocal supervenience is endorsed such that intentional types supervene upon the physical properties both within and beyond the body of the subject (see, e.g. 1990, p.404).

Since the individuation conditions of intentional state tokens are given by their physicalistic descriptions, and these conform to the Solipsism Claim, Macdonald's thesis counts as a version of token internalism.

Before we proceed to look at her arguments for type externalism, it is worth stating briefly her reasons for holding (3) and, hence, for rejecting token externalism (see also ch.10 sec.3 for arguments against token externalism). She offers two main reasons. The first reason seems to be that token externalism appears to be incompatible with a token event identity theory of the relationship between mental and physical events (e.g. 1990, pp.402-403). For example, if token externalism is true, the following argument appears to follow: if (i) (by token externalism) mental events are essentially individuation-dependent on features beyond subjects' bodies; and if (ii) neurophysiological events are not essentially individuation-dependent on features beyond subjects' bodies; then (iii) mental events cannot be identical with physical events.[19]

Macdonald's gives a second reason for holding (3).[20] This stems from the view that classification of (at least some) natural kinds is not determined by properties evident to unaided perceptions of instances of them. Standardly, the identities of such kinds are determined by their microstructures (e.g. the genetic make-up of the members of such kinds). The situation concerning the classification of natural kinds is contrasted with the situation concerning the classification of types of psychological states. She suggests that "[The basis of classifications of psychological states] namely intentional behaviour or action, and introspection, is one that we cannot conceive of as being systematically replaced by any other" (1990, p.403). Hence, in the case of phenomenal states, for example, the manner in which such states manifest themselves to their subjects seems essential to their individuation. But this seems not to be the case with respect to kinds such as gold and water; these types need not be determined by their observable properties.

It should be clear, then, that Macdonald's view cannot be regarded as full-blown (i.e. type and token) internalism since she claims that externalism is true for intentional types - type externalism. It is to her motivations for this view that we now turn.

Macdonald's explanatorily motivated (type) externalism

In Macdonald (1992), she sets out an argument against the view that types of psychological states are reducible to types of physical states. Her argument for that conclusion trades upon her version of externalism. It is her account of type externalism which is of most interest for purposes here, so I now turn to an exposition of her argument for that thesis as it is set out in Macdonald (1992).

She points out that internalism can be maintained in the face of Twin Earth cases via the proposal of a distinction between narrow and broad psychological states (cf. ch.1 above). In an internalism motivated by explanatory concerns it may be held that it is narrow psychological states which perform an explanatory role; psychological states individuated broadly, on the other hand, are not envisaged as having an explanatory role. Macdonald suggests that broad states concern "what is represented" whereas narrow states concern "how it is represented" (ibid.,p.137). So, from the internalist perspective as described by Macdonald, narrow states are said to characterise how agents conceive of states of affairs; and, further, to be the states referred to in explanations of action.

With respect to Twin Earth cases, Macdonald attempts to set aside one externalist response to the internalist claim that the Twins undergo token of the same types of psychological states. The response referred to is to deny that the actions of the Twins are of the same type, e.g. on the grounds that S, say, performs an act of the type *drinks water* but S* performs an act of the type *drinks water**. This response is ascribed to Evans (1982, p.203). Macdonald claims that the response does not work due to the plausibility of distinguishing between acts narrowly construed and acts broadly construed. Examples of the former include drinking and washing; examples of the latter include drinks water and drinks water*.

Macdonald concludes that the broad/narrow act-type distinction is a genuine one and so externalists cannot oppose internalism on the grounds that it is not. She writes,

What externalists must argue is that, even in cases where the act-types invoked in the explanans of intentional psychological explanations are narrowly construed, the types of which their causes are tokens,to do their explanatory work, must be individuated by reference to objects that exist beyond the confines of individuals' bodies (1992,pp.139-140).

The proposal is that externalists need to show that where narrow act types such as washing are recruited in adequate explanations of actions, explananda comprising only of narrow act types succeed as adequate explanations only in so far as they refer, perhaps tacitly, to features beyond the body of the subject.

In arguing for such a view, she then turns to an argument designed to show that explanation of action is essentially normative (as opposed to essentially causal (ibid., p.140)). The argument involves consideration of three kinds of explanations of action: (a) standard cases; and two kinds of nonstandard cases: (b) cases of actions based upon misperception, and (c) cases of actions based upon hallucinatory experiences.

With respect to (a), consider actions such as washing or eating. Macdonald denies that

[It is] plausible to say that the psychological types invoked in the explanans of any such explanation are ones whose referential components are idle (ibid.,p.141).

She argues that the intelligibility of explanations of such acts depends upon the existence of objects or kinds which occur beyond the body of the subject (cf. ibid.). The reason for this is, at least for some narrow act types, when they feature in explanations of action (e.g. washing), the explanations owe their intelligibility to the fact that they involve certain features of the subject's environment. So explanations of acts of washing considered as a narrow act type are intelligible given that subjects employ stuff in their environment to wash in. Washing can thus be regarded as a narrow act type; the intelligibility of explanations of acts of washing depends upon the availability of broad act types (e.g. washing in water) specifications of which involve reference to some stuff or other - e.g. the liquid subjects use to wash with.

The relationship between at least some narrow act types and the objects they involve is held to be normative. This is due to the fact that rational subjects can be expected to use, for example, water for washing given (i) that they believe that water gets things clean, and (ii) they desire to get things clean. So the narrow act type washing involves "not only beliefs and desires about the activity of washing,but also [beliefs and desires] about the kind of substance that it is appropriate to wash with" (ibid.).

With respect to (b) and (c), nonstandard explanations of actions, here Macdonald contends that how subjects conceive their immediate environment to be is not independent of how it actually is. She considers two examples to lend support to this contention. The first involves a case of misperception and the second involves an hallucinatory experience undergone by a subject.

Regarding (b) we are invited to consider a subject S who mistakes hydrochloric acid to be water. It is suggested that internalists will hold that S's action - say she places a hand into a sink of acid believing it to be water - will be explained by reference to how S conceives of the acid. The same claim may be made with respect to (c): it is how S conceives of the scene in front of her which explains her actions.[21]

In opposition to the internalist view, Macdonald proposes that "Even in cases like these [i.e. nonstandard action explanations]...the referential components of the relevant psychological types are not idle" (1992, p.142). This is due to the fact that the actions of the subjects must be categorised. Once this is done, given that the intelligibility of narrow act types requires the existence of an object appropriate for that kind of activity, reference to features of the environment of the subject is presumed (i.e. given that the intelligibility of the narrow act type washing depends upon the existence of something to wash with - e.g. water).[22]

So the claim is that in the case of misperception described above tacit reference is made both to water and to hydrochloric acid. This is due to its being the case that S's action is explicable due to certain of the properties of both these liquids. Since hydrochloric acid looks like water, it is possible to understand how a subject might be acting rationally and yet place her hand in some hydrochloric acid. And to explain her action, two act-types seem to be required; one which characterises what she intends to do (wash in water), and the other which characterises what she actually does (places her hand in some hydrochloric acid).[23]

With respect to the case where the subject has an hallucinatory experience, again, the act of the subject is explicable given that she believes that water is present in the sink.[24]

Given acceptance of her claims with regard to the need for a referential component in the explanations of action, Macdonald suggests that the possibility of drawing a plausible broad/narrow act distinction need not prohibit (type) externalism. To show why, she considers the Twin Earth case.

She distinguishes two responses to the internalist claim that the Twins undergo states of the same psychological type when they respectively desire water/water* (ibid., p.144). Macdonald provides two arguments for type externalism with respect to Twin Earth cases; let us consider these.

(1) In the first, it is proposed that Twin Earth cases are to be regarded as standard cases of action explanation. Further the possibility is considered that "[The] referential components of [S and S*'s] psychological state types play different explanatory roles in the explanations of their acts narrowly construed" (ibid.).

For example, suppose that the chemical differences between water and water* are such that the two liquids have different causal powers and this is revealed at high temperatures (cf. also Putnam, 1981, p.23) - say water* evaporates much more rapidly than water. If this were so, it can be envisaged that although water* may be the appropriate liquid on Twin Earth in which to wash, it would not be appropriate to make hot drinks with. Macdonald writes,

> [Even] though [S's and S*'s] acts of washing, narrowly construed, are type-identical, the role that XYZ plays with regard to other activities (such as drinking hot drinks made with it) justifies attributing an explanatory role to the referential component of psychological state types, broadly construed, involving XYZ, since it affects other activities which [S*] would be apt to engage in with that substance and inferential connections between beliefs which cause washing acts and beliefs which cause drinking acts (1992, p.144).

That is to say, differences in the causal properties of water* affect the suitability of water* to be involved in certain kinds of act (e.g. drinking hot drinks). Such differences would emerge when explanations of other kinds of action are undertaken. For example, suppose S* pours some water* into a kettle, mistaking it to be some other liquid, call it L*, which is normally used for making hot drinks on Twin Earth. S*'s act of pouring water* into a kettle would count as an act based on a misperception. This indicates that S mistook water* for L*.

S's performance of similar acts employing water would clearly not count as acts based on misperception since, on Earth, water is the liquid most used for making hot drinks with. So the respective narrow act types engaged in by S and S* are plausibly held to be typed by reference to different types of liquids - i.e. given the different causal properties of water and water*.

Hence, even when S and S* engage in the narrow act type washing, the referential components of their respective psychological states are not explanatorily idle. This is due to the fact that attributions of such narrow

60

act types are not independent of broad act types; these, in turn, are individuated by reference to an appropriate substance.

Consider Macdonald's second argument. (2) This proposes that Twin Earth cases be construed as nonstandard explanations of action - specifically that they be regarded as examples of actions based on misperception (ibid., p.145). Macdonald's proposal is that externalists need to motivate the view that even though the narrow act types engaged in by S and S* are of the same type, their referential components differ. She suggests that,

> The key to a solution is to see that the type identity of those actions is determined, not just by [S's and S*'s] actual behaviour in their actual environments, but also by their counterfactual behaviour across environments (ibid., p.145).

Thus, consider that S* is transported to Earth and S to Twin Earth. Suppose they each take their environments to be identical to those they have just left. It seems clear that S would behave in the same way towards water* as he did towards water, and that the same may be said of S* with respect to water. But what seems to be occurring in such a case is that S mistakes water* for water, and S* mistakes water for water*. Again, this is due to the perceptually discernible properties of the two liquids. So again, it seems plausible that explanations of the actions of S and S* will involve reference to two distinct liquids, and not just one.

The above two arguments, plus the more general considerations concerning explanation of action described above constitute the core of Macdonald's defence of (type) externalism in the face of Twin Earth cases. But she also recruits the points concerning action explanations to argue that Pierre-type cases are also best explained externalistically contrary to the claims of internalists (e.g. Loar, 1988a).

Macdonald on Pierre cases

Recall that in ch.1 above the Pierre case was said to motivate internalistic individuation of psychological states (types and tokens). From the internalist perspective, it is argued that Pierre's behaviour warrants ascription to him of two types of psychological states each of which capture how he conceives of London, and neither of which are individuation-dependent on factors beyond the body of Pierre.

Macdonald points out that to defeat internalism with respect to Pierre type cases, all the externalist needs to do is to show that the conceptions of London which are referred to in explanation of Pierre's actions (or, more correctly, his inaction) presuppose some reference to London. Externalists need not hold that "sameness of referential component is sufficient for sameness of psychological types" (1992,p.149). So room can still be made, within externalism, for subject's conceptions of e.g. cities to be individuation-dependent upon the object of those conceptions (cf. our earlier discussion of McDowell,1986).[25]

Macdonald's claim is that,

> [In] order to explain [the] mismatch between Pierre's actions and his beliefs, we need not only to refer to the differences in cognitive components, but also to represent those components as being traceable to a *single* object (1992, p.148).

The proposal is this. It can be acknowledged that Pierre conceives of London in different ways, but the fact that both his conceptions are of London explains why he fails to act in the way one would expect him to as a rational subject. So it is the fact that Pierre's conceptions of London are conceptions of London that explains his failure to act.

This, then, completes my exposition of Macdonald's explanatorily motivated (type) externalism. In the next chapter we give a brief recap of Macdonald's argument, then consider some internalist responses, and finally defend Macdonald's position against an objection from Burge-type thought experiments. For now we turn to consider responses to logico-semantic motivations for externalism.

Notes to chapter three

1. Frege writes, "[A] sentence expresses a thought" (Frege, (1892) p.36, in Salmon and Soames, 1988, p.36).

2. For the sake of brevity I will not address the question of what the sense and reference of predicative expressions (e.g. "...is red") are for Frege; I will presume that the reference of a predicate is its extension and that its sense is the way of thinking of that employed by a subject. It should be said though that the question is rather thorny but is not central to our immediate concerns. For information on this issue see Frege's letter to Husserl 24/5/1891 quoted by Wiggins in Wright (ed) 1984 p.126. Wiggins argues that the reference of a predicate is a concept and takes Frege to be denying that the reference of a predicate is its extension. Dummett insists that the reference of a predicate is a function and that Frege

assimilates concepts and functions (Dummett, 1981, pp.234-236, p.253).

3. These include singular terms, predicates, complete sentences, expressions capable of standing as complete sentences, and sentential structure. The gloss on the Principle of Compositionality provided here is intended to cover two components of the Principle: (a) that the reference of a sentence is a function of the reference of its semantically relevant component parts; and (b) that the sense of a sentence is a function of the senses of its semantically relevant component parts.

4. Of course, the latter second-level function can be defined in terms of the former.

5. I am indebted to McCulloch (1989, ch.1) for this way of explicating Fregean semantics.

6. McCulloch refers to "Thoughts...which essentially concern or contain the object which would be referred to by the thinker of the Thought in giving an accurate expression of it. In other words, the [view] is that such a Thought only exists...if the object exists" (McCulloch,1989, p.193).

7. According to Evans, a further perceived merit of Fregean theory is that a reference based Fregean semantic theory allegedly meshes well with a Davidsonian theory of natural language meaning (see Evans, 1982, ch.1; McDowell, 1977). Both place considerable emphasis on the Principle of Compositionality since it has the consequence that the truth conditions of sentences are determined systematically by the semantically relevant components of those sentences (cf. McDowell, 1977, p.141). The Davidsonian theory seeks to define meaning in terms of truth, and truth in terms of satisfaction. Named objects satisfy or fail to satisfy predicates accordingly as the object named has the property ascribed to it or not. The point being that the Davidsonian theory is perceived as being reference based in a way which is congenial to a Fregean semantic theory. Davidson makes use of Tarski's work in defining truth for extensional languages. Both Tarski and Davidson employ the idea of sequences of objects which are, in a way analogous to Frege's use of functions, presented to predicates which they satisfy or not. With regard to the question of the place of sense in such a theory, Evans and McDowell say that the axioms of the theory will include clauses such as ""a" stands for a"; ""b" stands for b"...and so on for the singular terms of the language. But such a theory is supposed by Evans and McDowell to be bound up with the attempt to provide "a theory knowledge of which would suffice

for understanding a language" (McDowell, 1977, p.141). However, a speaker may be aware that "a" names a without being aware that "b" also names a. His lack of knowledge of this may be displayed in his behaviour and his failure to make certain inferences. Evans and McDowell say that clauses such as "a" stands for a will "display" the sense of such expressions. McDowell says that clauses stating the references of names "...give - or as good as give - [their] sense[s]" (ibid., p.144; also Evans, 1982, pp.26, 35). These, remarks may be charged with being obscure but they are supposed to allay any ontological scruples one might have concerning the ontological status of senses, but their import will not be pursued further here.

8.   There are of course objections to Russell. For example the suggestion has been made that the utterance "The present King of France is bald" is neither true nor false (see Strawson, 1950).

9.   For Russell, examples of logically proper names are "I" and "This" (1917, p.214) - though in a note on the same page Russell says only "This" counts as a logically proper name.

10. Not necessarily their own acquaintance: Russell holds that so-called knowledge by description is dependent upon knowledge acquired from acquaintance with things (see e.g. 1917, p.207).

11. It is not wholly clear to me how Russell intends his constituency claims to be taken. See for example, (1917, pp.210-211). Reading of this suggests that Russell means by "constituent" something other than what it might literally be taken to mean; for example Russell might just mean "words" by "constituents". (But see Sainsbury (1986, p.225) who rejects such a suggestion.)

12. Macdonald (1990) suggests that such views on the nature of the relationship between the thoughts and the brain are incompatible with physicalism (both type-type and token-token) with respect to mental states.

13. It is worth making a comment at this point concerning the relationship between what has been described here as Russell's Constituency Thesis and Russell's Principle of Acquaintance. The constituency thesis conjoined with the Principle of Acquaintance can be said to result in a nonconceptual theory of mind (cf. Russell, 1917, p.212; Sainsbury, 1986, pp.227ff.) in which there is no role for posits such as concepts, mental representations or ideas. This means acquaintance is nonconceptual for Russell. The difficulties with his view include the criticisms of the Constituency Thesis which have just been discussed and further difficulties concerning the evident capacity of subjects to think of one object

in two ways (e.g. S thinks of Robson as Captain of Manchester United; T thinks of Robson as Captain of England). But perhaps more seriously, it has the consequence that the acquaintance relation seems insufficiently constrained since, on the nonconceptual construal, it means animals to whom we would not necessarily wish to ascribe thoughts are ascribed thoughts simply by virtue of their perceiving objects. In the Principle of acquaintance Russell, links perception and understanding (e.g. 1912,p.32; 1917, p.200), On the nonconceptual construal of Russell's overall theory of mind (i.e. conjoined with the Constituency thesis) what should clearly be a contingent connection between perception and higher cognitive faculties such as understanding, becomes a necessary connection; thus whereas, say, perceiving O should be a necessary but not a sufficient condition for having thoughts about O and understanding the term "O", the construal of Russell's view presented here has the consequence that perceiving O is sufficient both for having thoughts about O and for understanding the term "O". Evans (1982) construes Russell's principle so that conceptual elements are required in subjects if they are to be deemed capable of entering into the acquaintance relation with objects. In Evans' hands perceptual acquaintance is not sufficient for satisfaction of the acquaintance relation; but on one construal of Russell perception does appear to be sufficient.

14. Recall that this was the case for Russell since the objects thought of are sense data (cf. Russell, 1956, p.130).

15. I concentrate largely on visual perception in this discussion.

16. Of course, in a way, Burge may be thought to beg the question here. He takes "...this sort of perceptual representation" to be doing the main referential work in the internalistic expression cited. It might be objected that the quantifier expression "whatever normally causes..." also does referential work. But Burge can be defended. Recall the point that quantifier-expressions and singular terms refer to distinct types of entity (cf. McCulloch, 1989, pp.12-17); and ch.3, section 1 above.

17. In the way that, for example a duck/rabbit line drawing may be said to cause instances of the same type of retinal state but the perceptual content which arises from such a state can be said to represent a duck or to represent a rabbit.

18. Crudely, Fodor holds (i) (see his 1987); Burge holds (ii) (see, e.g. Burge, 1986a); Macdonald holds (iii); and Forbes holds (iv) (e.g. Forbes, 1987). Also, see note 1, ch.1 for McGinn's strong/weak externalism distinction.

19. I.e. since if two particulars are identical they must share all properties, but a mental event M may be individuation-dependent on features beyond the body of the thinker, whilst the neurophysiological event N with which M is identical is not - assuming that neurophysiological events do not have individuation conditions which make essential reference to features beyond the bodies of their subjects.

20. She also describes (3) as the view that "[No] physical event is essentially an exemplification of an intentional (or any other) mental property" (Macdonald, 1990, p.402).

21. Internalists may appeal to the notion of conceptual role here (cf. ch.1 above). Hence, if a Twin Earth case is set up in which S is faced with a sink containing acid and S* with a sink containing water, it could be held that their respective psychological states are of the same type due to their instancing the same type of conceptual role. Alternatively, mind-brain supervenience may be appealed to in support of the same conclusion; as indeed might epistemic motivations for internalism.

22. Macdonald writes "The issue of what type of action is being performed, even when narrowly construed, is not independent of the issue of what kind of substance, phenomenon, or object is typically appropriate for that type of activity" (1992, p.142).

23. Another example may be this. A subject S lives in a house in which the bathroom has white walls. Periodically, small insects enter the bathroom and attach themselves to the bathroom walls. The paintwork in the bathroom is far from perfect and there are many black dots on the bathroom walls; these are around the same size as the insects. S intends to swat an insect but instead strikes a black dot. His act is explicable given that the insects look like black dots on the paintwork.

24. Analogously, the actions of a subject who swats the bathroom wall having hallucinated that there is an insect there, are explicable by reference to what it is he is trying to do.

25. A thesis which did claim that identity of referential component is sufficient for identity of psychological type would be vulnerable to the criticisms which beset Russell's constituency thesis.

4 Responses to motivations for externalism

1. Responses to logico-semantic motivations for externalism

Fregean theory as recruited by McDowell (1986) and Evans (1982) (plus McCulloch, 1989) combines a reference-based semantics with the view that Thoughts ascribed to (and entertained by) subjects in explanations of their actions are themselves reference-based in a way congenial to externalism. There are a number of worries which a theorist unsympathetic to an externalism motivated in this way might have so far. Four of these will be discussed now.

First, what is the relationship between the two parts of the one overarching Fregean theory? Recall that it is the alleged systematicity and the theory of logical validity which are foremost among the presumed virtues of the Fregean account. Let it be conceded that these virtues apply to extensional languages: languages in which the Principle of Compositionality applies relatively unproblematically (e.g. the language of set theory). An essential characteristic of extensional languages is the rule that expressions which refer to the same objects can be exchanged without disturbing the truth value of the expressions in which they occur; call this the Substitution Principle.[1]

So the truth value of the sentence "Russell is the author of "On Denoting"" is preserved if "The author of Introduction to Mathematical Philosophy" is substituted for the name "Russell". But clearly, the Substitution Principle is bound to failure when we introduce cognitive terms such as believes, desires, fears and so on - so-called propositional attitude verbs (Russell, 1950, p.65). Subjects are not omniscient about, say, the life and works of Bertrand Russell and so when essential aspects of the cognitive theory are subjected to the constraints which are operant in the semantic theory it turns out that systematicity breaks down.

Further, the Principle of Compositionality appears to fail in contexts in which one belief is embedded in another, e.g. as in S believes that W believes that p. On the standard construal of Fregean theory contexts such as these are a sense short since, allegedly, the customary sense of p becomes the referent of "W believes that...". This leaves the whole expression "S believes that W believes that p" short of a sense and so threatens the Compositionality Principle where this is construed as including the principle that the sense of sentence is a function of the senses of its component parts.

It seems evident, then, that severe problems for the Fregean arise when constraints to which the semantic part of the overall theory are applied to the cognitive part of the theory.

Here is a second apparent difficulty for the Fregean theory. Another virtue, besides its systematicity, of Fregean semantic theory is its account of logical validity (cf. McCulloch, 1989, ch.1). But it is clearly the case that human subjects do not reason validly when cognitive verbs are employed to characterise their thoughts. For example, from (i) "S believes that all politicians are selfish"; and (ii) "S believes that Major is a politician"; it cannot be concluded that (iii) "S believes that Major is selfish" since S might simply have inconsistent beliefs: (i) and (ii) might both be true and (iii) false.

Thirdly, the Fregean account relies upon an objectual interpretation of quantification, one which is necessarily object-invoking. But there is at least one other theory of quantification which is not object-invoking - namely, a substitutional interpretation of quantification (see, e.g. Haack, 1978, pp.42-43).

And fourthly, internalists might suggest that epistemic motivations for internalism combined with some of the features of Russell's views actually serve to motivate internalism rather than externalism. For example, consider the following internalist response to the logico-semantic motivations offered above (ch.3 sec.1).

What is at issue between internalists and externalists is the question of whether what lies outside the head of the subject bears any constitutive relevance to the psychological states of the subject: internalists say no; externalists say yes. By way of an attempt to establish a rough criterion of when psychological states could be said to be the same, three test situations were outlined earlier in discussion of what was described as Russell's Constituency Thesis. Let us briefly reconsider those three situations - three possible worlds: (a) the actual, (b) the counterfeit, and (c) the empty.

Suppose S in (a) is perceptually acquainted with O at t; and in (b) is acquainted with O' at t; and in (c), in an empty world where the only occupant is S, S has a perceptual experience as of O at t. It seems at this stage to be open to an internalist to say that there is indeed something in common, psychologically, in S in each of the three situations. If that is correct, then it seems that in the cases of acquaintance and pseudo-acquaintance (i.e. in the empty world) described above there is a type of psychological state instantiated by S the nature of which is not constitutively determined by aspects of the world which S inhabits - namely, the presence of O.

But if acquaintance with O, is indeed a necessary condition for entertaining a thought in which a name for O appears, by the principle of acquaintance, it should not be possible for S in cases (b) and (c) to have a thought about O - that is, assuming O does not exist in their respective worlds and has never existed there and no inhabitant of their respective worlds has ever come into contact either with O or with anyone who has been in perceptual contact with O (of course, in case (c) the latter provisos are rather redundant).

These considerations can be taken to suggest the possibility that S thinks in the same kind of way in cases (a), (b) and (c) (cf. Blackburn, 1984, ch.9; Forbes, 1987). Internalists who make such a move may even be tempted to recruit Fregean Thoughts, construed in such a way that they are not object-dependent, but designed to characterise S's psychological state in each of the three cases referred to.

Some theorists have described Fregean Thoughts construed in such a way as descriptive thoughts, universal thoughts, or object-independent thoughts (cf. Blackburn ibid.; Peacocke, 1983, p.188; McDowell, 1986). These terms are intended to describe the claim that there is something psychologically constant instantiated by S throughout (a), (b) and (c). Let us describe such thoughts as "descriptive thoughts"; why are they so-called?

Recall that in ch.3 (section 1) it was seen how Russell analyses singular terms (with the exception of logically proper names) via the employment of his theory of descriptions. It was noted in that discussion that names, in effect, are parsed into descriptions which objects in the domain concerned satisfy or not. Characterisations of so-called descriptive thoughts do not contain expressions which have the logical form of singular terms. Rather, characterisations of descriptive thoughts contain only predicate expressions, the identity sign, connectives, quantifiers and variables. In other words, descriptive thoughts are, or approximate, instantiations by subjects of types of narrow contents (see ch.1 section 3).

The proposal that descriptive thoughts can be employed to supplant object dependent Fregean Thoughts may usefully be described as The Descriptivist Strategy. Such a strategy may be deployed to defeat externalism motivated by logico-semantic considerations of the kind described so far in this chapter. Consider how the strategy might be thought to work in the consideration of two types of thoughts, natural kind thoughts and demonstrative thoughts.

With respect to natural kind thoughts, consider cases (a) and (b) (ignore (c) since this would complicate the discussion unnecessarily). Suppose cases (a) and (b) are construed as the Twin Earth example outlined in chapter one. We have S on Earth who perceives O, where "O" refers to a natural kind, say, water; and we have S* on Twin Earth who perceives O', where "O'" refers to water*. A descriptive thought-type employed to characterise the thoughts - e.g. desires - of S and S* might be the following: S (S*) desires the stuff, whatever it is, that quenches thirst, is transparent, washes clothes...and so on.

The description, ideally, from the internalist perspective, should just determine water/water*, and not, say hydrochloric acid, and should be a finite description. Schematically it may be expressed thus S (S*) desires $(\exists x \ Fx \wedge Gx \wedge Hx...)$ (where "...F" stands for "...is thirst-quenching", "...G" stands for "...is transparent", and "...H" stands for some other property satisfied both by water and water* (cf. Fodor, 1981, p.111; Peacocke, 1981; Forbes, 1987).[2]

With respect to demonstrative thoughts: Suppose S thinks demonstratively of a vase O on Earth, a duplicate of O on Twin Earth, and that in the Empty World, S takes himself to be thinking demonstratively of O. We saw in chapter one above that there are epistemic motivations for regarding S's thoughts as of the same type in these three kinds of case. The Descriptivist Strategy provides a formal characterisation of the type of psychological state S may be said to undergo. E.g. Blackburn suggests that S's psychological states could be of the following type: "(D (MP) is F)" where "F" stands for "...is pretty" and the expression preceding "F" stands for "'the determinant of this mode of presentation'" (Blackburn, 1984, p.315). Alternatively, S's psychological state may be said to instance the type "$(\forall x) \ (Fx \wedge Gx) \rightarrow Hx$" where "...F" stands for "...is the cause of this psychological state", "...G" for some property which the experience instances (e.g. "...is red" if the vase is red), and "...H" stands for "...is pretty".

The main point here is that alternative formal characterisations of S's psychological states seem to be available. Further, and crucially, they do not feature singular terms, but descriptions and so are states which favour internalism and not externalism.

Also, since such descriptivist characterisations of thoughts seem better able to cope with situations in which subjects entertain thoughts about non-existent objects, it seems that,if anything, logico-semantic

70

considerations favour internalism rather than externalism. What externalists require are motivations other than those which stem solely from logico-semantic considerations.

The intention in these elaborations of the internalist response to logico-semantic motivations for externalism has been to show how internalist responses to externalism may make use of the notion of a descriptive thought. Further, it might be noted that these descriptive thoughts are themselves motivated by aspects of theses proposed by Russell and Frege. This indicates that the work of these theorists cannot be regarded as the sole preserve of externalists.

The view that there is a class of object-dependent thoughts enters the conception referred to by McDowell in two ways: first via Fregean semantic theory construed in such a way that referring expressions cannot have sense in the absence of their having reference; and second, via the Russellian notion of singular thoughts.

A significant problem with recruiting the Fregean considerations as a motivation for externalism arises when the semantic theory is conjoined with the cognitive theory. Employment of sense in the latter, though necessary from the viewpoint of explaining the actions of subjects, creates problems for the systematicity of the semantic theory (e.g. the substitution principle fails etc. - it should be said that some responses to such problems are available to defenders of the Fregean account (see Forbes, 1990)).

The attempt to recruit Russell's conception of object dependent thought - applied outside Russell's Restriction - faces problems similar to those faced by Fregean semantic theory shorn of the notion of sense when it comes to the explanation of action; namely, how to account for failures of inference on the part of subjects when they are faced with co-referential expressions. Other problems also beset what was described above as Russell's constituency thesis.

Finally, it has been noted that internalists may recruit aspects of Russell's own response to difficulties presented by empty names for the Fregean semantic theory. The internalist suggestion is that the contents of psychological states can be characterised and individuated without the use of singular referring expressions. Such characterisations of psychological states can be aligned with narrow content as this was described earlier (ch.1).

71

2. Explanatory motivations I (Burge's argument): two criticisms, and two defences

As might be expected Burge's argument has not met with universal acceptance and it has been subjected to a number of criticisms (see Matthews, 1988; McGinn, 1989, pp.58-99; Segal, 1988b). Two of these criticisms seem particularly powerful and it is these which will be considered next. The first criticism may be termed The Disjunctive Content Objection (the term is borrowed from Davies, 1991). And the second criticism is set out by McGinn (1989, pp.58-99), call this, simply, McGinn's Objection.

The first criticism levelled at Burge's argument points out that Burge's example does nothing to motivate the claim that the intentional perceptual states of S differ in the actual and counterfactual situations (Matthews, op.cit. p.83; Segal op.cit.). That is to say, Burge's third premise, as it stands, might well look attractive to a fully paid up externalist but opponents require a motivation for adopting such a view. Such opponents might point out that a more general disjunctive perceptual type such as an O/C or a "crackdow" could be employed to specify S's perceptual content (Segal, op.cit.; Matthews, op.cit. p.83).

The disjunctive content objection

Segal (1989b) mounts just such an argument against Burge's externalism with respect to perceptual content. The suggestion is that Burge has not done enough to show that the perceptual content of the subject differs in the counterfactual situation. It was noted above (ch.3 section 2) that all Burge needs to show is that the perceptual content of the subject does vary across actual and counterfactual situations; Burge claims that he does not need to specify what the perceptual content of the subject would be in the counterfactual environment (Burge, 1988a, p.96). But since Burge claims that his proposals are supported by the scheme of individuation employed in Marr's theory of vision (Marr, 1982), it might reasonably be expected that the difference in perceptual content posited by Burge would be supported by explanatory practise. Segal argues that when this is done the theory of perceptual content discussed by Burge in support of his claim that psychology as practised is not internalistic - Marr's theory of vision (Marr, 1982) - motivates a position for which internalism is true and externalism false.

Segal's criticism amounts to a query of Burge's second premiss: "[We] have perceptual representations...that specify particular objective types of objects as such" (Burge, 1988a, p.69). For Burge, in his Os/Cs

72

example, since the subject S and his fellows regularly interact with Cs and since Os do not occur in the counterfactual environment S's perceptual types are specified with reference to Cs. Segal claims that a plausible case can be mounted for the view that the perceptual types of S should be individuated with respect to a more general type - a disjunctive type - O/C.

Segal's case begins with a recapitulation of Marr's theory. In this, 3-D representations of objects are said to be constructed by the visual system from retinal states where these consist of light patterns falling on nerve cells (receptor cells) in the eye. These light patterns are arranged in a particular way - e.g. so that edges are emphasised. This representation of light patterns is described by Marr as a "primal sketch" (Marr, 1985, pp.103-126). From the primal sketch a 2.5D sketch of the likely shape and depth of the object causing the retinal stimulation is constructed (cf. ibid. p.124). And from the 2.5D sketch a "3-D model representation" (ibid.) of the object is constructed.

At each stage, more restrictive interpretations are made by the visual system in an attempt to narrow down the range of possible causes of the stimulus. As Segal puts it:

> At each stage what is inferred from the information explicit in the representations [i.e. in stages one, two and three] that are operated upon goes beyond anything available from that information alone (1989b, p.192).

Marr explains this aspect of the visual system by positing the presence of "a priori assumptions" (Marr, 1982, p.219) which are built (hardwired) into the system.[3] The following is an example of such an assumption,

> [(i)] The visible world can be regarded as being composed of smooth surfaces having reflectance functions whose spatial structure may be elaborate (Marr, 1982, p.219; see also p.46; and Segal, 1989b, p.193).

Segal makes the point that since the theory of vision is an empirical theory it will be subject to empirical constraints - e.g. it generates predictions which can be tested. A central feature of the evaluation of a theory of vision will involve testing the ability of subjects to discriminate between types of distal stimulus (Marr, 1982, p.326; Segal, 1989b, p.197). The implication is that if normally functioning human subjects fail to discriminate (i.e. in a test situation) between two distinct types of distal stimulus then the perceptual contents experienced by the subjects are of the same type. If the subjects tend to discriminate between two types of distal stimulus, then it can plausibly be conjectured that the subjects employ distinct types of perceptual representation when they are presented with these stimulii.

The latter claim seems more easily accepted than the former. Where subjects do detect a difference this indicates that they are representing a difference in the nature of the distal stimulus; but where subjects do not detect a difference it is not clear that they should be ascribed the same perceptual types without some kind of further behavioural evidence to support that claim. The question is whether it can ever be well-motivated to ascribe differences in perceptual content to subjects even where they do not discriminate between distinct types of distal stimulus (cf. Segal, 1989b, p.197).[4]

Having outlined some of these preliminaries, Segal sets out his strategy (he employs the Twin Earth scenario as opposed to Burge's employment of counterfactual cases). He intends, (a) "[To] make a general point about what we may legitimately suppose to vary across Twins" (ibid. p.199). (b) To expose the reasons why Burge concludes that externalism is true for perceptual content; and attribute to Burge a "restrictive interpretation" of Marr's theory (Segal, ibid.). (c) To provide a "liberal interpretation" of Marr's theory. (d) And then "[to] argue that Marr's theory, restrictively interpreted, would be unmotivated and methodologically suspect, and defend the liberal interpretation" (ibid.). (Let us follow Segal and conduct the debate in the Twin Earth setting rather than by the employment of counterfactual cases.) In accordance with his stated intentions, concerning (a), Segal points out rightly that the retinal images of the subjects are conceived by Burge to be of the same type even though their (eventual) representational contents are said to differ. Segal concludes that "The representational content derived by a given computation thus depends, in part, upon the innate assumptions" (ibid. p.200; also Burge, 1986a, p.33).[5] So, he claims, it is the innate assumptions operant in the two types of case - i.e. on Earth and on Twin Earth - which are responsible, at least partly, for the difference in representational content between the Twins. Thus Segal's answer to (a) is that the innate assumptions are what vary between the Twins in the Twin Earth case.

With respect to (b), Segal concurs with the account of Burge provided here: the perceptual contents of the Twins reportedly differ due to the types of entity with which they respectively regularly interact. This construal of Marr's theory, by Burge, is said to employ a restrictive interpretation of what constitutes a perceptual type in the theory. That is, even where a distal stimulus causes instances of the same retinal image type in S and S*, a theorist proceeding within the dictates of the theory could legitimately ascribe to the subjects distinct types of perceptual contents.

The problem is, Segal takes this to suggest that the innate assumptions operant in S and S* must differ; for Segal a difference in representational content results from a difference in operant innate assumptions. (I think Burge would reject this claim. I will say why once exposition of Segal's argument is completed.)

With regard to (c), by Segal's "liberal interpretation" of Marr's theory, it is legitimate and well-motivated to ascribe to the Twins instances of the same type of perceptual content, e.g. of type O/C. On Burge's restrictive interpretation, the Twins would be ascribed perceptual contents of either type O or type C depending upon whether the subjects regularly perceive Os or Cs.

Segal then proceeds to state why it is that Burge's restrictive interpretation is not well-motivated whilst Segal's own liberal interpretation is well-motivated. What Segal does is to invite us to consider what would happen if S* is transported to Earth from Twin Earth. Imagine further that S* and S are presented with the distal causes of type O and type C where Cs are thin cracks and Os are thin shadows. Segal points out what is surely the case - i.e. that neither S* nor S will prove better able to discriminate cracks from shadows. Therefore, he concludes, there is no behavioural motivation to ascribe to S and S* distinct types of perceptual content when they are presented with a distal stimulus which could either be a crack or a shadow. Segal suggests that the perceptual contents of S and S* are better characterised by the more general perceptual type O/C or "crackdow" (1989b, p.208). He points out that principles of theoretical parsimony dictate that we should not invoke "two contents where one would do" (ibid. p.206). Further, Segal asserts that he is unaware of any plausible way of individuating perceptual kinds other than by reference to "a behaviourally testable capacity" (ibid. p.208).

Defence of Burge against the disjunctive content objection

There is a plausible response which seems open to Burge at this point. The response involves contesting Segal's claim that a difference in perceptual content between S and S* must be the consequence of different innate assumptions (1989b, p.201). The examples of innate assumptions offered by Marr and quoted by Segal (1989b, p.193) are far too general to suggest that different information could be derived by the visual system when the distal stimulus is a thin crack or a thin shadow.[6]

75

Further, it might be said that if there were differences in the innate assumptions operating in the two subjects then this would constitute a physical (neural) difference between the subjects. If so, then the subjects are not physically identical and so cannot be employed in Burge-type thought experiments.[7]

However, perhaps more important than the last point is the point that Segal may simply be wrong when he implies that individuation of perceptual kinds must be by reference to "behaviourally testable capacity" (1989b, p.208); that is to say, behavioural evidence might not be all there is to the individuation of perceptual types. It seems plausible to argue that if, say, there are no Os on Twin Earth, then there would be no theoretical motivation for positing the perceptual kind "Crackdow"; that would seem to violate principles of theoretical parsimony. This suggests that ontological considerations are also a factor in the individuation of perceptual types - in addition to behavioural considerations.

Another example which may be recruited to make the same point might run as follows. As Segal notes, the fact that the human visual system is able to distinguish which objects stick figures represent suggests that edges are of particular significance to the human visual system (Segal, 1989b, p.196; Marr, 1982, p.326). Instead of Burge's Os/Cs example consider that on Twin Earth there are no rabbits, but there are ducks; and that on Earth there are rabbits but no ducks. Suppose further that S and S* are brought together in some experimental psychology laboratory somewhere and that they are presented with a duck/rabbit line drawing.

It should be agreed that the distal stimulus is the same for each subject and that the stimulus causes the same type of retinal image in each subject.[8]

Even prior to eliciting responses to the distal stimulus from S and S* it seems plausible to predict that S* will represent the stimulus as a duck and that S will represent the stimulus as a rabbit. Admittedly, these interpretations will be confirmed by the behavioural evidence but it seems reasonable to claim that their respective perceptual representations of the duck/rabbit line drawing may be judged to differ even prior to the confirmation by behavioural evidence. This can be taken to provide further indication that ontological factors are a consideration in the individuation of perceptual types; hence it can be seen considerations other than behavioural considerations are relevant to the determination of the individuation conditions of perceptual types.

An internalist might object that the example just provided (that of the duck/rabbit line drawing) in defence of Burge's position is more appropriate to the determination of the individuation conditions of conceptual content (e.g. judgements) rather than to perceptual content (i.e. nonconceptual states) (cf. Davies, 1992, p.24); if so, the internalist may continue, the example does not constitute a legitimate defence of Burge's position. (I will return to counter this objection shortly.)

Further,it could be pointed out that the kind-terms employed by Marr in his specifications of perceptual contents are much more general than kind-terms such as "crack" or "shadow". Marr indicates that perceptual types are to be typed by reference to "volumetric or surface shape primitives" (1985, p.124), e.g. those denoted by terms such as "cube", "cone", "square", "ellipse", and "circle" (cf. Humphreys and Bruce, 1989, p.46). But it seems to me that the externalist position can be defended from these objections.

The central consideration is that even though the kind-terms invoked by Marr are more general than crack or shadow, the perceptual types he deploys are individuated with respect to kinds which feature in the environment of the subject. Since, in Twin Earth cases, the environments of the Twins are so alike an internalist might take the view that mind-brain supervenience is true for perceptual types and that in Burge's cracks/shadows example, the Twins undergo perceptual states of a type such as that referred to by "Edge of length 1". But even if this is accepted, internalism may still be resisted. It is pertinent to suggest that the Twins do not instance perceptual states of the same type due to the truth of mind-brain supervenience. It is at least as plausible to hold that the perceptual states of the Twins are only coincidentally of the same type.

This strategy, deployed on behalf of the externalist, exploits the kind of difference present in the following two cases: (1) A meteor lands in a pond; (2) Lightning strikes a conductor (the example is borrowed from Peacocke, 1981, p.210). With respect to the first event, no physical explanation would be required of why the meteor landed where it did. The trajectory of the meteor is blind, so to speak, to its eventual destination. No properties of the pond are relevant to an explanation of why the meteor landed where it did. With respect to the second event, the properties of the conductor are relevant to an explanation of why the lightning struck at that particular location. It is evident that psychological explanations of perception are more akin to explanations such as those required by the occurrence of the second event (the lightning strike) rather than explanations such as those required of the first event (concerning the meteor). Hence, Marr writes "In the theory of visual processes, the underlying task is to reliably derive properties of the world from images of it" (1985,p.113). These considerations suggest that Burge's argument is not threatened by the observation that the perceptual types employed by Marr are more general than those suggested by Burge (at least in the crack/shadows example). And, they seem to lend further weight to the externalist position in general.

The other possible internalist objection mentioned above concerned the employment of the duck/rabbit example. Davies (1992) has recently put forward an example in support of Burge's position which exploits, in its typing of perceptual states, types individuated by reference to ellipses and circles. I will close this section by briefly describing Davies example which is being taken here to lend further support to the externalist position.

Davies invites us to consider a perceiver P on Earth. When P sees "ellipses as ellipses" (ibid., p.38) he undergoes perceptual states of type T1. When P perceives round things, he undergoes perceptual states of type T2. These attributions are confirmed by behavioural evidence.[9]

On Twin Earth, P's twin P* undergoes perceptual states of type T1 when he perceives circles; in the example, "behaviour is squashed along the vertical axis so that input-output harmony is preserved" (ibid.). According to externalism, P's perceptual states of type T1 are individuated with respect to ellipses, and P*'s perceptual states of type T1 are individuated with respect to circles. It is to be assumed in each case that both P and P* are "well adapted" (ibid.) to their respective environments.

Davies points out that if the perceptual states of the Twins are individuated by a disjunctive type "ellipse-or-circle" (ibid.), the view that P sees ellipses as ellipses is rejected - i.e. on the grounds that P supposedly perceives an ellipse-or-circle. But since P behaves differently when faced with circles and ellipses it seems implausible to claim that these distinct types of behaviours stem from perceptual states of the same type.[10] Having defended Burge from Segal's objection, we now move onto consider an objection to Burge proposed by McGinn (1989).

McGinn's criticism of Burge

As we have seen, for Burge, the individuation conditions of perceptual types are determined by objects (etc.) with which subjects regularly interact perceptually. Hence, where two subjects, S and S* (or one subject in counterfactually distinct worlds), experience tokens of the same type of proximal stimulation, if these token states are regularly caused by different types of distal stimulus, then S and S* should be ascribed tokens of distinct types of perceptual content. Thus, suppose that both subjects instantiate tokens of proximal stimulus type PST, for S instances of PST are caused by Os; but for S* instances of PST are caused by Cs. According to Burge, the perceptual type instantiated by S is of type O;

and the perceptual type instantiated by S* is of type C. (It can be supposed that on Earth, S sees Os, whilst on Twin Earth S* sees Cs.)

McGinn constructs a Twin Earth thought experiment which purports to present a convincing challenge to Burge's claim (McGinn, 1989, pp.58-99). Suppose we employ the schema $S \rightarrow O$ to characterise the relationship of perceiving. It is clear that S may have a perceptual experience as of perceiving O whether or not S, at t, is actually perceiving O - the experience is not sufficient for satisfaction of the perceiving relation. Suppose further that it is these perceptual experiences which are being said by externalists to have perceptual content. Let perceptual experiences typically caused by the required kind of perceptual contact with square objects on Earth be called experiences of type S1; and let perceptual experiences typically caused in the required way by perceptual contact with round objects on Twin Earth be called experiences of type S2.

McGinn asks us to consider a situation in which on Twin Earth, square objects systematically produce perceptual experiences as of round objects even though, hitherto, they had caused experiences as of square objects; that is, on Twin Earth, type S2 experiences are caused by square objects. So it seems to the subject S that he is perceiving something round when he is really perceiving something square (McGinn, 1989, p.60). Meanwhile, on Earth, experiences of type S2 are caused, unsurprisingly, by round objects.

According to an externalist account of perceptual content of the kind set out by Burge and described above, the content of S's perceptual experience is determined by the "types of objects, properties and relations" (Burge, 1988a, p.70 (i.e. premise 3 above)) which feature in S's environment. If this is accepted, then it would appear to have the following consequence. When Twin Earthers think they see round objects they are really having perceptual experiences which derive from square objects. This seems to follow from Burge's premise 3: according to which, as McGinn puts it, "[The] distal dominates over the proximal" (1989, p.75).

The cracks/shadows example did not appear to have any dramatic consequences for the explanation of the actions of the subjects concerned. But McGinn's example seems potentially damaging to Burge's case. McGinn suggests that explanation of the actions of the Twin Earthers forces the conclusion that the perceptual content of the subjects is as of round objects and not as of square objects.[11] For example, suppose a Twin Earther is visually presented with a cube (he is not allowed to touch it) and asked to describe it. However such a description may sound, it will not sound like a description of a cube since, presumably,

79

the Twin Earther will perceive the cube as something like four discs (i.e. with two other discs hidden from view).

Suppose further that such a subject is asked to walk around the object immediately in front of him; and, that the object is, say, a cube with sides which are six feet long. Again, in such a case, it seems plausible to conjecture that the subject will trace a circular path around the object and not a rectangular one.[12]

It would seem to follow from these reflections on McGinn's thought experiment that a person who has the task of explaining the actions of the Twin Earthers, and is not subject to the illusion to which they are subject, would be forced to the conclusion that the Twin Earthers systematically misperceive square things as round things. If so, this conclusion conflicts with externalism regarding perceptual content since, as has been seen, that thesis has it that perceptual content is individuated by the properties of the distal stimulus.

So in McGinn's thought experiment there is alleged physical identity between S on Earth and S* on Twin Earth. But on Earth instances of a proximal stimulus type PST typically result in visual experiences as of a square. On Twin Earth, due to some environmental condition (McGinn suggests "some trick of the atmosphere" (1989, p.60)), instances of a different proximal stimulus type PST* are caused by square objects. Further, instantiations of PST* in Twin Earth subjects typically result in visual experiences as of round objects.

Defence of Burge against McGinn

Let it be agreed that McGinn has successfully constructed a case in which the subjects S and S* are indeed physically identical. Thus S and S* experience instances of the same type of retinal stimulation but they construct perceptual contents of distinct types from those stimulations: S has perceptual experiences as of perceiving round objects when he in fact perceives round objects, and S* has perceptual experiences as of perceiving round objects when he in fact perceives square objects. Further, let it be supposed, there is behavioural evidence to suggest that the perceptual contents experienced by S* should be specified in a that-clause which ascribes to him perceptual experiences as of round objects and not as of square objects (recall the two behavioural tests outlined earlier in this section) even though he has never encountered round objects since as in Burge's thought experiment, they do not occur in S*'s environment.

There are two main conclusions drawn by McGinn from this example. The first is that it shows S*'s perceptual content cannot plausibly be individuated by reference to the distal cause of his perceptual experiences. This follows, it is claimed, since explanation of S*'s behaviour would motivate the ascription, to S*, of perceptions as of round objects. So contra Burge perceptual content which has explanatory power need not be individuated by reference to its distal cause.

McGinn's second main conclusion stems from his attempt to consider what responses might be available to an externalist about perceptual content given McGinn's first conclusion. Each of these points can be responded to.

Consider McGinn's first conclusion. It is certainly the case that ascription of perceptual content, for Burge, centrally involves considerations related to the explanation of action; that is why we turned to McGinn's discussion in the first place. However, it may be that Burge's thesis is weaker than McGinn takes it to be. It is open to Burge to say that he is unable to say what the perceptual content of S* perceptual states will be on Twin Earth, or, in Burge's own thought experiment, in the counterfactual case. Indeed, Burge says of his argument concerning externalism for perceptual content "The argument is not committed to any particular attribution of perceptual states" (Burge, 1988b,   p.96). All that Burge needs in order to strongly suggest externalism for perceptual content is that such contents differ when nonintentionally individuated states remain the same. He does not need to specify what the natures of those states would be. Recall Burge's third premise,

> [Some] perceptual types that specify objective types of objects, properties, and relations as such do so partly because of relations that hold between the perceiver (or at least members of the perceiver's species) and instances of those objective kinds (1988a, p.70).

Burge's reference to "instances of objective kinds" (ibid.) means types of objects (or properties of objects etc.) that occur in the environment of the subject and/or his fellows. If there are no instances of the property round on Twin Earth can it be right to ascribe to Twin Earthers perceptual contents with the content round (i.e. it is not being said that their retinal images etc. are literally round)?

To put the point differently, it is true that S* perceives an instance of the property roundness only if S perceives an instance of that property. But on Twin Earth that property is not instanced anywhere (this is what must be assumed if McGinn's experiment is to parallel Burge's). In the light of this, it seems highly implausible, at least to me, that an ascriber of perceptual content - specifically, one unaffected by the illusion to which the Twin Earthers are subject - would ascribe to Twin Earthers perceptual contents specified in that-clauses including the phrase "as of round". It seems plausible that such an ascriber would simply be at a loss as to how to describe the actions of the Twin Earthers with respect to square objects.

Also, consider that the atmospheric change which McGinn refers to which is the cause of the illusion to which Twin Earthers become subject happens overnight or gradually over a period of a week. So at t square things look square and at a later time t* square things look round. It is surely obvious that the Twin Earthers will employ other senses (specifically their sense of touch) in their judgements about square things. Further, they will probably tell the ascriber of perceptual content who is not subject to the illusion that square things look circular to them. Alternatively, if square things had always looked round on Twin Earth it seems clear, again, that the sense of touch would be relied upon that much more to compensate for the unreliability of vision. These considerations strongly suggest that McGinn's case against Burge's externalist account of perceptual content does not succeed.

The second main conclusion drawn by McGinn from his discussion of perceptual content and the construction of a Twin Earth case for it concerns the question of first person authority (McGinn, 1989, p.61). Suppose, contrary to what has just been argued, that an externalist responds to McGinn's first main conclusion by conceding that although the Twin Earthers might say that they are having perceptual experiences as of round things (and, recall, McGinn requires us to agree that they behave in a way consistent with this) they are really having experiences as of square things; this is so whether they know it or not.[13]

In Burge's own thought experiment, as we have seen, although in the actual environment subjects interact with Os and occasionally with Cs, Os do not occur in the counterfactual environment although Cs do. Using Burge's Os/Cs notation rather than McGinn's square/round example, McGinn appears to make the following claim. On Twin Earth the Twin Earthers take themselves to be perceiving Os when they are really perceiving Cs. By externalist principles concerning the individuation of perceptual kinds, since the Twin Earthers regularly interact with Cs their perceptual kinds should be individuated by reference to Cs. But McGinn asserts that the perceptual kinds of the Twin Earthers should be individuated with respect to Os and not Cs. McGinn points out that the externalist account appears to threaten the idea of first person authority. As he says,

> We may not be completely infallible about our experiences, but
> surely we could not be quite so fallible - never getting it right at
> all! (1989, p.61).

The externalist line appears, indeed, to carry the implication that the
Twin Earthers are wholly wrong about how things seem to them. But
perhaps McGinn's claims can be queried again here.

It is open to an externalist to question the motivation for ascribing to a
subject a perceptual experience concerning a type of object which is
never instanced on Twin Earth. Why should an ascriber ascribe to a Twin
Earther a perceptual experience as of an O when Os do not occur on
Twin Earth? McGinn might say "Behavioural evidence" but the force of
this suggestion has been seen to be weak. More to the point, why should
a Twin Earther take himself to be perceiving an O when Os do not occur
on Twin Earth?

In short, there seems no motivation for the suggestion that a Twin
Earther would claim to be having a perceptual experience as of an O
when he is perceiving a C. Again, it can plausibly be suggested that the
Twin Earther is not sure what the content of his perceptual experience is
since he lacks the conceptual resources to characterise it - since Os do
not occur on Twin Earth and neither he nor his fellows have heard of Os.
This suggests that McGinn's claim that first person authority is
compromised under the externalist account of perceptual content is itself
dubious or at least, incapable of resolving the issue.

McGinn might respond by suggesting that behavioural evidence can be
taken to indicate that the Twin Earthers are having perceptual experiences
as of Os rather than as of Cs - think of the square/round example again.
But this move was discussed above and found not to be adequate. So it
may be concluded that McGinn's case against externalist individuation of
perceptual content is not successful.

It might be said that the line of response just given in defence of Burge
presumes an overly empirical account of concept acquisition. This is a
fair charge. But pause to consider what appeals to a rival account might
sound like. Suppose, in the Radical Translation situation (Davidson,
1984), a subject S claims to have thoughts about Bryan Robson. S is also,
let it be supposed, able to state facts about Robson which are all true.
Yet, S claims never to have had any perceptual contact with Bryan
Robson nor with anyone who has had such contact; nor has S been in
contact with anyone who has seen media coverage concerning Bryan
Robson and S himself has never been exposed to any such coverage. It
seems plausible to say that the Radical Translator would be reluctant to
ascribe to S thoughts about Bryan Robson; or else, the Translator would

be completely bewildered. These reflections on such a case suggest (they do not establish the fact) that thoughts about objects are anchored in causal commerce with them. This thought experiment does not constitute a valid argument to that effect, but it strongly suggests the claim just ventured (at least with respect to thoughts about material things).

Consider now the square/round example provided by McGinn. It does not seem plausible to suppose that a subject could have an experience as of round without ever having had some perceptual acquaintance with an instance of that property. This possibility seems implausible in the same way that it seems implausible to say that S has thoughts about Bryan Robson.

If these considerations are correct, they suggest, at least, that a subject would not be in a position to have a perceptual experience as of round unless he had acquaintance with that property; and, the subject would not be in a position to claim to have had such an experience unless he had had acquaintance with an instance of the property round.[14]

There is one further issue which needs to be mentioned here. It has been presumed throughout the discussion of ascription of perceptual content that the position of the ascriber is distinct from that of the subjects. This came out most clearly in discussion of McGinn's thought experiment when it was suggested that the ascriber was not subject to the illusion to which the Twin Earthers were subject (perhaps he wore some compensating lenses).

The question of the status of the ascriber raises consideration of a case in which the subjects whose actions are being explained and perceptual content ascribed to them have a perceptual capacity which is lacking in the ascriber. An example of such a case is provided by Churchland (1979, pp.8-9).

He describes the possibility of a race of subjects who perceive temperature rather than colour. Their ascriptions of perceptual content to each other make references to temperatures of the surfaces of the perceived objects rather than to their colour.

The possibility of such a case, though, is still not incompatible with externalism concerning perceptual content. Provided that the natures of objects are independent of the natures of human subjects there is no obstacle to the claim that perceptual types are to be individuated with respect to their distal causes. Let us turn, now, to consider Macdonald's position.

3. Responses to explanatory motivations (II)

There seem to me to be four main steps in Macdonald's argument. (i) Individuation of types of psychological states is bound up with the explanation of behaviour. (ii) Explanations of action are essentially normative. (iii) (a) There is a distinction between narrow and broad act types. (b) The intelligibility of explanations which recruit narrow act types are dependent upon the intelligibility of explanations which recruit broad act types. (iv) The view that contextual factors enter into the determination of the individuation conditions of broad act types. (v) Hence, externalism is true for at least some types of psychological states.

Consider each of these steps. (i) Though not explicitly stated in her 1992 paper, Macdonald's argument is based on the presupposition that the individuation of psychological states is at least intimately, if not essentially, tied to the conditions under which they are ascribed to subjects - specifically in explanations of their behaviour.

This presupposition might be vulnerable to Searle's charge of tailoring the ontology of psychological states to suit epistemological considerations (Searle, 1992, p.23, p.77). For example, the presupposition seems to lead one to the view that behaviour is a necessary condition for the exemplification by subjects of psychological properties. This is a position which has seemed attractive to some philosophers (e.g. Campbell, 1980, p.75), but it has been denied. (For example, Searle writes "[As] far as the ontology of the mind is concerned, behaviour is simply irrelevant" (1992, p.77).) It is logically possible that entities which do not exhibit behaviour do undergo psychological states; if accepted, it follows that behaviour is not a necessary condition for being a subject of psychological states. Nor, of course,is behaviour a sufficient condition for undergoing psychological states: planets behave but do not think, feel pain etc.

Since Macdonald's view does seem committed to the position opposed by Searle, adoption of the presupposition described above requires some defence. Such a defence might run as follows.

It was noted in the introduction to this essay that commonsense belief/desire psychology is an explanatory enterprise engaged in the task of ascription of psychological states to subjects. It is clear that this enterprise can only get off the ground when movement occurs - otherwise there is no data to explain. This might constitute one defence of the adoption of the presupposition.

A second is this. The explanatory enterprise just referred to is required to apply some principles of organisation over the phenomena it attempts to explain. This inevitably involves dividing the data into kinds in accordance with certain principles of individuation. This latter project, it seems plausible to suppose, again, can only begin once subjects behave in some way. Otherwise there appear to be no grounds to claim that a subject is thinking that p as opposed to that q.

Third, one can simply agree with Searle that behaviour is neither a necessary nor a sufficient condition for the instantiation by a subject of psychological properties but point out that behaviour plus a certain kind of complex constitution provides evidential support for the ascription to subjects of psychological properties. Conversely, the absence of behaviour and the absence of a certain kind of complex constitution provide evidential support for not ascribing psychological properties to individuals.

These three considerations seem to me to lend not inconsiderable weight in support of the adoption of the presupposition described in (i) above.

With respect to (ii) (explanations of action are essentially normative). The considerations Macdonald offers concerning action explanation and described above seem not to need any further support here. Two other reasons which she offers in a footnote are these. (a) Explanations of action cannot be causal since causes are logically independent of their effects and reasons for action are not logically independent of their effects. (b) The actual contents of beliefs and desires are appealed to in explanations of action and it is these contents which explain the actions of subjects rather than the causes of the actions (Macdonald, 1992, p.140, fn.13).

Consider, now, the third step in Macdonald's argument. This was divided into two components: (a) The narrow and broad act types distinction. (b) The claim that the intelligibility of explanations which recruit the former are dependent upon the intelligibility of explanations which recruit the latter.

(a) Macdonald seems to me to have done enough to establish the plausibility of a distinction between narrow and broad act types, but at least three kinds of qualifications should be pointed to.

First, it might be objected that Macdonald's argument is directed at explication of act types but that claims made about these do not support claims made concerning the individuation conditions of types of psychological states.

However, this objection can easily be resisted. In explanation of S's act of washing in water we ascribe to her desires to engage in that kind of behaviour, together with relevant beliefs (e.g. that water gets things clean (cf. Macdonald, 1992,p.141)). So the taxonomy of act types connects up with a taxonomy of psychological states since in explaining the actions of a subject one recruits (e.g.) the desires of a subject to engage in certain types of act, and also beliefs concerning the acts.

Second, narrow act types such as reading, eating, running, and cooking seem to have no one specific kind of object associated with them. It should be said, though, that there do seem to be limits to the kinds of objects which can intelligibly be associated with each act type. E.g. one can only read things which have words or some other kinds of symbols on them; one cannot eat tall buildings; one cannot run on water; and one cannot cook ice.

These examples indicate that these act types may not be associated with just one kind of substance. The internalist might seek to exploit this point by conceding the general object-dependency of certain types of psychological states, whilst resisting the conclusion that the types are individuation-dependent on contextual factors.[15]

Third, with respect to the broad/narrow act type distinction, it should be pointed out that there seems to be a possibility of broad act types which may not involve any appropriate object. A possible example here is praying.

These qualifications can be made without any consequent weakening of Macdonald's position since, clearly, she does not need to claim that externalism is true for all types of psychological states, only that it is true for at least one type.

(b) With respect to the relationship of intelligibility between explanations which recruit narrow act types and explanations which recruit broad act types, recall that the claim here is that at least some narrow act types are intelligible only given the intelligibility of relevant broad act types (1992, p.141, 1990, p.391). Unfortunately, she does not spend much time spelling out further the nature of this dependence relation between narrow and broad act types, but it is clearly crucial to her overall position.

One way in which the relationship may be elaborated is as follows. In a general discussion of dependence relations McGinn identifies linguistic dependence and conceptual dependence (McGinn,1989, p.4). These can plausibly be employed to supplement Macdonald's position.

For example, according to McGinn, a relationship of linguistic dependence obtains between two types of particulars if "reference to Fs requires prior reference to Gs" (ibid.). Suppose that Fs are instances of the narrow act type washes and Gs are instances of a broad act type which specifies a substance which subjects use to wash in (e.g. washes in water, sand etc...). It could then be proposed that a relationship of linguistic dependence obtains between Fs and Gs since reference to the activity of washing seems to involve "prior reference" (ibid.) to the act of washing with a particular substance.

With respect to conceptual dependence, it is claimed that "possessing the concept of an F requires prior possession of the concept of a G" (McGinn, ibid.). Suppose Fs and Gs are construed as before. Again, it seems reasonable to conjecture that a subject could only possess the concept of washing, if he understood that washing involves the use of certain kinds of substance to get things clean. In fact, the strong claim that it is a necessary condition of a subject's possessing the concept of washing that he understands that it is an activity which involves the use of some particular kind of substance to get things clean seems highly plausible here.

These remarks on dependence relations seem to usefully supplement Macdonald's claims in this area and can be recruited in support of her version of type externalism.

(iv) The view that contextual factors enter into the determination of the individuation conditions of broad act types. An internalist might be prepared to concede that Macdonald's argument establishes that certain kinds of psychological states are constitutively bound to certain features beyond the body of the subject. But, it may be argued, that does not yet establish that type externalism is true for such states since it does not show that types of psychological states are constitutively bound to features in the environment of the subject - e.g. are not individuation-dependent upon features to be found specifically on Earth or specifically on Twin Earth. So what is required is a strategy for binding psychological states to contexts.

There are at least three plausible ways to do this. First, one can point out that the physical properties of substances at least partly determine the kinds of activity which they can plausibly be involved in. Thus, water is the appropriate stuff to wash in, but one could not intelligibly use water to dress in.[16] So it seems that the physical properties of substances in the environment of the subject will enter into the individuation conditions of psychological types via the relations between broad act types and relevant kinds of substances.

Secondly, what was described above as Macdonald's second argument for externalism in the face of Twin Earth examples can also be recruited to fend off the kind of internalist response just described. That is, that if S is transported to Twin Earth, it would be fair to say that he mistakes water* for water and that two explanatory types are required to explain his actions. A third way to support Macdonald's line is as follows.

Logical space of explanation versus evidential space of explanation

A determined internalist might allow that these points are inviting but not yet compelling. To defeat such an internalist the notion of a logical space of explanation might be appealed to and contrasted with an evidential space of explanation. Crudely, the contrast is between (i) a view which regards any logically possible event as relevant to the explanation of a particular state of affairs or event; and (ii) a view which imposes constraints based upon empirical and other evidential considerations with respect to the range of data relevant to the explanation of a particular state of affairs or event. Although certain explanations of phenomena are logically possible, certain other explanations are more likely. (Of course, evidential space, so to speak, is a sub-class of logical space.)[17]

Quine's Radical Translation scenario (Quine, e.g. 1960) and its development into Radical Interpretation by Davidson (e.g. 1984) can be exploited here to indicate the relevance of the above distinction to the present issue (cf. also section 2 of the present chapter). In translating native utterances and explaining native behaviour the subjects are ascribed thoughts about kinds of objects etc. they interact with and regularly single out for attention. In translating the utterances of subjects who have never ventured outside some remote part of Papua New Guinea and who have had no contact in any form with people beyond that region, it would be theoretically unmotivated to ascribe to them thoughts about a particular street, Any Street, in Oldham. Of course it is logically possible that the natives do have thoughts about Any Street but the possibility is so remote, given what the translator knows about the natives, that the possibility need not enter into his hypothesising with regard to the contents of the thoughts of the natives.

Ascription of thoughts to subjects in the conditions envisaged in the Radical Interpretation scenario may be said to be constrained by two kinds of factors. First, actual contextual factors; these will include consideration of the sorts of entities with which subjects usually come into contact with, and the kinds of activities with which such objects are associated in the context under consideration. Second, conjectured contextual factors. Selection of these is constrained by what might be termed the evidential space of explanation as opposed to the logical space of explanation.

Certain possibilities concerning thought ascription lie beyond the evidential space of explanation. For example, suppose an anthropologist is attempting to identify the point of a particular ritual. It is a logical possibility that the ritual is designed to pay homage to the English footballer Bryan Robson. But although this is a logical possibility it is not an explanation which the anthropologist - if he is a good scientist - will consider (i.e. assuming no members of the tribe have had any contact with Robson or with anyone who has). Put another way, Robson does not lie within the evidential space relevant to the explanation of the event to be explained - in this case, the strange ritual. This suggests that there are criteria operant which are employed to sift out facts that are relevant and from facts that are not relevant in explanations of phenomena.

Such pragmatic strategies seem equally justified in the case of translating the language of the natives and explaining their behaviour. It may be logically possible that the natives perform some kind of ritual which is directed at a particular street in Oldham but it is not an explanatory possibility which would be considered unless well-motivated; such motivation might be derived from the possibility that a man from Oldham visited the tribe and made a big impression on them. But such a motivation is underpinned by plausible constraints on theory formation (e.g. the distinction between evidential and logical spaces of explanation) which suggest that one should not ascribe thoughts about objects to natives if they have not had any contact with those objects nor any contact with any other subject who has had such contact.[18]

An internalist response

Consider two cases, in one a subject A mistakes hydrochloric acid for water; in the second a subject S mistakes gold for fool's gold.

In an internalist account of the cases it would be held that it is the way the subjects A and S conceive of what is before them (i.e. hydrochloric acid, and fool's gold) which serves to explain their actions (e.g. Fodor, 1987; McGinn, 1982a; Loar, 1988a). To see this, simply reconstrue the examples in the Twin Earth idiom. So we have Alice and Twin Alice (Alice*) and S and Twin S (S*).

Suppose Alice acts as described above. The sink perceived by Alice*, on the other hand, really does contain only water. Analogously, suppose S acts as described above, but the ring S* purchases is in fact a gold ring.

Consider the psychological states of Alice and Alice* just prior to their placing their respective hands in the sinks they perceive. An explanatorily motivated internalism should be committed to the view that the psychological states of the Twins are type identical; this follows since, it is reasonable to suppose, by the lights of the internalist, the narrow states of the Twins will instance the same type of conceptual role (recall how this was individuated (ch.1 above)). Alternatively, from the perspective of an ontologically motivated internalism, it is reasonable to suppose it to be held that the psychological states of the Twins will be type identical due to the fact that their physical states are type identical (due to mind-brain supervenience).[19]

In fact it seems that even at the time the Twins place their respective pairs of hand in the liquid in the sinks they respectively perceive, the internalist must maintain that their respective psychological states are of the same type.

So, contrary to Macdonald's claims, from the internalist perspective it may be argued that the actions of the Twins can be explained by ascribing to the subjects psychological states which (a) do not include a referential component - they are descriptive thoughts; and (b) the internalist may claim that only one explanatory type is required to explain the actions of the subjects where the type externalist requires at least two.

For example, consider a case in which a subject, S, purchases a ring made of fool's gold but which he believes to be genuine. An internalist attempt to explain S's action could involve the attempt to construct descriptive thoughts which are adequate to perform the explanatory task required. This may look as follows:

(i) S desires a ring which satisfies the predicates "...is pretty to look at", "...is valuable", "...looks yellow".[20]

(ii) S believes the ring in the jewellers satisfies the predicates which occur in (i), so (iii) S buys the ring.

When S later discovers that the ring fails to satisfy "...is valuable" his return to the jewellers shop and subsequent annoyance can be explained by the thought: "S believes that the ring he bought fails to satisfy the predicate "...is valuable"".

Macdonald would clearly reject the claim that the kind of response suggested on behalf of the internalist is in fact available to such a theorist. That internalist response involves the claim that subjects entertain psychological states of the same type when they encounter gold or fool's gold (or, analogously, when they encounter water or water*). But according to Macdonald such a response is not explanatorily adequate. She would claim there are at least two types of psychological states involved in such cases, and not one.

In support of Macdonald's position it can be said that her points to the effect that act-types trade upon the notion of an appropriate object can be recruited in support of the claim that it is appropriate to spend a large sum of money on a gold ring but not on a fool's gold ring. This motivates the suggestion that there are two types of intentional states involved in S's case and not just one. In saying there are two distinct types of such states involved it seems possible to explain both S's purchase of the ring (he believed it to be a gold ring) and his subsequent disappointment (upon realising it to be a fool's gold ring).

In saying, with the internalist, that only one type of psychological state is involved it is problematic to account both for S's initial purchase of

91

the ring and his subsequent disappointment; behavioural evidence for the latter being, say, S's returning the ring to the jeweller in an angry state.

These cases of misperception seem to indicate the need for at least two explanatory types in nonstandard explanations of action; one of which is typed with respect to the kind of stuff which particular acts normally involve (e.g wash in water); and a second in which the stuff the subject mistook to be water (or gold) is referred to. Since hydrochloric acid looks like water, it is possible to understand how a subject could be acting rationally and yet place their hand in some hydrochloric acid; similarly, since fool's gold looks like gold, S's actions are explicable.

4. A problem for Macdonald?

It was pointed out above that Macdonald's type externalism has an ontological foundation in her version of token physicalism. And, it was also noted earlier, that Macdonald holds a position on the supervenience relation according to which "[Mental] properties supervene on physical properties of persons' bodies *and their environments*" (Macdonald, 1990, p.404, my emphasis). That is to say, the mental properties of subjects do not supervene just on the physical properties exemplified by the subject, but supervene on those physical properties together with the physical properties of the environment inhabited by the subject; hence she holds a version of nonlocal supervenience (note 9, ch.1). But, as will now be seen, this ontological foundation of her version of externalism seems vulnerable to a problem which stems from Burge's "Arthritis" thought experiment described above (ch.1) (Burge, 1979a).

Macdonald's view of the supervenience relation is perfectly compatible with Twin Earth cases. Since the Twins inhabit distinct physical environments - one contains water, the other contains water* - one would expect to discover, on Macdonald's view of supervenience, that the psychological properties of the Twins differ also. So far so good.

But consider again Burge's Arthritis thought experiment and various others he constructs in 'Individualism and the mental' (Burge, 1979a). Here Burge provides examples of cases in which the physical environment of the subject does not change, yet, according to Burge, the psychological properties of the subject do change; indeed, it may seem that even in the arthritis/arthritis* case, outlined earlier, it is the case that the physical environment of the subject is unchanged in both the actual and the counterfactual situations. Surely, if nonlocal supervenience is true, and if the physical environments are the same in both actual and the counterfactual cases (as Burge seems to say), then it should turn out to be the case that the mental properties instanced by the subject in both actual and counterfactual situations remain the same. But it does not. As we have heard, it appears to be the case that the subject's intentional states differ in the actual and the counterfactual situations.

The nature of this difficulty which is caused by Burge's thought experiments for Macdonald's thesis can be put more generally as follows: Macdonald's strategy is compatible with her understanding of the supervenience relation when there are differences in the physical environment of the subjects. But her strategy faces problems in cases, like those apparently described by Burge (in 1979a), where the physical environment remains the same but the social environment differs.

Nonlocal supervenience and Burge's arthritis case

The problem is this: How is Macdonald's view of the supervenience relation to be reconciled with cases in which there are no differences in the physical environment of the subject but where there are differences in the social environment which lead to differences in psychological states in physically identical subjects in physically identical environments? The difficulty stems from Burge's Arthritis case in which it appears that there may be changes in the identities of psychological states in the absence of changes in the physical environment. If accepted, this threatens the view that psychological properties supervene upon physical properties.

There is a strategy which Macdonald might adopt in opposition to Burge. This is simply to query the plausibility of Burge's "Arthritis" thought experiments, and, hence, the acceptability of conclusions drawn from them. A justification for such a query might run as follows.

According to Burge, there are no physical differences in the subject in the actual and counterfactual situations in his Arthritis thought experiment. But suppose that the utterances of subjects cause sound waves; these latter form part of the physical environment of the subjects and can be characterised nonintentionally.

In the counterfactual environment it will be, largely, instances of inflammation of both muscle and joint tissue which prompt utterances such as "I think I've got arthritis doctor" or "My arthritis is giving me terrible pain". In the actual situation only inflammations of joints generally prompt such outbursts.

This suggests at least the plausibility of the claim that where two terms have distinct extensions then the physical environments in the actual and counterfactual cases will differ because different stimulii will prompt utterances of the kind exemplified above (e.g. "My arthritis hurts" etc.). This will result in a physical difference because the spatio-temporal locations at which arthritis-prompted utterances are made will not, it seems reasonable to assume, be coextensive with the spatio-temporal locations at which arthritis*-prompted utterances are made. In Burge's arthritis example, according to the medical classificatory scheme employed in the two situations (the actual and the counterfactual) different types of events (i.e. inflammation of muscle or joint tissue, inflammation of joint tissue only) are classified as either arthritis or arthritis*.

In the actual situation events such as inflammation of the joints prompt, in general, arthritis utterances. In the counterfactual case events such as inflammation of the joints and/or muscles prompt, in general, arthritis* utterances. It seems fair to say that events of these distinct types will on at least some occasions occur at distinct spatio-temporal locations. If this is accepted, then it seems plausible to say that the physical states of the subject may differ in the actual and the counterfactual situations because, let it be supposed, subjects will be prompted to make arthritis* utterances at distinct spatio-temporal locations in the actual and the counterfactual cases. Suppose that S has one acquaintance who is affected by arthritis*. Suppose he occasionally complains to S* that he is in pain due to his arthritis*. The acquaintance will be prompted to make such complaints by differing stimulii in the actual and the counterfactual situations: in the actual situation he is prompted by inflammation of joint tissue, and in the counterfactual situation he is prompted by inflammation of muscle and/or joint tissue. It seems plausible to conjecture that S*'s nonintentionally individuated physical states will differ in the actual and the counterfactual situations since sound waves initiated by S*'s acquaintance, and prompted by his arthritis or arthritis*, will occur at different times. This suggests that contra Burge the physical environments differ in the actual and the counterfactual cases, and so too do the physical states of S in the actual and counterfactual cases. This is enough to salvage nonlocal supervenience and, hence, to subvert the threat to Macdonald's type externalism from that aspect of the ontological foundation for it.

5. Conclusion

Two kinds of motivations for externalism have been considered: logico-semantic, and explanatory motivations. Consider logico-semantic motivations first. These are so-called due to their origins in the logico-semantic theories of Frege (e.g. 1892) and Russell (e.g. 1956). First, it is important to note that these motivations derive from a controversial interpretation of Frege and a rejection of much of what

Russell held true concerning referring expressions. But even when these considerations are set aside, problems remain. The formal problems set out earlier seem at least to temper any initial enthusiasm one might have for the intriguing combination of views proposed by McDowell (1986). Also, as noted earlier, the work of Frege and Russell can be recruited in ways which are congenial to internalism rather than for externalism. The objection to externalism which recruits three possible situations - actual, duplicate, and empty (ch.1 above) - again seems more congenial to internalism than to externalism. Given these problems, it seems that, at best, logico-semantic considerations, taken alone, provide only weak motivation for externalism.

Burge's explanatory motivations, as seen, exploit an example of theorising within cognitive psychology in support of the claim that this enterprise individuates psychological states externalistically (Burge, 1986a). Burge's proposals were defended from two objections to them (from Segal (1989b) and McGinn (1989)). Discussion of these objections seemed, in fact, to strengthen Burge's position. Burge's argument is directed at perceptual states (states containing nonconceptual information (Evans, 1982, e.g. p.123-124)), but his proposals require to be set in the context of a position which argues externalism for other kinds of intentional states - states which characterise subjects' judgements and reasons for actions (cf. Evans, 1982, p.124). Macdonald's arguments for externalism were then turned to in order to show how a more general externalist position might look. Macdonald's position was set out and defended from objections to it - including one generated by Burge's "Arthritis" thought experiment.

In the light of the case made against ontological and explanatory motivations for internalism it seems that we are now in a position to endorse type externalism. But at least one serious difficulty remains: that of reconciling the thesis with the view that subjects have first person authority with respect to the contents of their intentional states. This task is to be undertaken in the next part of this essay. For now I propose to end this first part of the essay with some remarks which are intended to lend further support to externalism with respect to at least some types of psychological states.

It can be pointed out that psychological states as these are individuated in the commonsense scheme comprise the bulk of the data which psychologists seek to explain. And, it seems that the commonsense scheme supplies the tribunal against which the success or failure of psychological theories is evaluated. For example, in the field of cognitive pain management, it is subjects' reports relating to pain states which comprise much of the data which the psychological theorist is concerned with (e.g.

Tollison, 1982). And, it is these reports which constitute the tribunal by which a theory of pain management is to be evaluated. If many patients report no difference in their capacity to manage pain, in spite of the interventions of the psychologists, then the strategies suggested by them will be deemed to have failed.[21]

The last point is not adversely affected by the observation that theorising in the natural sciences seeks to explain (some) phenomena as these are individuated in the commonsense scheme (e.g., water freezing, the solidity of tables, that objects fall when dropped, and so on). Explanations in natural science can and do conflict with common sense (e.g. in claiming that apparently solid tables are really composed of vast numbers of moving particles). But as the pain example indicates, the pattern of individuation employed in commonsense belief-desire explanations of behaviour constrain psychological explanations; this is not true of explanations in natural science.

Notes to chapter four

1.   The principle allegedly follows from two rules of identity theory (a) things are self-identical (a=a), and (b) if two things a and b are identical then whatever is true of a is true of b. The latter rule is described by Newton-Smith as the Identity Elimination rule (Newton-Smith, 1985, p.146). Quine and Russell take the rule to be indistinguishable from the Substitution Principle (see e.g. Quine, 1961, p.138; Russell, "On Denoting" p.47 (in Marsh (ed) 1956).

2.   As it stands this schematisation may be open to the charge of inadequacy since it just says S (S*) desires that some stuff satisfies the predicates ...is thirst-quenching, ...is transparent...etc. It should say S desires the stuff, whatever it is, that is thirst-quenching, transparent...etc. E.g. $(\forall x) (Fx \wedge Tx \wedge Wx) \rightarrow$ [Self s] desire x.

3.   These can be understood to be innate assumptions (cf. Segal, 1989b, p.192).

4.   Burge is explicit that it can (e.g. 1986a, p.27).

5.   Segal uses "representational content" to denote what I have been denoting by "perceptual content". We both mean to indicate a perceptual state which represents a feature or features of the subject's environment.

6.   Recall the example given earlier: (i) "The visible world can be regarded as being composed of smooth surfaces having reflectance

functions whose spatial structure may be elaborate" (Marr, 1982, p.219; see also p.46; and Segal, 1989b, p.193).

7. This is what is wrong with Segal's thought experiment (1989b, p.205).

8. If it is objected that the retinal images differ due to differences in the primal sketch, then these differences can only be due to different innate assumptions, and, that would suggest a neural difference between the two subjects. If that is the case, then the objection stated above in the first part of this response, on behalf of Burge, succeeds against Segal.

9. This example is a variant of one provided by McGinn (1989) which we discuss in the next section.

10. Davies labels internalist responses to Burge's argument which recruit disjunctive types as "revisionary", and contrasts these with "conservative" responses (1992, p.28). In conservative responses it is claimed that, e.g., P and P* undergo perceptual states of the same type when they perceive (e.g.) cracks or shadows. Hence, by the conservative response, both P and P* are claimed to undergo perceptual states of type T1 (i.e. the type individuated with respect to ellipses). This strategy commits the internalist to the view that P* misperceives round things as ellipses. But given that P* and his fellows are well adapted to their environment, this is not a motivated position.

11. Hence McGinn can be seen to adopt the conservative response to Burge's position - see last note (10).

12. It must be said that there is some artificiality about this last point; subjects tend not to trace rectangular paths when they walk around rectangular objects but do, in fact, trace something approximating a circle or ellipse. Perhaps the first example suggested is enough to secure the objection being raised.

13. It should be noted that this response is not one an externalist need resort to if the arguments presented above against McGinn's conclusion are accepted.

14. This empiricism about mental content faces problems concerning, e.g. universal quantification, and thoughts abut remote parts of space and time; see Peacocke (1986, chs. 3 and 5) for suggestions in this area. For further explication of the sort of "grounding" in perception which is suggested in the text see Evans (1982, pp.77-78) and Peacocke (1986, e.g. pp.15-22).

15. Macdonald's first argument against Twin Earth cases is, it can be supposed, designed to subvert such an internalist claim.

16. E.g. Macdonald writes, "[The] physical properties of an object are

not unnecessary to the determination of which activities it is appropriate for" (1990, p.393; also,1992, p.153).

17. The term "logical space of explanation" was used by Newton-Smith in lectures at the University of Manchester in 1985. But I have not seen it feature in his published writings.

18. These considerations apply less easily to religious thoughts but these might plausibly be set aside for special treatment. It is more important here to emphasise the role which is envisaged for objects in the environment of subjects in the most basic types of case of thought ascription.

19. The same points may be made from the perspective of an epistemically motivated internalism: since the Twins, Alice and Alice*, each believe themselves to be about to wash in water/water*, their psychological states will be of the same type.

20. E.g. for any x, if x is pretty to look at, and is valuable, and is yellow, then S desires x. Borrowing from Blackburn (1984, p.315), it can be said that S desires the object (i.e. the ring) determined by the mode of presentation type $((\forall x) (Px \wedge Vx \wedge Yx))$.

21. The point does not apply exclusively to theories concerning sensation states. Eysenck and Keane point out that first person reports of psychological states are presumed to be reliable data in psychology - though not, necessarily, reports concerning past states (see Eysenck and Keane,1990, pp.38-39).

Part II
FIRST PERSON AUTHORITY

5 The problem and two solutions to it

In this chapter we first outline the nature of the alleged conflict between externalism and first person authority; briefly consider and reject the possibility of abandoning the view that subjects have first person authority; and then examine solutions to the problem offered by Burge (1988c) and Davidson (1984b,1987).

1. The problem stated

It has been noted in previous chapters (esp.ch 1) that there is an alleged conflict between externalism and certain intuitive, Cartesian views concerning the nature of thought when this is considered from the perspective of the person who entertains the thought - the first person perspective. Further, it has been suggested by some commentators that compatibility with Cartesian intuitions about first person thinking amounts to a condition of adequacy on a theory of mental content (see e.g. Heil, 1988a, p.238; Boghossian, 1989).

For example, explanations of action make essential reference to agents' conceptions of what is the case. If a theory of the nature of mental content has the consequence that agents do not know what they think, then it would be difficult to account for the centrality accorded to agents' conceptions of what is the case.[1] Externalism has been considered by some commentators to carry such a consequence and thus to be false (e.g. Georgalis, 1990). Hence the need to address the charge here.

Put baldly, the nature of the supposed conflict between externalism and certain Cartesian aspects of first person thinking is this. It is assumed, in the Cartesian view, that subjects both know the contents of their own occurrent intentional states and are authoritative with respect to knowledge of the contents of those states. But according to externalism the individuation conditions of these occurrent intentional states are determined at least in part by factors outside the head of the subject (e.g. in the case of intentional states the individuation conditions of which are determined by natural kinds). This can be seen to generate two problems. The first concerns subjects' epistemic warrant to claim to know what they think. And the second concerns first person authority (cf. Macdonald, 1991a).

The first problem stems from the fact that the acquisition of knowledge of the natures of things outside the head requires empirical investigation; such knowledge cannot be obtained apriori - where this means without the need for recourse to empirical information ("from the armchair" as it is sometimes put). But, typically, knowledge of the contents of one's own occurrent intentional states is considered to be obtainable without the need to resort to empirical evidence. Such knowledge, again typically, is regarded as being direct - can be obtained without the need for inference based upon evidence (cf. Alston,1971).[2]

If the above claim concerning the individuation conditions of intentional states is true, in what sense can subjects be said to know the natures of their intentional states (to know what they think)? - assuming that subjects do know what they think and given that the conditions which determine the identities of at least some of those states cannot be known without recourse to empirical evidence.

The second problem concerns first person authority and arises in two ways. First, externalism appears to compromise first person authority since, at least in part, what makes for that authority is the fact that subjects are regarded as knowing the contents of their own occurrent intentional states. But, as seen, the epistemic right of subjects to that knowledge appears to be threatened by an externalist pattern of individuation; and so too, it would seem, must the authority accorded to subjects concerning their own occurrent intentional states if this rests upon the claim that subjects do have direct knowledge of the contents of such states. The second difficulty concerning first person authority is this. Assuming that subjects do know the contents of their own occurrent intentional states, and that that knowledge is direct (does not require an inference) a query arises as to why knowledge claims not based on evidence should be regarded as authoritative when they are contrasted with knowledge claims which are based on evidence. This is a difficulty brought out by Davidson (e.g. 1984b). It should be stressed that this latter difficulty is not one which is peculiar to externalism but is one which must be faced by any account of first person authority which affords a central role to subjects' direct knowledge of the contents of their intentional states.

The view that subjects both know the contents of, and are authoritative with respect to the contents of, their own occurrent intentional states is widely held and intuitively plausible: S might be mistaken when he takes a fool's gold ring to be a gold ring, but, it seems, he can be sure that he thought that the ring was gold. But according to externalistic schema of individuation, S's conception of the ring - what he believed the ring to be composed of (i.e. gold) - is itself determined by the nature of S's environment. Since, as noted, S is not authoritative with respect to the nature of the environment; and since features of that environment determine the contents of S's thoughts; it appears that certain intuitions concerning the particular authority available to the first person perspective on thought are compromised.

One further preliminary point here is this. The references made above to "occurrent" intentional states concern states which are currently undergone by subjects. These can be first-order or second-order states (cf. Burge, 1988c, p.654). S's thought that water is wet can be described as a token first-order intentional state; and S's thought that he is presently thinking that water is wet can be described as a token second-order occurrent intentional state. Second-order states can be said involve the adoption of a certain perspective upon one's own first-order states. Subjects are commonly regarded as being both knowledgeable and authoritative with respect to the contents of such states.

Of course second-order states can be construed as occurring just after first-order states; and subjects are standardly regarded as knowledgeable and authoritative with respect to such second-order states. But it can plausibly be suggested that subjects' authority with respect to occurrent thoughts is a prior issue since when subjects give voice to their thoughts in ordinary, everyday discourse they are generally regarded as authoritative and knowledgeable with respect to the content of such states.

It needs to be added that the present debate does not concern long-standing psychological states such as attitudes. For example, a subject might claim to know that he does not have a sexist attitude to women. But it may be shown that, contrary to what the person believes, he acts in a way which is justifiably describable as sexist and so might reasonably be ascribed the belief that women are inferior to men. Such states are not of concern here.

We turn, shortly, to consider Burge's attempt to render externalism compatible with the epistemic aspects of the Cartesian conception of mind (see ch.1 above), but it may be worth spending a little time considering the possibility of abandoning the view that there is first person authority.

2. Abandoning authority?

What, then, of the possibility not considered by either Davidson or Burge, that subjects are not in fact authoritative with respect to the contents of their own first-order intentional states?

It should be said that McCulloch (1989, p.212) does, briefly, consider that subjects are not authoritative with respect to the contents of their thoughts. In his example, a student believes he has grasped Descartes' argument for the existence of God but when asked to explain the argument is unable to do so. McCulloch's example seems to me to be beside the point here. The view that subjects are generally authoritative with respect to the contents of their thoughts is compatible with the occurrence of lapses of the kind he describes. And also, the construal of authority which we have been considering is one in which subjects have an epistemic advantage, so to speak, when it comes to determining the contents of their thoughts. Again, this construal of authority is compatible with lapses of the kind described by McCulloch.

Suppose it is presumed that (type) externalism is true. Thus, the natures of at least some intentional types are determined in part by the nature of the physical environment of their subjects. Why might subjects take themselves to be authoritative with respect to the contents of their first-order intentional states?

Three considerations in support of the view that subjects actually possess first person authority are these. The considerations are intended to indicate that relinquishing the view that subjects have first person authority leads to problematic consequences.

First, it is evident that in legal and moral discourse subjects are taken to be authoritative with respect to the contents of their thoughts. For example, it is plausible that the notion of someone's telling a deliberate untruth is one which rests upon the presumption that subjects are authoritative about the contents of their thoughts. If a subject is, say, charged with deliberate deception and denies the charge the task of the court appears to be to decide whether the defendant knew himself to be performing an act of deceit. Whilst it may be up to the court to decide whether the defendant actually did deliberately deceive the relevant third party, the presumption throughout the proceedings is that the subject knows authoritatively the truth of the matter. The task of the prosecution is to try to entice the defendant into admitting that he performed the dastardly deed knowingly. It seems that such a procedure is intelligible only in the light of the presumption that subjects are authoritative with respect to what they think. And, perhaps, the notion of deliberate deceit becomes unintelligible in the absence of there being the presumption of first person authority.

Second, consider the following situation. A subject signs a consent form - say, to undergo a particular operation. The subject signs the form knowingly having read and understood the relevant information. Just before the operation is due to take place the subject refuses to undergo the operation. When it is pointed out to him that he signed a consent form he argues that he signed the form but didn't really intend to give his consent. So at the time of signing the form he had doubts about whether to undergo the operation. The medical staff regard it as intelligible that although the person signed the form he is authoritative about what he was thinking at the time of signing it. Why should they do this? Again, such a situation only seems intelligible in the light of the presumption that subjects possess first person authority.[3]

The third consideration in support of the proposal that subjects are authoritative with respect to the contents of their own thoughts simply points to the phenomenon that being regarded as not being authoritative with respect to the contents of one's own thoughts (either by oneself or by others) may be taken as a sign of thought disorder. Consider the psychopathological phenomenon of thought broadcasting. In this

> [The] patient knows that as he is thinking so everyone else is thinking his thoughts in unison with him and is [consequently] aware of his most intimate contemplations (Clare, 1976, p.95).[4]

The situation described by Clare, thus, is one in which the language of first person authority is particularly helpful in describing what is wrong with the patient. For most of us the situation seems to be one in which we do appear to occupy an epistemically advantageous position when it comes to determining the contents of our own thoughts. When this breaks down - as in cases of thought broadcasting - this is symptomatic of the presence of mental illness in the subject.

Finally, to someone who remains unpersuaded that we do in fact possess first person authority all that can be said further is that all participants in the internalism/externalism debate seem agreed upon the view that subjects do in fact possess first person authority. The dialectical situation would be much simpler if it could simply be relinquished! Thus I appeal to such a sceptic to indulge, for the sake of argument, those who do think there is first person authority.

3. Burge's solution

At the start of this chapter, two main areas of conflict between externalism and the Cartesian conception of first person thinking were identified. The first concerned subjects' epistemic warrant to claim to know the contents of their occurrent intentional states when these are individuated externalistically. The second concerned the explication of subjects' authority with respect to these states when they are individuated externalistically. Burge has attempted to address both of these issues.

The first area of conflict derives from the observation that subjects are supposed to have direct knowledge of the contents of their first-order occurrent intentional states. But according to externalism the individuation conditions of such states are determined in part by contextual factors. The problem lies in explaining how subjects can have direct knowledge of the contents of their own occurrent intentional states when the conditions which serve to individuate those states cannot be known directly but requires empirical investigation. So how can subjects know, directly, the contents of, e.g., their natural kind thoughts when they cannot know, directly, the conditions which serve to individuate such kinds? Let us deal with Burge's attempt to address this problem before we proceed to examine his attempt to deal with the problem concerning authority.

Burge and the problem of subjects' direct knowledge of the contents of their occurrent intentional states

Burge is in broad agreement with the epistemic aspect of the Cartesian conception of first person thinking as that was described above (ch.1; Burge, 1988c, p.649). So what Burge needs to do is (a) to show how subjects can know the contents of their occurrent first-order intentional states (for example, those concerning natural kinds) without their knowing the individuation conditions of the relevant kinds; and (b) to show how knowledge of the contents of one's occurrent first-order intentional states can be obtained directly - without the need for inference based upon evidence. Before we look at Burge's attempt to deal with these problems it is necessary to outline a distinction exploited by Burge in pursuance of his overall end.

The distinction referred to is a distinction between first- and second-order intentional states. As noted earlier, a second-order state is a state in which a subject thinks about the contents of a first-order state. Such second-order states include instances of what Burge describes as "basic self-knowledge". Instances of basic self-knowledge are said to be self-verifying in that simply thinking the relevant thought at a particular time guarantees its truth (Burge, 1988c, p.649). A paradigmatic example of such a thought is the thought "I am now thinking"; thinking this thought, at a particular time, is sufficient both for that thought to be true and for the thinker to know it to be true. (Such a thought counts as a second-order thought by virtue of its reflexive nature.)

Burge provides another example but one in which the content of the first-order thought includes components which may be claimed to be individuated externalistically. The example is: "I judge (or doubt) that water is more common than mercury" (Burge, ibid.). This, according to Burge, is self-verifying in the same way as is the previous example. But what is significant about this claim for our purposes is that the thinker is able to know the content of the first-order thought directly without his knowing the individuation conditions either of water or of mercury.

Further, the claim is supposed to be generalisable to all second-order thoughts which take occurrent first-order thoughts as their contents, and which include reference to natural kinds in their specifications.[5]

Concerning (a), then (i.e. the problem of showing that subjects can know the contents of their thoughts without their having knowledge of the relevant individuation conditions), it is noted by Burge that his way of reconciling externalism with epistemic aspects of the Cartesian conception of first-person thinking exploits a distinction between (i) "knowledge of one's own thoughts" (1988c, p.650), and (ii) knowledge of the principles which determine the individuation of those thoughts (ibid.,p.51; also Burge, 1988b, p.92). It is held to be possible for subjects to possess the first kind of knowledge without possessing the second kind. Subjects can know that p without knowledge of all the conditions which are required for it to be the case that p; and this general point is applied by Burge to the question of whether one can be said to know the contents of one's own occurrent first-order intentional states. Burge writes, "...to think the [second-order] thought, one need not know the enabling conditions.It is enough that they actually be satisfied" (1988c, p.654).

For example, to be said to know the truth value of a claim such as "That table is red", the subject is not normally required to know all the conditions which contribute to its being the case that the table is red; he need not know, for example, optical laws concerning the speed of reflected light, the neurophysiology of perception and so on (Burge, 1988c, p.654; Heil, 1988a, p.246).

It is claimed by Burge that just as the subject is not required to know the kind of empirical conditions just referred to, so the subject is not required to know the kind of conditions which make basic self-knowledge possible. Simply reflecting upon one's own occurrent first-order states is sufficient, it seems, for one to possess knowledge of the truth value of the relevant second-order state.

Radical scepticism aside, Burge's claim seems acceptable here. Standard attributions of intentional content do ascribe knowledge that p to subjects; and it is not required of such subjects that they know all the conditions which contribute to its being the case that p. Even with respect to natural kind thoughts a subject may be said to know that he wants a gold ring or a glass of water in the absence of the subject's knowing the individuation conditions of either of those kinds. (Burge notes that his argument proceeds on "the unargued assumption that skepticism is mistaken" (1988c, p.655).)

So Burge may be said to deal adequately with the first problem involved in reconciling externalism with epistemic aspects of the Cartesian conception of first person thinking. He simply draws attention to attributions of knowledge to subjects - e.g. knowledge that p - in which subjects are not required to know the conditions necessary for it to be the case that p. Further, commonsense attributions of intentional content to subjects which concern their knowledge of the contents of their own intentional states - e.g. thoughts about thoughts about natural kinds - do not appear to require that the subject knows the individuation conditions of the relevant kind.

Let us turn, now, to (b) (i.e. how can subjects know the contents of their occurrent intentional states directly - without the need for conscious inference?) Burge writes of instances of basic self-knowledge,

> In basic self-knowledge, one simultaneously thinks through a first-order thought...and thinks about it as one's own. The content of the first-order (contained) thought is fixed by nonindividualistic background conditions. And by its reflexive self-referential character, the content of the second-order judgement is logically locked (self-referentially) onto the first-order content which it both contains and takes as its subject matter (1988c, pp.659-660).

When one occurrently thinks a token of the second-order intentional type "I am thinking that p" the content of the first-order state p is determined externalistically. It is a thought of the type p due to "nonindividualistic background conditions" (ibid.); by this Burge means, at least the nature of the subject's physical environment. In spite of this, Burge claims that the subject is not required to know the conditions which are necessary for it to be the case that he is thinking that p. say, as opposed to that q (where p and q respectively stand for, e.g., "water is wet", and "water* is wet"). The empirical conditions which determine the identity of the first-order thought, also determine the identity of the second-order thought. This, Burge claims, is due to the fact that the second-order thought "contains" the first-order thought; the second-order thought "inherits" (ibid. p.656) the content of the first-order thought. So in cases of basic self-knowledge subjects can be said to know directly the contents of their first-order intentional states.

It needs to be stressed that for it to be true that the subject S knows the content of his first-order thought (where this is individuated externalistically) S is required to know what type his thought is an instance of (cf. Burge, ibid., p.653) - otherwise S would not know whether his thought is a thought that p or a thought that q.

The reference to "containment" in the quoted passage might usefully be construed as analogous to the set-theoretic relation of the same name. In that, as in Burge's use of the containment metaphor, there is a relationship of dependence between the contained set and the containing set. That dependence relation has two aspects each of which Burge might usefully exploit.

First, the identity of the containing set is dependent upon the identity of the contained set; call this individuation-dependence. And second, the dependence just referred to suggests an ontological dependence between the containing set and the contained set such that if the contained set were to be removed then the containing set would cease to exist - i.e. trivially, it would be a different set; call this "existence-dependence" (cf. McGinn, 1989, p.7). This is something like the kind of dependence Burge is attempting to point to. The second-order state would not exist unless the first-order state existed; and the identity of the second-order state would differ if it contained a different first-order state.

Simply reflecting upon one's own occurrent first-order states is sufficient, it seems, for one to possess knowledge of the truth value of the relevant second-order state. Such knowledge is direct in the sense that it is not based upon inference (it is "immediate, not discursive" (Burge, 1988c, p.656)).

Burge is claiming, thus, that first person thinking at the second-order level affords direct knowledge of the contents of one's own occurrent first-order states; the knowledge is not based upon evidence - it is direct; and, generally, no justification for the knowledge is required other than the facts (a) that ones intentional states are one's own (Burge, ibid., p.658), and (b) that one is contextually related to instances of the relevant kind. As indicated, radical scepticism aside, there is a precedent in epistemology for the view that knowledge that p is possible in the absence of knowledge of all the conditions which make it the case that p

(cf. the example given above concerning a subject's knowing that a given table is red.)

As noted, Burge claims that subjects' knowledge of the contents of their first-order intentional states is knowledge of their types. Second-order states are typed, in part, by virtue of the type of the first-order state they "contain".

To remove the temptation to suggest that subjects' knowledge of the contents of their intentional states stems from some introspectible difference between them he refers us to the Twin Earth idiom (Burge, 1988c, p.652). Burge suggests that if a subject S is unknowingly transported to Twin Earth from Earth, then given time to establish causal relations sufficient for his being able to entertain thoughts about water*, it will be true to say that when S thinks that he is thinking that water* is wet, he knows what it is he is thinking.

We are to suppose that a subject S is, unbeknownst to him, transported to Twin Earth. Then, providing S is on Twin Earth long enough "to establish environmental relations necessary for new thoughts" (Burge, ibid.,p.652), S should have thoughts other than those he would have had in the event of his being left on Earth.[6] It is Burge's view that, given sufficient time and opportunity to develop the right relations, S's thoughts are to be individuated by reference to water* and not to water. This, Burge holds, is the case in spite of the fact that, phenomenally, things may well seem the same from the point of view of the subject:

> The idea is that [the subject] could not, by making comparisons, pick out the the twin periods from the 'home' periods.I [Burge] grant these ideas.The person would have no signs of the differences in his thoughts...The upshot of all this is that the person would have different thoughts under the switches, but the person would not be able to compare the situations and note when and where the differences [i.e. the transfers] occurred (Burge, 1988c, p.653).

So, the picture is this. First, things seem the same to the subject when he introspects. Second, given enough time to establish the right relations with the environment S's thoughts are individuated differently; instead of being individuated by reference to water they are individuated by reference to water*. Third, this does not threaten the idea of basic self-knowledge: Burge continues the passage just quoted with: "We know which thoughts we think" (ibid.).

Even though the subject cannot discern a difference when he introspects, Burge claims that during his stay on Twin Earth S can be said to have basic self-knowledge that his second-order judgements are judgements that water* wet; and that when he returns to Earth S can be said to have basic self-knowledge that his second-order judgements are judgements that water is wet. So runs Burge's attempt to account for subject's knowledge of the contents of their occurrent first-order intentional states when these are considered from the perspective afforded by second-order intentional states.

Before moving on to discuss Burge's strategy for reconciling externalism and the view that subjects are authoritative with respect to the contents of their occurrent first-order intentional states, a tension in his strategy for reconciling externalism with the claimed directness of subject's knowledge of those states needs to be mentioned. The tension stems from the requirement on theory that if a subject S knows the content of one of his occurrent intentional states he knows which type it is. Burge's externalism commits him to a view in which the individuation conditions of intentional types are determined in part by contextual factors. But of course Burge wants to allow that subjects can be mistaken in the judgements they make on any particular occasion - at least judgements concerning external states of affairs (Burge, 1988c, p.657). Put metaphorically, it may be said that on an externalist pattern of individuation the outer facts (e.g. the nature of the physical environment) partly determine the nature of the inner facts (intentional types). But since on any particular occasion there is the possibility of error a subject may mistakenly take himself to be thinking of F when he is really thinking of G. It can be concluded, then, that the typing of any particular token intentional state on that particular occasion isn't fixed by the nature of the object thought about. (The quote from Burge, (ibid. pp.659-660) may have led one to the interpretation being set aside here.)

Thus, since the subject knows which thought he thinks, and therefore knows which type it is an instance of, there must be a way other than that just described of accounting for this in Burge's theory. The other way - that which Burge must intend us to adopt - is a way in which the subject simply employs a type, so to speak, in thought with which to type the relevant token intentional states. Since, on Burge's account, the content of the first-order thought fixes the content of the second-order thought the subject knows the content of his first-order thoughts - where he employs a type with which to type these first-order states. Recall that a subject can do this (type his first-order states) without knowledge of the conditions which determine the identity of the relevant intentional type (at least in thoughts about natural kinds).

This latter interpretation of Burge's strategy makes sense of his employment of the containment metaphor. It was noted earlier in the

111

reference to the set-theoretic relation of containment that the containing set is both existence-dependent and individuation-dependent upon the contained set. This is directly analogous to the nature of the dependence between first-order and second-order intentional states as this is conceived of by Burge.

In the light of this, let us turn now to look, briefly, at Burge's attempt to render externalism compatible with a further key aspect of the Cartesian conception of first person thinking; namely, the view that subjects are authoritative with respect to the contents of their thoughts - recall that our concern is with first-order occurrent intentional states.

Burge's attempt to account for first person authority

The fact that Burge has successfully accounted for subjects' knowledge of the contents of their first-order occurrent intentional states does not yet show why subjects are claimed to know the contents of such states authoritatively. However, it does seem to be the case that Burge takes himself to have accounted for authority in his account of the nature of subjects' knowledge of the contents of their own thoughts (see e.g., 1988c, pp.658-659). The fact that subjects have a perspective available to them alone on their own first-order states, together with the special epistemic character of the containment relation seems, for Burge, to be sufficient to explain the authoritative nature of subjects' knowledge of the contents of their first-order intentional states. For Burge, simply thinking the thought from the second-order perspective guarantees that one knows its contents: there is no room for error so to speak (cf. Burge, ibid.,p.658). Just as "I am now thinking" is self-verifying, so too it seems does Burge take thoughts such as "I am now thinking that water is wet" to be self-verifying.

Having, now, considered Burge's strategy for reconciling externalism and first person authority,let us turn to consider the proposals of Davidson in this area; these can be divided, roughly, into negative and positive proposals; consider the negative proposals first.

4. Davidson: the negative story

Davidson provides two main statements of his views on the reconciliation of externalistic individuation of intentional states and first person authority (1987; 1984b). His arguments are mainly negative and directed at criticisms of rival accounts; his positive arguments are stated extremely briefly in the two papers referred to. In this section I focus on

Davidson's negative proposals, and in the next consider his positive proposals. I concentrate largely on the arguments presented in Davidson 1987. (It should be added that Davidson discusses a bewildering number of views in both papers and this makes it particularly difficult to summarise his overall claim.) It can safely be said, however, that his two main aims are (i) to show that relational individuation of intentional states is compatible with the view that mental states occur within the head; and (ii) that Cartesian introspectionist, or relational models of thought cannot account for first person authority.[7]

Davidson begins (ibid. p.441) by stating that, for him, it is true that subjects are authoritative with respect to the contents of their own intentional states. Further, this is due to the fact that there is a difference in kind - an asymmetry - between first and third person claims to know the contents of thoughts. Then (ibid. p.442) he runs quickly through and rejects the attempts of Wittgenstein (1958) and Ryle (1949) to account for first person authority. Ryle fails to account for the inferential asymmetry which Davidson takes to be present in first and third person claims to know the contents of thoughts. Wittgenstein's criterial account in which the criteria which form the basis for attributions of content to others (e.g. actions etc.) differ from the criteria for self-attribution is criticised for failure to explain why we should take S's attribution to A of (e.g.) the thought that London is nearer to Paris than Manchester to be a token of the same type of thought when S attributes this to himself. Davidson suggests that if two concepts have distinct evidential criteria (e.g. in the case of self-attributions of content versus attributions of content to others) they are distinct concepts. So since first-person attributions of content have a different evidential basis than do third person attributions of content, S could have no reason to suppose that the belief he ascribes to himself that, say, London is nearer to Paris than is Manchester, is the same type of belief as the belief he ascribed to A even if the same that-clause is employed.

It is then noted that his own account of the attribution of intentional states (cf. Davidson, 1984a) has been considered to threaten first person authority since the radical interpreter may ascribe intentional states to subjects which the subjects do not know they have. But Davidson points out that threats to first person authority have an origin stretching back at least as far as Russell's logical atomism (recall our earlier discussion of Russell's Constituency Thesis in ch.3 section 1). In that thesis (on one interpretation at any rate) external objects are constituents of intentional states. Since subjects have no special authority when it comes to knowledge of the natures, properties and relations of such objects, first person authority is threatened (call this the Russellian Difficulty).

113

But Putnam (1975) is singled out for special mention due to his thesis that the meanings of some terms are determined by contextual factors and the further claim that this context-dependence transmits to intentional states themselves (cf. ch.1 above).

Davidson then wonders why such an externalistic pattern of individuation of intentional states should be thought to threaten first person authority. It is noted that, in the Twin Earth case, there is no introspectible difference between S's thought that water is wet and S*'s thought that water* is wet (1987, p.445; also, Burge, 1988c); so no amount of introspection will reveal differences in type between the thoughts of S and S* concerning water/water*. The reason first person authority is allegedly threatened is the same as that referred to earlier concerning the threat to first person authority presented by Russell's logical atomism (i.e. since subjects have no special authority when it comes to knowledge of the natures, properties and relations of such objects, first person authority is threatened).

Having noted this, Davidson offers the observation that some theorists who allow that the commonsense scheme of individuation of intentional content is not compatible with mind-brain supervenience respond by positing narrow content (notably Putnam (1975), Fodor (e.g. 1982), and McGinn (1982)). It is then allowed by such theorists that subjects are authoritative over such narrow states. So subjects are authoritative about the contents of narrow states but not about intentional states as these are individuated in the commonsense scheme. (So a subject may be authoritative about the fact that he desires some liquid which satisfies the predicates "...is transparent", "...is thirst-quenching" etc., but not over states such as "I desire water".)

Davidson proposes that "any theory" (1987. p.447) which involves the positing of inner objects or abstract objects (e.g. Fregean propositions) will not be able to effect the desired reconciliation. The reason being, again, the familiar one that there will always be properties or relations of such objects (the individuation conditions of which are determined by external relations) which are at least as well-known or knowable from a third person point of view as from the first person perspective. As one would anticipate, Davidson's own view is one which does not rely on any inner or abstract objects.[8] Davidson seeks to rule out of contention any theory which involves an attempt to account for first person authority by positing "...entities that the mind can "entertain", "grasp", "have before it" or "be acquainted with"" (ibid., p.454) - i.e. any kind of inner object (e.g. narrow contents, ideas, inner propositions) or, it would seem, abstract objects (e.g. in the sense that numbers and Fregean propositions may be considered as abstract objects). Such theories might usefully be said to employ relational models of thought in their attempts to account for first person authority. (We will consider other relational models below (ch.6).)

Consider the attacks on these two theories separately (each of which employs a relational model of thought); first, that which appeals to inner objects, e.g. ""appearances", sense data, qualia, what is given in experience" (ibid. p.453). One objection to this move (i.e. to explain first person authority by appeal to these inner objects) is that it leads to scepticism. For familiar reasons, since Locke, Berkeley and Hume, the problem has always been to show how these inner objects are related to the outer objects which cause them.

Another objection recruited by Davidson stems from Hume's observation that such theories have difficulty explaining the notion of a self; crudely, the self may have ideas according to this general picture, but cannot gain an idea of itself (Hume, *Treatise*, bk.1, pt.4, sec.6).

Clearly, there are responses to Davidson's swiftly stated objections to the inner object theory, for example from theorists who really do take scepticism to be a genuine problem; also, it is unclear that anyone, as yet, has come up with a satisfactory explanation of selfhood. But rather than pursue these difficult problems, we can simply take the escape route and just presume, along with the other theorists which are the main focus of Davidson's account, that there is an external world about which we can have knowledge; and also that there are selves about which a satisfactory account can be given.

It is the second theory, according to which intentional states are relations to objects - abstract or otherwise (e.g. sentences of mentalese) - which Davidson suggests is a more important target to criticise due to the appeal it has among contemporary philosophers (esp. e.g. Fodor, 1982, 1987). Davidson proposes that the problem of explaining first person authority with respect to intentional states as these are individuated in the commonsense scheme will remain intractable as long as intentional states are regarded as relations to objects "public or private, abstract or concrete" (1987, p.455). It is intractable due to the Russellian Difficulty (p.212 above). With this stage-setting complete, let us now turn to Davidson's own solution.

5. Davidson: the positive story

Davidson aims to show that externalistic individuation of intentional states is compatible with the view that subjects are authoritative with respect to the contents of their first-order intentional states.[9] Since Davidson's solution to the problem is stated so briefly (1984b, pp.110-111; 1987, p.456) I will attempt to elaborate it here on his behalf. Four key claims can be identified:

(1) "...all thought and language must have a foundation in...direct historical connections [between the subject and her environment]" (1987, p.450).
(2) "...what a person's words mean depends in the most basic cases on the kinds of objects and events that have caused the person to hold the words to be applicable; similarly for what the person's thoughts are about" (1987, p.456).
(3) Only in the light of these claims is it possible to explain "how language can be learned and how words and attitudes can be identified by an interpreter" (ibid.).
(4) Davidson's solution appeals to, "...a presumption that speakers, but not their interpreters, are not wrong about what their words mean. The presumption is essential to the nature of interpretation" (Davidson, 1984b, p.110).

In short, it might be said that Davidson requires us to accept that when it comes to ascribing thoughts to others, we are in the position of the Radical Interpreter; and that we should accept an account of first person authority which is derived from constitutive constraints on radical interpretation.

Concerning (1), "all thought and language must...[etc.]"; that is to say, there has not, is not, and never will be a single thought or an item of language which does not have its "foundation" in empirical relations between the subject and the world. Does this mean simply (a) that it is only possible for a subject to entertain thoughts and to use language if the subject exists? If so, it is compatible with a crude language of thought hypothesis in which thoughts are wired in so to speak in the brains of subjects. Or does it mean (b) that the natures of intentional states are necessarily determined by the nature of the relations between subjects and their environments. That (b) is the intended interpretation is shown by (2).

The second claim renders Davidson's position a version of externalism. In this it is proposed that the natures of intentional types are determined by the environments of their subjects; specifically by the objective types which are instanced in the environment of the subject and to which the subject applies semantic tokens.

With respect to (3), a theoretical assumption of the nature of that proposed in (2) is, allegedly, necessary for the possibility of explaining

116

both how subjects learn languages, and how it is possible for intentional states to be ascribed to subjects from the third person perspective. I employ the term "theoretical assumption" since it is not clear that Davidson is making an empirical claim; it possible that he means something stronger than that - e.g. to the effect that the "theoretical assumption" is necessary for the possibility of interpreting the actions of others.

With specific reference to first person authority, in (4) it is claimed that ascription of intentional states to others, from the third person perspective, requires that such subjects are supposed to be authoritative with respect to the contents of their thoughts.

So "in the most basic cases" (ibid.) a person, on the basis of regular interaction with certain types of object, regularly applies the same word(s) - semantic types - to refer to that object or kind of object. The use of semantic types in such a regular way serves to individuate the person's intentional types; that is, semantic types employed by the speaker may be used by an interpreter to individuate the intentional types he (the speaker) instances.

In keeping with other aspects of Davidson's views (see 1984a), it can be supposed that subjects do not do this entirely unprompted and that language learning involves some degree of training and so on. (This point is important, as will be seen shortly.) It may plausibly be suggested that Davidson's argument is a transcendental argument of approximately the following form.

(i) Language is a going concern - communication is effected.
(ii) For it to be the case that (i), it is necessary to assume (a priori) that subjects apply semantic tokens in a regular manner to significant features of their environment.
(iii) It is necessary for interpreters to assume that (ii) is true for the possibility of ascribing thoughts to speakers.
(iv) The theoretical assumption appealed to in (ii) is an assumption that, in general, subjects know and are authoritative about what they think.

The interpreter's initial attitude to the speaker is one which includes a "presumption" (Davidson, 1984b, p.110) that the speaker is authoritative about the contents of his own thoughts. It appears that the "presumption" is neutral on the question of whether subjects actually are authoritative. Possibly because attempts to answer the latter question inevitably commit the error which Davidson identifies (i.e. allocating a special epistemic property either to the objects introspected or to the faculty of

117

introspection).

Hopefully, it can be seen, then, that Davidson's attempt to account for first person authority is wholly distinct from attempts to explicate first person authority in epistemic terms. Specifically, Davidson's solution is entirely distinct from all relational accounts. Recall that such accounts seek to explicate first person authority by appeal to an epistemic advantage which subjects have merely by virtue of being the subject of their own intentional states; this metaphysical fact brings with it epistemic advantage due either to the special nature of the introspective "view" of introspected objects; or due to the special nature of the introspected objects themselves.

A term which might usefully serve to distinguish Davidson's solution from the type of solutions just mentioned is this: it may be said that Davidson's is an Explanatory solution whereas the other solutions constitute Epistemic solutions.[10]

In Davidson's solution, then, it is claimed that since the sole evidential base for interpreting other subjects is their behaviour and their environments, some guiding principle(s) is necessary for the possibility of interpretation. Where the interpretations of behaviour are to be couched in intentional language, there will be so many possibly correct ways of interpreting the behaviour of other subjects (*pace* Quine (1960)) that some guiding principle(s) is required to distinguish plausible from implausible interpretations. In undertaking such a task the interpreter applies the criteria of rationality which are his own (or those of his fellows). Since it is held not to be possible to interpret the behaviour of other subjects without applying some criterion to enable the selection of some intentional states rather than others - from an indefinitely large number of possible (e.g.) beliefs and desires - in explanations of action, the status of the "guiding principle(s)" mentioned above, must be construed as constitutive rather than simply as "guiding". The said principle is not optional but is necessary for the possibility of interpretation. Unless it is adopted, problems concerning the inextricability of meaning and belief, ensure that it is not possible to interpret the utterances of others. (Roughly, it is necessary to assume that they believe what they say to be true otherwise one cannot determine what they mean (cf. Ramberg, 1989, pp.68-69).)

The principle referred to can be described as The Principle of Charity (Davidson, 1984, p.xvii). Though Davidson is coy about what it actually means, the above attempt to indicate some of its import does not seem obviously objectionable. Due to the inextricability of belief and meaning, the interpreter must presume that most of the utterances made by the interpretees are true. The upshot, for our purposes here is that the

Principle of Charity, ultimately, seems to rest at the bottom of Davidson's explanatory account of first person authority. The very act of interpreting the utterances of others is said, by Davidson, to involve both the presumption that the speaker does in fact intend to utter something and intends to be understandable; and the presumption that in general speakers believe that what they are saying is true. These fundamental parts of Davidson's radical interpretation program seem, for him, to be all there is to first person authority.

Having set out the proposals of Burge and Davidson, we turn now to criticism of them.

Notes to chapter five

1. Think especially of moral culpability here. That notion directs specific attention to the question of whether an actor did X deliberately. This requires that the actor knows what he is thinking at the time of his doing X.

2. A note concerning the use of "typically" in the last two sentences. It is meant to indicate a subject who may be regarded as a normal subject, a subject who has a causal history which is standard for humans, e.g involves some interaction with other humans and with instances of natural kinds, e.g. water. So a brain in a vat would not be a typical subject on this account.

3. Recall that first person authority is intended to denote a position of epistemic advantage. In this example one imagines that the medical staff will defer to the patient on the grounds that he is better placed than they to know what he thinks.

4. See also the phenomenon of thought alienation as described in Clare op.cit. p.95.

5. It is important to emphasise here that for Burge a subject can be said to know that he is thinking that F is more common than G (where F and G refer to natural kinds) without his knowing what it is that serves to individuate instances of F from other natural kinds - the same applies for knowledge of G.

6. Recall our earlier discussion (ch.2, section 2) concerning the relevance of causal histories to the identity conditions of entities.

7. The second aim is the most important for purposes here. The version of token physicalism described in ch.3 above shows how Davidson's first aim can be met.

8. By "inner objects" or abstract objects Davidson means "propositions, tokens of proposition...representations [or external

objects or events considered as constituents of thoughts]" (ibid.).

9. Davidson appears to concur with Burge concerning the problem of reconciling subjects' knowing the contents of their first-order states with externalism (Davidson, 1988, p.654).

10. It can be noted that there is some discomfort in the labels just suggested since Davidson's explanatory solution stems from the epistemic problem of determining the intentional states of other subjects. Nonetheless, it seems sufficiently clear that Davidson's strategy is radically different from other strategies considered so far in this chapter and does warrant a different label.

6 Responses to Burge
and Davidson

1. Response to Burge

(i) Knowledge

Having tried to make explicit Burge's strategy for dealing with the two problems identified at the start of ch.5, two possible difficulties need to be mentioned. The first concerns his disregard of scepticism. A sceptic is likely simply to reject Burge's claim that there can be knowledge that p without knowledge of the conditions necessary for it to be the case that p. This move is crucial to Burge so is there any response that he can bring against it? Well, the obvious response is simply to point out that Burge takes the tribunal for resolving the question of the truth or otherwise of externalism to be ongoing psychological explanation (see, e.g. 1986a, p.8, p.24). As we noted in ch.2 above psychological explanations also presume that scepticism is false. So the sceptical response to Burge here can be said to be inappropriate.

The second possible worry concerns the obscurity of the notion of containment. It might be wondered how literally Burge wants to be taken here. For example, it may be suggested that a brain state A described in neurophysiological terms literally contains a brain state B where B also is described in neurophysiological terms. This is not how Burge intends to be understood because, as we have heard, he proposes that there is more to the individuation of intentional states than their descriptions in neurophysiological terms. Rather, it seems that Burge is appealing to a notion of containment as may occur when it is claimed, say, that the sentence (1) "Major believes that Thatcher has a sister" contains the clause (2) "Thatcher has a sister". The content of (1) seems dependent upon the content of (2) in the way brought by the set-theoretic elaboration of Burge's use of the notion of containment provided above in that (1) is both individuation- and existence-dependent upon (2). So again it seems to me that Burge can be defended here. Hence, Burge's account of how it is that subjects know the contents of their first-order intentional states is being endorsed here. However, as will now be seen, this does not yet show that the knowledge subjects have of such states is authoritative.

(ii) Criticism of Burge's account of first person authority

A criticism of Burge's account which might be raised here is this. It can be pointed out that given that the nature of the relationship between first-order and second-order intentional states is as Burge suggests, it is still possible that subjects know the contents of their first-order intentional states but do not do so authoritatively. For example, if it could be shown to be possible that other subjects can share the first person perspective on the first-order intentional states of others, then presumably it would follow that it is possible to know authoritatively the natures of the intentional states of other subjects. Such a possibility will not be pursued here. The intention is simply to point to a metaphysically possible case in which the second-order perspective on one's own thoughts is shared, or intruded upon by another subject. Such a possibility indicates that there is at least a logical gap between Burge's account of the nature of subjects' knowledge of their own intentional states and subjects' authority with respect to such states.[1]

A more serious objection is the following. To say that subjects know the contents of their thoughts authoritatively - when authority is construed as an epistemic privilege - should imply that subjects are in a better position than others to know what the contents of their thoughts are. As noted, this is a claim which applies to intentional states at the level of types: to know that one is thinking a particular thought one has to know what type it is. But it would appear that subjects are not in an epistemically privileged position to determine the identities of the intentional types they instance. Other subjects seem at least as well-placed to do this; they might do this, for example, by observing the types of entities with which the subject comes into contact.

Consider the Twin Earth idiom again; this time S is transported to Twin Earth without his knowing that the transfer has occurred. Given time to establish causal relations sufficient for his being able to entertain thoughts about water*, Burge's model of basic self-knowledge has the consequence that when S thinks that water* is wet, he knows what he thinks. Granting this, though, does not make it clear how S could be regarded as being authoritative with respect to the contents of his

122

first-order states. The mere fact that the first-order state is contained in the second-order state might well serve to show how S can be said to know what he thinks, but it does not appear to show that S is authoritative with respect to the contents of his first-order states - where authority indicates a position of epistemic privilege. Observers of S who are aware of S's predicament seem, in fact, better placed to type S's thoughts.[2]

We might label this criticism of Burge "the Burgean circle". This is because, in Burge's account, subjects' knowledge of the contents of their first-order states is explained by reference to subjects' typing of these states. It is problematic then to seek to explain subjects' authority in terms of subjects' knowledge since the latter explanation does not show why we should accept that a subject is authoritative at the level of intentional types. In short, Burge explains subjects' knowledge of their intentional states by their employment of types. And then he seeks to explain authority by making use of points made about subjects' knowledge. But there is no explanation of how subjects are authoritative with respect to the relevant types.

It can be proposed then that the Burgean circle constitutes a serious objection to Burge and so he cannot be taken to have shown externalism to be compatible with first person authority (i.e. even though his account of how subjects can be said to know the contents of their first-order states has been endorsed here).

2. Relational models not considered by Davidson

Before considering Davidson's positive proposals, it is worth commenting on an inadequacy in his negative proposals. The inadequacy centres on his failure to consider certain other kinds of relational models for explicating first person authority.

Davidson clearly takes the available options to effect the reconciliation between first person authority and externalistic individuation of intentional states to be these: (a) adopt some form of relational model; (b) adopt some other view (e.g., his own). Theories of type (a) are ruled out, Davidson believes, due to their vulnerability to the Russellian Difficulty (the difficulty that subjects are required to know everything about the object thought of). However, it is worth making explicit one other option not considered by Davidson: (c) A type of relational model which is not vulnerable to the Russellian Difficulty.[3]

A first point to make here concerns the very idea of a relational model; that is, of a model in which intentional states are considered to consist in relations to objects. Davidson complains that such a model is radically misguided and amounts to a "dogma" (ibid., p.455) - "the dogma that to have a thought is to have an object before the mind" (ibid., p.455). The principal reason why the dogma should be relinquished, according to Davidson, is the Russellian Difficulty; but that is only a reason for relinquishing the dogma if subjects are in fact authoritative with respect to the contents of their thoughts. Since, however, we are presently presuming that subjects do have first person authority it can be agreed that if a relational model is vulnerable to the Russellian Difficulty (see last note) then its retention amounts to a dogma.

It should also be said that Davidson's point that the relational form of attributions of intentional states does not, by itself, license an inference to the ontological nature of intentional states is sound; but it can be countered that it is, at least, a preliminary motivation for such a proposal. So to consider the very idea of a relational model of intentional states need not be seen as involving commitment to a dogma.

A second worry is this. On the Cartesian conception of intentional states considered earlier (ch.1) the natures of those states were wholly insulated from the context of the subject of the states. An externalist pattern of individuation of intentional states, as we have heard, is not compatible with such a Cartesian conception of intentional states.

In chs.3 and 4 above our discussion of the position articulated by Macdonald (e.g. in Macdonald, 1992) with respect to the relationship between mental and physical properties suggested that that relationship can be described as one of nonlocal supervenience. If that is accepted, a position in which the natures of mental items are not independent of the nature of the physical environment of their subjects becomes possible.

Suppose, then, it is proposed that intentional states are relational in nature, and that the natures of the objects of those states are not independent of the nature of the physical environment of their subject. Can such a model avoid the Russellian Difficulty?

Such a model could only avoid the Russellian Difficulty if a subject could know directly, just by introspecting, the type identity of the relevant thought. Even if such a model is plausible, it would need to be able to explain how a subject could be said to know authoritatively that his thought was a water-thought as opposed to a water*-thought. It would have to be explained how a subject could possess such knowledge in spite of the phenomenal similarity of the two thoughts and of the syntactic similarity of the two thoughts. (Recall that both Davidson (e.g. 1987, p.445) and Burge (1988c, p.653) allow that there is no "basis" upon which a subject could distinguish between the two thoughts.) Also, more would need to be said about the nature of the relation between the thought and the mental object. Let us turn to these tasks.

How, then, could it plausibly be claimed that a subject knows the content of a particular thought? First, it needs to be shown that there may be direct knowledge - i.e. since first person authority is to be grounded in the availability of such knowledge to subjects when it comes to consideration of the contents of their own intentional states. And second it needs to be shown that there can be direct knowledge of relational facts - i.e., since the objects, if there are any, of intentional states will be individuated relationally if externalism is true.

Can there be direct knowledge? Recall that direct knowledge is knowledge obtained without the need for inference. To accept that there could be direct knowledge it first has to be accepted that there may be knowledge per se. We are assuming that scepticism is false so it is being allowed here that it is possible for a subject to know that p where p is some proposition.

One characteristic of direct knowledge proposed by Heil (1988a, p.239) is that it can be problematic to provide evidence for such knowledge. So, for example, if S claims to know that the table he is presently looking at is brown and S is asked to provide evidence in support of that knowledge claim, according to Heil, S would not know what to do "beyond indicating the item in question" (ibid.); the same proposal is made with respect to S's claim to know directly that, say, his legs are crossed (Heil, ibid.).

It could be said against Heil that these two examples are not analogous. Consider the first example. It seems plausible to suggest that if a bystander B asks S to provide evidence in support of the claim that the table is brown S would be able to provide evidence. For example he could ask B what colour the table appeared to him. If B denied that it was brown they could invite the judgments of other perceivers. So in respect of colour judgments it does seem to be the case that some evidence could be provided in support of a knowledge claim to the effect that a particular object is a particular colour.

The situation is less clear with respect to Heil's second example (i.e. his knowing directly that his legs are crossed). It would indeed be problematic to offer evidence to show that one's legs were in fact crossed if B were to ask S how he knows that his legs are crossed.

Assuming that one can possess direct knowledge of facts of the two kinds just described, then, little weight can be attached to the claim that typically it is problematic to provide evidence in support of claims for direct knowledge.

Claims for the existence of direct knowledge often appeal to visually identifiable properties such as colours (e.g. Heil, ibid.; Macdonald,

1991a, p.3); and whilst it can be agreed that the fact that a particular object is a particular colour can be known directly, the fact that evidence could be recruited to settle any disputes is important to bear in mind. In fact that point takes us onto the second question identified above; namely, can there be direct knowledge of facts the individuation conditions of which are relational?

Can there be direct knowledge of relationally individuated facts?

We have just mentioned and allowed the possibility of direct knowledge of visually identifiable properties such as colour properties. It can plausibly be claimed that colours are in fact relationally individuated. This claim can be motivated by the proposal that some properties are mind-dependent (e.g. being in pain) whilst some are not (e.g. being square-shaped) (cf. McGinn, 1983, pp.9-11, 119; and of course Locke's *Essay Concerning Human Understanding*). If this distinction is allowed it may be proposed further that application of colour predicates, e.g. "...is red", is dependent upon there being a group of perceivers with a particular type of sensory equipment. The property of being red then consists in looking red to a significant number of normal perceivers (members of of the relevant species) under normal lighting conditions. Colour predicates are then describable as relational since the true ascription to an object of such a predicate implies the existence of a group of perceivers with a particular type of sensory apparatus (cf. McGinn, 1983, p.119).

Having said something about direct knowledge and, hopefully, indicated that relational individuation is not prima facie incompatible with direct knowledge (i.e. that facts which are relationally individuated may be known directly) let us continue. What needs to be done now is to try to construct a relational model which is not vulnerable to the Russellian Difficulty, making use of our recent deliberations.

The points about direct knowledge and relational individuation were made with the example of properties which are visually open to view, so to speak. An observational metaphor may go some of the way towards explicating a relational model of thought when the introspected objects are construed along the lines of colours; i.e. their individuation conditions are open to view, roughly, if it looks red, it is red (so the story might run).[4] But plainly, even if this observational metaphor is accepted with respect to colour-thoughts there is much more work to be done to say how the metaphor will operate in the case of natural kind thoughts. In the case of water-/water* thoughts these liquids both look the same. So the observational model does not enable any progress to be made towards explication of authority with respect to natural kind thoughts; nor to any thoughts about entities whose individuation conditions are not open to view in the way that (perhaps) the individuation conditions of colours and sensations are open to view.

Desperate times call for desperate measures. What if we worry an old phrase of Quine's and attempt to claim that the relata of introspection wear their identities on their sleeves (1960, p.42); and, that they do so in such a way that that subjects' knowledge of the contents of natural kind thoughts is directly analogous to their knowledge of e.g. pain states and perhaps colour-thoughts. Such a view would not be vulnerable to the Russellian Difficulty since subjects would know which properties of the inner object constituted its identity conditions. The subject could tell just by introspecting that a particular thought is a water-thought rather than a water*-thought because water-thoughts would display their identity conditions and water*-thoughts would display theirs. So although any number of properties may be displayed, so to speak, by the inner object, those which comprise its identity conditions shine forth most prominently - again, so to speak.

There are two great difficulties with this particular avenue however. The first is that, as noted earlier, phenomenally, both water and water* have the same properties. So construing introspection as directly analogous to observation would not provide a basis in thought for a distinction to be drawn between water- and water*-thoughts. Further, as the Twin Earth story is told (chs.1 and 2 above), the Twins speak languages which are syntactically and phonetically indistinguishable. So if the introspected items are construed as syntactic items no difference would be discernible from the first person perspective between the thoughts of the Twins S and S*.

The second difficulty is that it becomes problematic to explain how subjects can be said to lack knowledge of the individuation conditions of natural kinds. At the start of this chapter it was suggested that subjects can legitimately be ascribed thoughts about natural kinds without their knowing the individuation conditions of such kinds. We may ascribe to S a desire for a gold ring, where "gold" occurs in oblique position, without that implying that S knows the individuation conditions of gold. Presumably, it would be absurd to allow that subjects have such knowledge of empirical matters at birth; and it is difficult to explain, on the account presently being considered, why subjects would possess knowledge of the individuation conditions of natural kinds at some stage but not at birth.

These reflections seem to indicate that there is little to be gained from attempting to pursue the Quinean metaphor any further - at least with respect to natural kind thoughts (i.e. it may be possible to pursue the metaphor further for other kinds of thoughts).

The very idea of a relational model

We have attempted to characterise a relational model of introspection which is compatible both with externalism and with first person authority. The attempt has not been successful, at least as far as natural kind thoughts are concerned. To cast further doubt on the possibility that such a model will prove viable, let us consider some remarks made by Burge (1988c,p.660).

In strategies such as that just suggested - employing the Quinean metaphor - Burge claims that an attempt is made to render the introspective faculty infallible. Such attempts either (a) allocate properties to the introspective faculty such that it cannot provide false data; or (b) allocate to the objects of introspection a property which renders them incapable of being misperceived. This second strategy is that exploited in the Quinean metaphor strategy and which was unsuccessful for natural kind thoughts.

Further, Burge points out that strategies which seek to exploit an analogy between perception and introspection are guilty of overlooking two fundamental differences between the two faculties (1988c, p.657). First, in the case of perception the possibility of error - of misperception - is always present. The nature of the introspective faculty which has featured in our recent discussion (and in the Cartesian conception outlined in ch.1 above) is one according to which that faculty cannot deliver false information (at least with respect to natural kind thoughts and colour thoughts). This puts the appeal to metaphorical similarities between perception and introspection under some pressure. And second, the objects of perception are, obviously, open to public view. But this is not the case for the objects of introspection; as we have heard, these are allegedly private, inner objects. So again, the appeal to relevant similarities between perceptual and introspective faculties can be queried.

Although our recent considerations do seem to rule out attempts to account for first person authority with respect to natural kind thoughts - where, in effect, appearances can deceive - the possibility still remains of first person authority over states which do, less controversially, display their individuation conditions. A possible example of such a state may be pain states: plausibly, a subject can tell just by feeling the relevant sensation that he is in pain. If this is accepted, a limited construal of first person authority may be got off the ground - authority over phenomenal but not propositional states (cf. McGinn, 1982c, pp.8-9;

128

and see below, ch.7).

But even if such a range of properties can be identified that still leaves the problems identified by Burge concerning attempts to exploit analogies between perception and introspection.

Although, as we have heard, Burge has indicated how dubious attempts to exploit analogies between perception and introspection really are, he was seen earlier to exploit a containment relation to characterise the relationship between first- and second-order intentional states: second-order states literally contain first-order states and the individuation conditions of the latter determine those of the former. Suppose it is suggested that this type of relationship may be appealed to in attempts to account for first person authority. In this case the metaphysical relationship between first- and second-order states may not necessarily involve attributions to the introspective faculty of any special properties. An attempt to recruit this notion of containment to explain first person authority may claim that a subject instances a first-order intentional type. Then it may be claimed that from the second-order perspective, the first-order state is typed. Macdonald (1991a, p.10) suggests that rejection of the kind of relational model of thought to which Davidson was seen to object - and to which Burge's points concerning the perception/introspection analogy apply - may still be compatible with a position in which subjects have a "perspective" on their first-order thoughts which is open to them but not to others. Our problem, though (as she recognises), is that even given the availability of such a perspective it is extremely problematic to account for first person authority with respect to, e.g., natural kind thoughts - specifically to any thoughts whose phenomenal aspect does not serve to individuate the thought.

In the light of the likelihood that a model of the kind just alluded to promises at most only limited success (since authority over natural kind thoughts seems ruled out), we move on now to consider further Davidson's view.

3. Davidson's Theory: comments and criticisms

Davidson's account helps to explain the widely held view that there is an inferential asymmetry between first and third person perspectives on thought (cf. Heil, 1988a, Georgalis, 1990, Boghossian, 1989, Burge, 1988c). In Davidson's view it is suggested that there is a difference between the utterer and the interpreter when it comes to the interpretation of speech. He indicates that the interpreter must hypothesise about contextual facts such as the social setting of the utterance, the background of the speaker, the kind of speech act the utterer is likely to be making on the occasion concerned and so on (Davidson, 1984b, 110).

Davidson's claim here is unremarkable but nonetheless plausible. There seems to be no doubt that even in the home case, contextual factors play a role in the determination of the kind of utterance a speaker is regarded as making. The reason that the interpreter's position with respect to the determination of the content of the utterance differs from the position of the utterer appears to be that there is a gap between meaning and belief which is present for the interpreter but which is not present for the utterer (Davidson, 1987, p.456; 1984b, p.111).

It may be seen, thus, that Davidson is going some of the way toward explicating the claimed inferential asymmetry between utterer and interpreter; and, analogously, between thinking from the first and third person perspectives. Further, Davidson seems to be going some of the way towards an explanation of why the third person perspective requires the making of inference to the determination of the contents of the thoughts of others. Such an inference is required due to the gap between meaning and belief; the gap exists for interpreters but not for utterers.[5]

It may be added that, empirically, it does seem to be the case that there is a presumption on the part of interpreters that speakers do know what they mean - as opposed to the opposite case. One can become persuaded that a person does not know what they think (e.g. in certain forms of thought disorder), but one's initial attitude to other speakers does seem to be that they know what they think.

Some remarks made by Heil (1992, pp.176-177) seem to me to clarify further the Davidsonian line. Heil refers to a situation in which a subject S is describing the Battle of Borodino with the use of a blackboard. S uses "Xs" to denote Napoleon's army, and "Os" to indicate the location of Kutuzov's forces. Heil points out that it would be bizarre to put a question such as the following to S: "What makes you think the Xs stand for Napoleon's troops and not Kutuzov's troops?" (ibid., p.176). Although S could be wrong about the exact location of Napoleon's troops in relation to Kutuzov's, he surely cannot be wrong in thinking that he intends the X's to stand for Napoleon's forces; and it is difficult to conceive of evidence which S could recruit in support of an answer to the question posed.

The point of the example is to indicate the asymmetry between the position of S and that of others with respect to the answer to the question posed in the last paragraph.

I propose, now, to consider some possible objections to the Davidsonian position as that has been outlined so far. A first worry is that of accommodating the kind of case described by McCulloch (1989, p.212) in which a subject takes himself to know, e.g. Descartes' Ontological Argument, but then discovers that, when asked to give an account of it, he is unable to do so. It might be thought that Davidson's account proves too much, so to speak, in that it cannot cope with instances in which it appears that subjects are not authoritative with respect to what they are thinking.

However, it should be clear that nothing Davidson says need commit him to the strong thesis that subjects are always - i.e. on every occasion - authoritative about what they think. As noted earlier, he claims just that there is a presumption on the part of the interpreter that the speaker is authoritative. It may be the case that on particular occasions a speaker turns out not to be authoritative with respect to the contents of his thoughts. But that possibility is, of course, compatible with the proposal that there is a general presumption on the part of interpreters that speakers are authoritative.

Second, it may be thought that Davidson's account falls victim to the objection which besets Burge's attempted solution (see ch.6, section 1 above). This was that authority at the level of token first-order intentional states cannot rest upon authority concerning the typing of first-order states at the second-order level. This is due to the suggestion that subjects are not authoritative concerning the typing of semantic types. For example, it can be agreed that subjects may apply words to features of their environment in a systematic way. But it seems reasonable to suggest that such uses of language are subject to the constraining influence of the linguistic community to which the speaker belongs; this suggestion is supported by the truism that mistakes can be made in linguistic usage. The mistakes are identified as such by virtue of their failure to conform to the rules governing the way the relevant term is employed in the linguistic community concerned. In effect, then, use of language by a subject is constrained by the linguistic community to which he belongs.

If it is correct, this claim invites the further suggestion that subjects' application of a sound in the presence of a particular type of object over a period of time is similarly answerable to the way that sound is employed in the subject's linguistic community; the subject is not, typically, authoritative about such matters.

Macdonald (1991a, pp.8-9) appears to claim that for Davidson the typing of intentional states follows from the typing of semantic types; typing of semantic types is accomplished by the application of certain sounds to certain environmental conditions on a regular, systematic basis. Subjects are alleged to be authoritative regarding the latter (in Macdonald's account of Davidson) due to the fact that agents are the subjects of their own causal histories. Authority at the level of semantic types transmits upwards, so to speak, to bring authority at the level of intentional types. But if subjects' authority at the level of semantic types proves questionable - as suggested above - then, presumably authority with respect to intentional states will be adversely affected. As I understand it, this is an objection to Davidson's account which is raised by Macdonald (1991a, pp.8-9). What Davidson says is

> The agent herself [in contrast to the interpreter]...is not in a position to wonder whether she is generally using her own words to apply to the right objects and events, since whatever she regularly applies them to gives her thoughts the meaning they have and her thoughts the contents they have (1987, p.457).

It seems to me that Davidson's claim here is consistent with the constraining role which the linguistic community has with respect to the determination of semantic types. In this passage it does not seem evident that what Davidson is saying is that the subject is responsible for the determination of semantic types; it seems to me, rather, that he is noncommittal. It can be suggested, therefore, that Davidson may not be vulnerable to the same objection to which Burge's account proved vulnerable (Macdonald seems to say Davidson's account is vulnerable to that charge, 1991a, pp.8-9).

The objection raised in this section seems to foist onto Davidson more epistemic baggage than is appropriate and lays insufficient emphasis upon the suggestion that Davidson's is an explanatory and not an epistemic account of first person authority. Heil's example (that concerning Napoleon and Kutuzov) helps to see how a subject may be answerable to his linguistic community with respect to matters of linguistic usage, whilst remaining in a position of epistemic advantage with respect to his own thoughts.[6]

Third, it may be said that the point in favour of Davidson's account identified earlier (concerning inferential asymmetry) can be successfully made within an epistemic model of first person authority. It was suggested above that Davidson's account helps to explain the inferential asymmetry commonly believed to be characteristic of the difference between first and third person perspectives on thought. But it is possible that the supposed asymmetry can be explained from within an epistemic model (i.e. a way other than one which involves positing special epistemic properties either of objects viewed or the introspective faculty itself). For example, suppose it is conjectured that, from the first person perspective, subjects learn inductively that they are more likely to be

132

correct about what they themselves presently think than are others. This does not seem implausible. The following, rather cruel, (hypothetical!) experiment might lend some support to the conjecture.

Suppose a child is brought up to believe that his parents know what he, the child, is thinking; in such a case, the infant might reasonably take his parents to be authoritative when it comes to determining what he thinks. So if the child is asked what he thinks, he is always prepared to defer to his parents since he takes them to be authoritative about what he the child really thinks.

It is reasonable to consider that such a child might devise some kind of test situation to test the hypothesis that his parents are, in fact, authoritative about what he himself thinks. Crudely, on a particular occasion the child might think to himself "I am four years old" and whilst thinking this, ask his parents what he is thinking. If they fail to determine that he is currently thinking that he is four years old, the child might begin to suspect that his parents are not, after all, authoritative about what he thinks. The child might subsequently construct similar test situations and inductively conclude that that he is authoritative about what he presently thinks.

This epistemic view of first person authority, it seems reasonable to say, is compatible with Davidson's claim that there is a "presumption" that speakers know what they think. The presumption might have an epistemic basis in the sense that subjects infer from their own case that just as they are authoritative about what they think, so too are others - generally speaking.

The epistemic account of first person authority gestured at in this section also helps to deal with what Davidson describes as the "strange idea that claims made without evidential... support should be favored over claims with such support" (1987, p.442). Typically, epistemic accounts of first person authority do not attempt to address this phenomenon; Davidson seems right to point out that it should be puzzling why knowledge claims not based on evidence (i.e. first person knowledge claims) should be regarded as having greater authority than claims which are based on evidence (i.e. claims made from the third person perspective).

However, an account along the lines just described does not discount the relevance of evidence altogether since, initially, the subject accumulates evidence that he is authoritative about what he thinks. But that does not entail that on every occasion the subject appeals to evidence in support of the view that he is authoritative about his own thoughts. Nor does it entail that it is strange that subjects be regarded as authoritative.

133

What needs to be distinguished here is (a) the claim that particular first person claims to know are authoritative when they concern the subject's own intentional states simply due to the fact that they are made from the perspective of the first person; and (b) the claim that evidence is of some relevance to the issue of first person authority. To return to the child recently described, initially, evidence is relevant to authority since the subject accumulates evidence that he is authoritative with respect to his own thoughts. But then, having arrived - inductively - at the conclusion that he is indeed authoritative, he presumes it to be the case that he is authoritative generally; so the question of the provision of evidence does not arise once the hypothesis that the subject is authoritative has been accepted by him. (Though it may arise in the future, e.g. if the subject develops some kind of pathological thought disorder and comes to doubt that he is authoritative.)

If these considerations are set against what Davidson takes to be a "strange idea" it can be said that under normal circumstances (i.e. a competent, functioning human member of a linguistic community) a claim to know made from the first person perspective can be regarded as being authoritative even though that particular claim to know is not based on evidence. That can be accepted without adherence to the further claim that evidence is entirely irrelevant to the authority attached to first person claims to know. The child in the earlier example, in effect, learns that he is authoritative about his first person claims to know.

These considerations, though conceived of within an epistemic model of first person authority, can be taken to suggest that from the third person perspective first person claims to know, made by cognitively competent humans, can be presumed to be correct. This is due to extrapolation from one's own case.

Although there are undoubtedly difficulties with the approach to first person authority gestured at in this section (e.g. concerning inference from one's own case, the paucity of empirical data supporting the suggestion and so on) it seems reasonable to allow the following: (a) that a model of first person authority which has epistemic aspects to it but in which there is a presumption that utterers have authoritative over the content of their first-order occurrent intentional states is, at least, not obviously incoherent; and (b) that such a model is able to cope with Davidson's point concerning the "strange idea" that certain knowledge claims not based on evidence be regarded as more authoritative than knowledge claims which are so based.

If accepted, these considerations do not necessarily show Davidson's theory to be wrong, they just indicate that an alternative position which has one of the advantages of Davidson's own position may be available.

So the point in favour of Davidson's account described above, is explicable within an attempt to ground first person authority in epistemic rather than explanatory factors. The upshot, then, is that Davidson's "presumption" or explanatory theory of first person authority, though apparently opposed to epistemic attempts to account for first person authority, may well be compatible with at least one such attempt.[7]

A fourth objection to Davidson may be the following. It is all very well Davidson telling us that epistemic accounts of first person authority are doomed to failure but it is so powerful an intuition that one's relations to one's occurrent intentional states are epistemic that no matter how plausible are Davidson's arguments, an explanatory account could not be accepted. This intuitive plea seems especially powerful when made in relation to second-order intentional states which include first-order thoughts concerning presently experienced phenomenal states.

It should be clear, then, that Davidson's view can be successfully defended against the objections from McCulloch and Macdonald. But the points made in thr third and fourth objections just given indicate that Davidson's rejection of the possible relevance of epistemic factors may require certain modifications to his account. The example given in the third objection seems to show how evidential considerations can be relevant to assessment of claims to be authoritative with respect to the contents of one's intentional states. More seriously, it seems clear that epistemic factors are relevant to the issue of first person authority with respect to phenomenal states. What I propose to do now is to comment further on the question of the relevance of the issue of first person authority with respect to phenomenal states. The purpose of this is to develop an account of first person authority which takes into consideration epistemic issues which Davidson omits to take seriously. Further, Davidson's account is so counter-intuitive in its apparent rejection of epistemic factors in the explication of first person authority that more does need to be said concerning the extent to which epistemic considerations are to be set aside.

Notes to chapter six

1. Perhaps a Parfitian account of personal identity would yield the metaphysical possibility suggested in the text (Parfit, 1984).
2. As I understand her, this is a criticism levelled at Burge by Macdonald (1991a), though it is not expressed in the way set out here.
3. The difficulty that "if to have a thought is to have an object

"before the mind", and the identity of the object determines what the thought is, then it must always be possible to be mistaken about what one is thinking. For unless one knows everything about the object, there will always be senses in which one does not know which object it is" (Davidson, 1987, p.455).

4. Perhaps thoughts which concern pain states are a better class of example here.

5. At least, the gap is ever-present for interpreters, but is not ever-present for utterers. ,

6. In short, it is being claimed here that Davidson can allow that subjects are answerable to members of their linguistic community when it comes to matters of correct usage of semantic tokens. This can be granted without conceding the further point that on particular occasions, subjects are presumed to be authoritative with respect to what they think.

7. It might be added that the attempt in this section to gesture towards an epistemic account of first person authority may well be similar to that proposed by Ryle - i.e. the ideal observer theory - (Ryle, 1949, ch.6); this theory is dismissed by Davidson on the grounds that it does not respect the intuition that there is an epistemic asymmetry between first and third person perspectives on thought. However, it has been indicated above that that such a theoretical position may well be available and may not be incompatible with Davidson's own view.

7 Towards a solution

1. An impure Davidsonian theory

McGinn (1982c, pp.8-9) draws attention to the suggestion that mental states can be divided into two categories: sensations and intentional states. As may be anticipated, the former states include "pains, tickles [and feelings of] nausea" (ibid.); intentional states on the other hand are states the ascriptions of which employ that-clauses.

There may be some artificiality in this way of dividing up mental states since a pain state can also be specified by the employment of a that-clause, e.g. Jones believes that he in pain; or that he is being tickled; or that he feels sick and so on. Further, descriptions of such states have logical properties (e.g. "S is in pain", if true, implies that at least one thing is in pain). But, as McGinn indicates, a significant difference between the two kinds of states is the relative importance of any phenomenal aspects of such states in relation to the determination of the individuation conditions of the states. In the case of sensation states the phenomenal aspects of such states are plausibly regarded as essential to their individuation conditions (McGinn suggests that the individuation conditions of such states are exhausted by their phenomenology). In the case of propositional attitude states any phenomenal aspects of such states are less important to the individuation conditions of the states; the that-clause employed to specify the content of the state bears the main burden when it comes to determining the identity of the state.

It should be stressed that as the taxonomy has been set out here it is perfectly possible for propositional attitude states to have a phenomenal aspect (as McGinn makes clear (ibid. p.9)): e.g. Smith's fear that he has to give a lecture may be said to have a phenomenal aspect. How, then, does this taxonomy bear on the first person authority issue?

Attempts to reconcile intuitions about first person authority with externalism which have been mentioned so far in this essay have been monistic in the sense that they have little or nothing to say concerning sensation states. Davidson, for example, appears to pay insufficient attention to the extremely powerful intuition that subjects are authoritative with respect to beliefs which concern currently experienced sensation states - perhaps due to some epistemic property instanced by those states.

In McGinn's discussion of the (admittedly crude) taxonomy just described, he points to a tension highlighted by the taxonomy. It is pointed out that sensation states seem best described from the first person perspective - i.e. since the phenomenal aspects of such states seem so relevant to their individuation conditions, and since such phenomenal aspects seem only to be experienced from the first person perspective. However, ascriptions of intentional states seem more comfortably characterised from the third person perspective. Such states are ascribed to subjects on the basis of what they say and do - in order to explain their actions. Of course, the claim that intentional states may have phenomenal aspects, if accepted, indicates that the first person perspective may not be entirely irrelevant to the ascription of intentional states, and so data from the first person perspective may be of some relevance to ascriptions of intentional states. Nonetheless, it is plausible to suppose that there are these two perspectives from which to consider mental states. By this account, an adequate characterisation of mental life would admit data obtained from both perspectives - first and third person.[1]

Suppose, then, that such a claim is taken seriously; namely, that a fully adequate account of the mental should admit data obtained from both the first and third person perspectives. Suppose further that we apply this claim to the problem of attempting to reconcile externalism and first person authority. Might a nonmonistic (so to speak) approach to the problem prove more adequate than a monistic approach? That is to say, suppose occurrent thoughts which concern presently occurring sensation states can be coped with by the proposal that their individuation conditions are transparent to their subjects. And suppose further that intentional states which do not concern presently experienced sensations can be coped with in something like the way Davidson describes. So, from the distinction between two types of mental states, the possibility of a nonmonistic approach to first person authority is opened up. Three positions now need to be distinguished.

First, position in which first person authority over a certain class of states stems from certain properties of those states; for example, sensation states the instancing of which by subjects is sufficient for subjects both to know and to be authoritative with respect to their

138

identities. For this type of approach to be accepted it is required that there are such properties. Further the view that taking a perspective upon one's own first-order psychological states is relevantly analogous to perception (e.g. visual or tactile) also needs to be taken on. Still further, it needs to be borne in mind that even if these two concessions are allowed the approach bears only a limited amount of fruit; this is due to familiar problems concerning thoughts about distinct types of objects which appear phenomenally to be of the same type, e.g. water and water* (and, recall our discussion of the Quinean Metaphor (ch.6, section 2)).

The second position is what might be described as "A Pure Davidsonian Position". In this, first person authority has nothing to do with epistemic factors stemming from appeal to a relation between the thinker and the object thought of - e.g. an introspected item. In the pure Davidsonian line, first person authority stems from a condition on the interpretation of the speech of other subjects. The condition requires the presumption that speakers are authoritative with respect to their presently entertained thoughts.

A third position may be described as "An Impure Davidsonian Position". As noted, the pure position does not seek to ground first person authority on epistemic factors - the presumption of first person authority stems solely from constraints on interpretation. The 'impure' Davidsonian position retains commitment to the view that the presumption of first person authority is a necessary component of interpretation; but its impurity stems from its acknowledging an epistemic basis for at least one class of psychological states - namely, occurrent thoughts concerning presently occurring sensations. So the impure Davidsonian position involves the said presumption plus a degree of epistemic baggage.

Since (at least to my knowledge) all participants in the internalism/externalism debate are in agreement that there is first person authority, it can reasonably be supposed that all agree with Davidson that there is a presumption of first person authority in interactions with most other (human) subjects. As noted earlier, when interacting with other speakers the presumption is, in normal circumstances, that they do know what they are thinking; of course, in some cases the presumption may need to be revised, say, when it is concluded that the other speaker is suffering from some manner of thought disorder.

The main point of disagreement between Davidson and critics of externalism centres on the basis for that presumption. As we have heard, for Davidson the presumption has no epistemic basis. In the Cartesian account the presumption has an epistemic basis via the introspective faculty. Again, as noted earlier, Davidson seems right to point out that such accounts appear vulnerable to the Russellian Difficulty (i.e. how can the subject know which of the properties displayed by the internal object determine its identity?). But if a range of properties which display, so to speak, their individuation conditions can be discerned (e.g. those involved in sensations of pain), then the possibility arises of there being a range of psychological states for which there is an epistemic basis for first person authority with respect to those states. For such states, the presumption of first person authority would have an epistemic basis. One suggestion is that properties such as those instanced when subjects undergo pain states may be plausible candidates for the range of properties required. But even if this is accepted, the difficulty remains of providing an epistemic basis for states whose individuation conditions are not plausibly accounted for in the same way in which at least some of those involving sensations may be accounted for (i.e. the problems relating to the Quinean metaphor (ch.6, sec.2)). An account of first person authority based on properties of the desired kind (i.e. those capable of displaying their individuation conditions) will provide only a limited epistemic basis for first person authority. Authority concerning (e.g.) natural kind thoughts could not be coped with along similar lines.

The situation, then, may be thought to invite the following two suggestions: Let it be accepted that there is an epistemic basis for first person authority with respect to certain states, namely, those concerning properties which display their individuation conditions to the thinker at the time they are thought about. And let it also be accepted that, for all other types of states there is no epistemic basis for first person authority; specifically, no basis which rests upon appeals to a special relation between thinkers and the objects of their thoughts.

Recall also what was said earlier concerning the presumption of first person authority - i.e. that just as in the English legal system those charged are presumed innocent until proven guilty, so (under normal circumstances) are other subjects presumed to be authoritative until reasons to suspect otherwise arise. It may be suggested, now, that the presumption referred to applies to states of the kind described in (1) and has an epistemic basis when applied to them. Also, it may be suggested that when applied to the kind of states described in (2) the presumption, strictly speaking, does not have an epistemic basis. This raises the question of why it is that the presumption applies to both types of state.

A diagnosis of why this may be the case is this. So impressive is the degree to which subjects are perceived to be authoritative with respect to their sensation states that this perceived authority carries over to other kinds of states also. An indication of the degree to which it is believed to be the case that subjects are authoritative with respect to their sensation states is provided by the fact that the appeal to the distinction between behaving as though one is in pain and being in pain is regarded as a serious obstacle to the acceptance of behaviourist attempts to reduce the mental to the merely behavioural. On such accounts of the relationship between the mental and the behavioural, certain sensory inputs when correlated with certain bodily outputs (responses) are capable of providing an exhaustive characterisation of pain states. However, the widely held belief that it is empirically possible for (say) a person to be subjected to the relevant stimulus-type (e.g. the person's foot being brought into contact with a hot coal) and display the relevant type of bodily movement without experiencing the sensation of pain casts doubt on (refutes?) the proposed behavioural reductions of mental to behavioural types. Presumably, the appeal could only have the force it does appear to have (cf. e.g. Churchland, 1989, p.23; Armstrong, 1968, pp.68-69) if it is accepted that claims about phenomena which may be experienced without being behaviourally manifested are to be taken seriously (e.g. first person reports about sensation states) and are regarded as authoritative.

It needs to be said that there is a response to this general line which may be made at this point. A familiar move by opponents of so-called folk-psychology is to attempt to cast doubt on the veridicality of the kind of first person claims to know just appealed to. For example, Churchland (1979, pp.97-99) suggests that there are occasions when subjects are unsure about the identities of their sensation states; e.g. although at one end of the pain-spectrum, so to speak, there are states where a subject will quickly, and with conviction, declare that he is in pain, there are states when it is not so obvious, and the subject may be unsure whether he is in pain or not. Similar points are made about sensations of hunger and thirst and so on.

However, it may said in reply that the issue under discussion here is first person authority, and this is taken here to indicate a position of epistemic advantage. So as long as it is allowed that subjects themselves are better placed than others to know whether they are in a state of a certain type or not then first person authority is retained. It is clear that the point raised by Churchland in the last paragraph can, thus, be accommodated in the position described here since it is possible to allow both that subjects may be unsure about whether they are currently undergoing a state of type A or a state of type B and that they are in an epistemically advantageous position to make that determination.

These last considerations seem to lend some support to the diagnosis of why it may be that subjects' authority over sensation states carries over to intentional states; and that this may be the case even if there is no epistemic basis for the presumption of first person authority in respect to states of the latter type.

2. Clarification of the impure Davidsonian theory

As noted earlier, at least two major points have to be taken on if the proposed epistemic basis for first person authority is to be accepted, these are first that some account needs to be given of the kind of properties concerned, and second, the question of the apparent appeal to an analogy with perception needs to be examined. Consider each of these tasks.

What kind of properties are being appealed to? Recall that what is required is some kind of basis for the claim that subjects have an epistemic advantage when it comes to typing their first-order occurrent states. One way to develop such a basis is to propose a range of properties the individuation conditions of which are transparent to the subject as these are viewed (so to speak) from the second-order level of the first person perspective.[2] Peacocke, in his account of observational concepts (1983, ch.4), suggests that they can be characterised in terms of "the absence of certain complex epistemic possibilities" (ibid., p.100). That is to say, the kind of epistemic possibility present in thoughts which concern (e.g.) natural kinds is the possibility that distinct natural kinds may appear phenomenally the same from the perspective of the perceiver - e.g. as is the case in perceptions of water and water*. But, for example, pain states seem to lack such epistemic possibilities. This feature of such states seems widely accepted. McGinn suggests that any "epistemic counterpart of pain must itself be pain" (1977, p.156; also Kripke, 1972, p.146). The phenomenal properties of pain states exhaust their individuation conditions. And the subjects of such states can plausibly be held to be in a position of epistemic advantage when it comes to the determination of whether or not they are presently undergoing a pain state. The thinker instantiates the property of being in pain and from the second-order perspective on first-order states is in an epistemically privileged position to type the first-order state due to the fact that the identity of the first-order state is exhausted by its phenomenal aspects. Perhaps the same may be said of hunger, thirst and so on for other types of sensation states.

But can we get any further? Macdonald tentatively suggests that thoughts about colours might also be subsumable within the kind of model which seems applicable to sensation states (1991a). If it is allowed that a subject can know directly that (say) his sweater is red, it may be said that

> [T]hat [colour property-] type is manifested to me through its instance. I access the property, as it were, by way of its instance through my sense of sight (ibid., p.12).

The view expressed here seems to be this. A subject perceives an instance of the relevant colour; suppose the subject's first order intentional state can be described as a demonstrative thought, e.g. "That's red". In this way, it may be said, the colour/property-type is manifested to the subject through its instance.

However, at the second-order level, surely, the colour itself is not what is taken to be instanced but a means of representing the colour. To say that the colour itself is instanced at the first-order level is like saying that the content of a first-order thought concerning the perceiving of an elephant would itself be elephant-shaped. To make this point clearer, contrast the story concerning perception of the colour of an external object with an experience of a sensation of pain. It is plausible to claim that the actual first order state is a pain state; the state itself instances the property: a subject could say "This is pain" referring to the state itself. Contrast this situation with that in which the subject perceives the red sweater. Clearly the subject could not refer to the first order state described (e.g.) by "That's red" and mean that the experience itself is red.

The crucial difference between the pain state example and the sweater example seems to be this: In the pain state example, the subject instances the property of being in pain; but in the sweater example, the subject does not instance the property of being red. This difference, it seems reasonable to assert, indicates that although sensation states may indeed manifest their type to their subjects it cannot be said of (e.g.) first-order states concerning instantiations of colours that they manifest their individuation conditions in the same way as sensation states.

Further, it may be pointed out that two particular classes of epistemic possibilities to which colour perceptions are susceptible do not seem applicable to sensation states. First, whilst there may be an epistemic gap between appearance and reality with respect to the perception of colours (relative to a group - e.g. members of a species - of perceivers), there does not seem to be an analogous epistemic gap in experiences of sensation states.

Second, whilst it seems possible to have an hallucinatory experience of perceiving a colour, it does not seem possible to have an hallucinatory experience of being in pain - presumably one would be in pain if one felt as though one was, though one might not be perceiving a red sweater even if one believed oneself to be.

If I understand her correctly, these differences of epistemic possibility constitute a significant problem for Macdonald's strategy. This is because, in her account, the (visual) perceptual system faithfully delivers the colour-property instanced by the relevant external object to the subject. But this account seems to face a difficulty when it comes to misperception of colours by subjects (if that is indeed an epistemic possibility). Also, there seems to be a difficulty in accounting for hallucinations. If in normal circumstances the subject's perceptual system merely instances the property perceived, what happens when there is no object present, e.g. as in hallucination. It is not clear to me that Macdonald's account of perception of colours is able to deal with these two epistemic possibilities.

This suggests problems inherent in attempts to identify a range of properties the individuation conditions of which are transparent to subjects in a way directly analogous to the way in which the individuation conditions of sensation states seem transparent to subjects; there seem to be significant differences between sensation states and other states (cf. e.g. the point that the experience of pain is itself painful but the experience of seeing red is not itself red).

The last point does not defeat the claim that colour properties may be such that their individuation conditions are transparent to subjects; it simply suggests that the way they are transparent (if they are) differs from the way the individuation conditions of sensation states seem to be transparent to subjects. In effect then, once an epistemic gap is opened up with respect to colour thoughts between how a thing seems and how it is, the analogy with sensation states breaks down in an important way.

What are required are properties the individuation conditions of which are transparent to subjects; but once the epistemic gap just referred to can be shown to apply to thoughts concerning instances of colours it seems to follow that colour properties are not the kind of properties which will meet our requirements.

In answer to our question, then, the answer is that what is required is a range of properties the individuation conditions of which are transparent to their subjects. But if colour properties do constitute such a range, they do not seem relevantly analogous to sensation states for the reasons stated here. Further, even if it could be shown that colours are such that they manifest their types to subjects, this goes only a very small part of the way towards accounting for first person authority due to the enormous number of thoughts which do not seem to have phenomenal aspects to them (or, at least, not in a way contributing to the individuation conditions of such thoughts). Having made this last point, I propose, now, to move on to the second task identified above, that concerning the appeal to analogy with perception.

The whole metaphor of transparency is one which is bound up with visual perception. But how far should this metaphor be taken. Recall Burge's points, first that perception is a faculty which may deliver mistakes, and second that the objects of perception are open to public view - in the sense that others can view them and can do so from (roughly) the same perspective as oneself. The second of these points seems not to apply to the contents of first order states when taken a perspective on from the second order level. Such first order states do not seem open to public view - though, of course, their behavioural manifestations may be.

With respect to Burge's first point, it should be said that the way first person authority has been characterised in this essay is as an epistemic advantage which subjects have. Clearly that is compatible with a position in which it is allowed that subjects make mistakes about the contents of their first order states. So perhaps this point of Burge's can be accommodated. But, possibly, what is more pertinent is to query the extent to which an appeal to analogy with perception is in fact being made. (Also, even if it is being made it can be pointed out that Burge's points are persuasive though not compelling.)

Recall that what is being appealed to in the account of first person thinking under consideration is the relevant relationship between first- and second-order intentional states. It was suggested (in the account of Burge's solution) earlier that second-order states involve the taking of a perspective upon first-order states. It may be claimed that this perspective is not one which is in fact wholly analogous to that taken in perception between the perceiver and the object. For example, as is commonly pointed out, a visual experience can occur in the absence of a stimulus which has the representational content of the experience - as in hallucinations (see, e.g. Searle, 1983, pp.57f). But it may be remembered that during our earlier attempt to elucidate the containment relation, said by Burge to obtain between second- and first-order states, appeal was made to the containment relation as that features in set-theory. It was claimed that second-order states are both individuation-dependent and existence-dependent upon first-order states. Thus if, at a particular time, from the second-order perspective there is no first-order thought, then there is no second-order thought; of course, this is what would be expected if second-order states are indeed individuation- and existence-dependent upon first-order states. Note, though, that this does not seem to be the case with visual experiences. At a particular time, a visual experience can occur in the absence of a state of affairs which corresponds to the representational content of the experience - again, e.g.

as in hallucinations.[3]

The latter argument seems to strongly indicate that the relationship between second-order and first-order states, thus, is not strictly analogous to the relationship between visual experiences and the objects of those experiences. Hence, the second of the two tasks to be addressed in this section has been addressed - albeit with more success than the first task.

3. Objections to the impure Davidsonian theory

Attempts to find an epistemic base for first person authority appear to have problems extending beyond thoughts which concern presently experienced sensation states. Yet, the presumption of first person authority identified by Davidson appears extremely plausible. But how can the presumption be justified, specifically in the case of thoughts which do not concern sensation states, and for which the "phenomenal properties" strategy seems bound not to work even in principle - and that is not to say that it has been made to look plausible in far less problematical cases such as colour thoughts.

One option towards which a Davidsonian might be tempted to lean would be one in which a challenge is issued: what more could there could be to first person authority beyond its presumption - at least with respect to intentional states which do not concern sensation states? Attempts to locate an epistemic basis for subjects' authoritative knowledge of the contents of their thoughts have been found wanting. Also, the claim that it is necessary to presume subjects to be authoritative with respect to what they think in order to understand what they say seems highly plausible. Such a presumption appears a necessary constraint on interpretation. Without the constraint, it seems, there is no data against which the interpreter's interpretations might bump up against, so to speak.

It seems to me that enough has been said in recent sections here to support the view that for at least some kinds of state there does seem to be an epistemic basis for first person authority. And it is perhaps a weakness of Davidson's account that such an epistemic basis is not allowed for with respect to those kinds of states. That said, the possibility opens up of a strategy which combines two approaches: one in which it is allowed that there is an epistemic basis for first person authority with respect to thoughts about one's own presently experienced sensation states; and another which applies to other kinds of states (e.g. beliefs about natural kinds), in which there is no epistemically grounded basis for first person authority - i.e. epistemically grounded in the first person

146

perspective.

Such a nonmonistic approach preserves the strong intuition that there is in fact an epistemic basis for authority with respect to sensation states whilst it accommodates the apparently severe difficulties involved in characterising an epistemic base for other kinds of intentional states.

With respect to intentional states which do not concern subject's own sensation states, the Davidsonian challenge can be taken to issue from the failure of (e.g.) relational attempts to account for first person authority (due to the Russellian difficulty (ch.6, note 3)) and from the apparent failure of attempts which recruit some epistemically special kind of properties. In the absence of a plausible rival account, a position which accommodates the intuition that there is first person authority - albeit in the absence of an epistemic base - and preserves the view that there is an epistemic basis for at least some types of states would seem to be at least worth taking seriously.

An initial, internalistically motivated, objection to the strategy is this. Why should such a nonepistemic approach to first person authority be accepted when there is an adequate internalist response awaiting? In the internalist rival, subjects are allowed a limited, watered-down conception of authority. As noted earlier, according to such an account, a subject may know authoritatively that he (say) desires some stuff which satisfies a number of predicates, e.g. "...is thirst-quenching", "...is a liquid", and so on.

But this account seems to be open to at least the following objections. First, in common with other views, the account still faces the problem of how the subject is authoritative when it comes to the identity of the particular first-order state. In addition to the predicates identified in the last paragraph there will be other predicates which the state satisfies, e.g. "...is the 1,000th undergone in the last ten seconds", "...is the 11th undergone in the last one second" and so on. Faced with an indefinite number of predicates which the relevant state satisfies (or, indeed, fails to satisfy) it is unclear how the subject could be said to be authoritative when it comes to the question of determining the identity of the state he is, in fact, undergoing. Second, when a subject claims to know that he is thinking about (say) water or gold, the subject just is taken to be thinking of those substances and not of a substance which satisfies an indefinite number of predicates; such intuitions lie behind the Putnam-Burge thought experiments described in chapter one above. Third, we discussed the motivations for internalism in part one above, and found these to be less compelling than the motivations for externalism. These objections seem to cast further doubt upon attempts to develop an epistemic basis for first person authority with respect to

147

states other than sensation states. More importantly, they seem to provide an adequate response to the internalistically motivated alternative proposal.

Further objections to the strategy suggested here seem likely to come from two camps. The first, being purely Davidsonian, think the strategy too impure - i.e. it allows too much epistemic baggage. The second, being generally hostile to the Davidsonian viewpoint, think the strategy not epistemic enough; they endorse the stance taken with respect to sensation states but find the stance taken with respect to other kinds of state objectionable.

The pure Davidsonians seem open to the serious objection that their account just ignores the strongly held intuition that there is an epistemic basis for authority with respect (at least) to some thoughts which concern presently experienced pain states.

Davidsonian objections to epistemically oriented solutions emphasised the points that in such solutions the introspective faculty is construed as directly analogous to the perceptual faculty, and that extraordinary epistemic properties are ascribed either to the introspective faculty or to its objects; these two views being open to objection.

However, as was seen above, a model of the relationship between second- and first-order perspectives on thought need not exploit a direct analogy between perception of external objects on the one hand, and the taking of a perspective on first-order thoughts in second-order thoughts on the other. As was argued earlier, there is at least one importantly relevant disanalogy between the two faculties (i.e. that concerning the existence-dependence of second-order states upon first-order states).

In addition to this last response to the pure Davidsonian his other worry can also be accommodated. That worry concerned the plausibility of ascribing extraordinary epistemic powers. But the thing about pain states (and perhaps other sensation states) is that they do seem to have such extraordinary epistemic properties such that their individuation conditions are transparent to their subjects. So it is reasonable to assert that the worries of the pure Davidsonian have been adequately addressed and that no real objection to the nonmonistic strategy suggested here survives from his perspective.

A further Davidsonian objection to the nonmonistic strategy is this. It may be recalled that one of Davidson's stated objections to the Wittgensteinian attempt to deflate the problem of other minds is that the attempt allows that first person ascriptions of psychological predicates have a different evidential base from third person attributions of psychological predicates (Davidson, 1987, p.442; ch.5 sec.4 above). This Davidson objects to on the grounds that "If two concepts regularly depend for their application on...different ranges of evidential support, they must be different concepts" (ibid.).

So, on Davidson's account, if I sincerely assert that I am in pain, and on seeing you wince, I ascribe to you the belief that you are in pain, the concept of pain as it occurs in each of these attributions - the first person attribution and the third person attribution - constitutes a different concept; this is due to the fact that the two applications of the predicate "...in pain" have different evidential bases: my application stems from my own experience of the sensation of pain, and my application of "...in pain" to you stems from the evidence of your behaviour.

But there is some room for objection here. One commentator, Root (1986, pp.297-298), amplifying Davidson's point, suggests that if there were these two ways of construing mental states, then "[(i)]...no first-person attribution of belief could have the same meaning as any third-person attribution. [(ii)]In speaking about my mind, you and I could never contradict one another" (ibid.). Hopefully, it can be seen that (i) is simply a reiteration of Davidson's own way of expressing the point, and that (ii) is intended to amplify it.

It can be pointed out, however, that (i) and (ii) are open to challenge. Take (i), if an interpreter attributes a belief to me of the form "Edwards is in pain", and I ascribe a belief to myself of the form "I, Edwards, am in pain", it is surely the case that these two attributions share the same truth conditions. They do this due to the extension of the predicate and to the referent of the subject-expression(s). Now, it is an important part of Davidson's views on interpretation that sameness of truth conditions is a necessary condition for sameness of meaning - so the two ascriptions meet that constraint. And, it seems plain that an adequate theory of interpretation would regard the predicate "...in pain" as having the same extension in each language - i.e. the home language and the language to be interpreted. Thus, it is difficult to see how (i) can be regarded as persuasive when applied to psychological predicates which concern pain states.

If the suggested response to (i) is accepted, then it should be easy to accept the force of this response to (ii); specifically, it appears that A could contradict B in the following way, A: "I am in pain"; B: "No you're not"!

With respect to objections from the other camp - namely that the nonmonistic account is insufficiently epistemic - it can be pointed out that subjects' authority over states which seem to constitute a paradigm case of states over which subjects possess first person authority has been preserved; an account has been provided of how it is that subjects may be considered authoritative with respect to certain of their sensation states. It has to be conceded that an epistemically based account of first person authority with respect to other states has been relinquished. But in the absence of a plausible rival account this option does not seem so objectionable.

In summary, it is not being claimed here that an adequate account of first person authority has been developed. It is being claimed that a position which is not obviously incoherent has been pointed to and shown to be plausible. The position is compatible with externalism, with the view that there is a presumption of first person authority, and that this has an epistemic basis with respect to subjects' thoughts concerning certain sensation states, but not for other kinds of states.

4. Postscript: McKinsey's argument

In this final section of this second part of the essay a recent challenge to attempts to render externalism compatible with first person authority will be reviewed and responded to. McKinsey (1991) attributes the following argument to Burge (1988c):

> (1) O knows a priori that he is thinking that water is wet.
> (2) The proposition that O is thinking that water is wet necessarily depends upon E.
> (3) The proposition E cannot be known a priori, but only by empirical investigation (McKinsey, 1991, p.12).

The suggestion is that Burge is committed to (1) by virtue of the fact that in his solution subjects have direct knowledge of the contents of their first-order intentional states; that he is committed to (2) by virtue of the externalist claim that (at least some) intentional types are individuation dependent upon (e.g.) natural kinds; and that Burge holds (3) by virtue of his refusal to allow that the fact that water is wet can be known a priori.

McKinsey points out that the kind of dependence appealed to in (2) is not made explicit by Burge, and so he (McKinsey) suggests two interpretations of "necessarily depends". The first is "metaphysical dependence", and the second is "conceptual dependence". It is then argued by McKinsey that the first kind of dependence is too weak bring externalism and that the second kind of dependence is logically incompatible with acceptance of (1).

Metaphysical dependence is interpreted by McKinsey as metaphysical necessity (op.cit., p.12). Thus it may be said that entity A is metaphysically dependent upon entity B if the existence of A is necessarily dependent upon the existence of B. When "necessarily depends" is interpreted in this way the argument given above in (1)-(3) involves no inconsistency. This is so since the metaphysical dependency of one class of items on another class of items brings with it no epistemic baggage, so to speak: to say that S's thought that p is metaphysically dependent upon the existence of (e.g.) As does not imply that the dependence is such that S's knowing that he is thinking that p entails that he knows that his thought that p is possible only given the prior existence of As.[4] However, as McKinsey points out, the kind of dependence involved in metaphysical dependence is too weak to bring externalism since O's thought that (e.g.) water is wet is metaphysically dependent upon a wide range of other facts, e.g. the existence of oxygen, of O's mother, of O's mother's mother and so on. So metaphysical dependence is too weak to bring externalism due to the fact that externalism requires the type dependency of (at least some) intentional types on (at least some) objective types (e.g. natural kinds). The general object-dependency of some intentional types on environmental conditions is not sufficient for externalism.

Consider, then, construing "necessarily depends" as it appears in (2) as conceptual dependence. By this, McKinsey means,

> [A] proposition p conceptually implies a proposition q if and only if there is a correct deduction of q from p, a deduction whose only premises other than p are necessary or conceptual truths that are knowable a priori... (op.cit., p.14).

So if the state of affairs described by p is conceptually dependent upon the states of affairs described by q, then q is deducible from p. If we plug this description of what it is that conceptual dependence amounts to into premise (2) above, it can be seen that (1)-(3) now display an inconsistency. (1) asserts that O can know a priori that he is thinking that water is wet. (2) asserts that the proposition that water is wet conceptually implies a proposition E - in McKinsey's terms, that E can be deduced a priori from that water is wet. And (3) denies what (2) asserts - hence the inconsistency.

McKinsey's description of conceptual dependence implies that according to externalism a subject can deduce the existence of water from his thinking to himself that he thinks that (e.g.) water is wet; and McKinsey ends his paper by pointing this out - he regards it as a reductio ad absurdum of externalism.

Are there any responses to be made against McKinsey? Well, there seem to be at least two related points which centre on objections to McKinsey's use of key terminology.

McKinsey makes extensive use of the term "a priori" in his argument, and his definition is this: "I will call knowledge obtained independently of empirical investigation a priori knowledge" (op.cit., p.9). Now, what is meant by "empirical investigation"? It is implausible that this means a rigorous scientific enquiry, so it must mean something less demanding. Perhaps it is meant knowledge obtainable "from the armchair" as it is sometimes put. But then it may be claimed the kind of subject deemed capable of obtaining knowledge in this way - by reflection - is not, strictly, obtaining knowledge independently of empirical investigation. Subjects plausibly deemed capable of obtaining a priori knowledge from the armchair have usually undertaken considerable empirical investigation into their environments during the natural process of growing up, learning a language and so on. This constitutes an empirical investigation, even if it falls well short of the standards of scientific investigation.

So when Burge is represented as claiming (1) that O knows a priori that he is thinking that water is wet, we may re-express this as (1)' O knows without the need for further empirical investigation that water is wet. Note that it need not be presumed that O has conducted a scientific enquiry into the chemical composition of water.

Given acceptance of the legitimacy of this complaint about McKinsey's use of "a priori" in (1), then (3) begins to look very odd: i.e. (3) The proposition E cannot be known independently of empirical investigation, but only by empirical investigation. This clearly demands that we investigate more closely what is meant by "E" before a proper assessment of McKinsey's argument is possible.

In (2) it is said that "The proposition that O is thinking that water is wet necessarily depends upon E". E is described by McKinsey as "the 'external proposition' whose presupposition makes Oscar's thought that water is wet a wide state" (op.cit., p.12). By "wide state" McKinsey means to indicate the kind of intentional state for which externalism is true. But the obscure expression in McKinsey's definition of "E" is "the external proposition"; to my knowledge this is not an expression employed by Burge.

It is reasonable to interpret E as referring to the theoretical presuppositions which makes O's state a wide state. This latter interpretation of E differs from that indicated in McKinsey's gloss. McKinsey makes it seem as though "E" would simply involve the statement of the proposition that water is wet. But this is too much of an oversimplification on McKinsey's part. As noted earlier (e.g. ch.2) the presence of water in the environment of the subject is not sufficient for the subject's thoughts to be individuation dependent upon water. The causal history of the subject is also a relevant consideration. Recall that this was the point of Davidson's Swampman example (ch.2). Davidson's spontaneously created replica cannot simply be ascribed the thoughts which were hitherto attributable to him, and this is due to the Swampman's lack of the right kind of causal history. Consideration of Davidson's example led to the proposal of the relevance of causal history to the determination of the individuation conditions of particulars.

Further, the fact that water exists in the environment of the subject may, in conjunction with other considerations (e.g.the cognitive capacity of a subject S) be sufficient for S's thoughts to be individuation dependent upon water. But, as Burge indicates (1988c, p.653) S may entertain water-thoughts even if water does not occur in S's environment. E.g. by being in "...a causal relation to other particular substances that enable one to theorise accurately about water" (ibid.). So it cannot be held to be necessary that S has causal interaction with water to be ascribed water-thoughts.

If these considerations are applied to McKinsey's gloss on E - if this does indeed mean the presuppositions which make O's state a wide state (a state which is an instance of a type for which externalism is true) - then E should have at least two components. One of which specifies that the cognitive capacity of O is such that he is capable of entertaining thoughts of a certain level of sophistication, and the other of which specifies relevant aspects of O's causal history.

If this response to McKinsey is accepted, it seems to expose a fatal inaccuracy in his characterisation of Burge's position which removes the plausibility of any points made on the basis of it. If (1)-(3) are recast in the light of the points just made concerning McKinsey's use of "a priori" and "E", the following results: (1) O knows without the need for further empirical investigation that he is thinking that water is wet. (2) The proposition that O is thinking that water is wet necessarily depends upon: (i) the fact that O possesses appropriate cognitive capacities necessary for entertaining water-thoughts, and (ii) the fact that O has a causal history of a certain type (one which involves actual causal interaction with water, or with the kinds which constitute water, i.e. hydrogen and oxygen). (3) (i) and (ii) cannot be known independently of empirical investigation but only by empirical investigation.[5] It now seems that the inconsistency induced by construing "necessarily depends" as conceptually depends is obstructed. It is obstructed due the presence of (ii) in (2). O cannot know a priori (in McKinsey's sense) that he does in fact have the relevant causal history. This is something he could only determine a posteriori.

153

The above treatment of McKinsey's argument seems to show that it does not present a fatal challenge to externalist attempts to render that thesis compatible with the view that subjects have first person authority.[6]

Notes to chapter seven

1. See also McCulloch (1986, p.82) for the claimed necessity to include the first person perspective in an adequate account of mind.
2. Perhaps a Lockean distinction between primary and secondary qualities may help here. With respect to primary qualities there is an epistemic gap between x looks F and x is F. But with respect to secondary qualities it is plausible to hold (at least relative to a group of perceivers) that being F amounts to being perceived to be F (cf. McGinn, 1983, ch.2 passim).
3. Note that externalists need to state the latter point with some care since they may want to claim that visual experiences are individuation- and existence-dependent upon the states of affairs they represent, or seek to represent. But as stated in the example given, such a position is consistent with a view according to which at a particular time the relevant visual experience can occur in the absence of the appropriate stimulus.
4. For example, S may know that he exists but not know that his existence metaphysically depends upon that of his mother.
5. This is a re-statement of McKinsey's original characterisation of Burge's position with the relevant terminology adjusted in the light of the considerations of this section.
6. A different response to McKinsey is set out by Brueckner (1992). He characterises McKinsey's objection as I have above. Then Brueckner agrees that Burge is committed to (1), but wonders how "E" is to be understood. According to Brueckner, by "E", Burge should be taken to mean E1: "O inhabits an environment containing H2O and not XYZ" (ibid., p.112). Since O's knowing apriori that water is wet does not conceptually imply E1, McKinsey's argument fails and Burge can consistently hold (1),(2) and (3).

Part III
THOUGHTS

8 Externalism and demonstrative thought

1. Introduction

In this, and two subsequent chapters we look at how the nature of demonstrative thought is explained within a type externalist account of content. A number of commentators have considered that externalism is true for demonstrative thoughts (e.g. McCulloch, 1989, p.193; Evans, 1982, e.g. p.64). But, typically, such theorists make no attempt to explain how their view of the individuation conditions of such thoughts bears on the problem of specifying the relationship between mental and physical events. It may be recalled that in this essay an attempt is made to provide an account of the individuation conditions of demonstrative thoughts which is constrained by a token physicalist theory of the relationship between mental and physical events. In accordance with the theory (see ch.3, sec.3 above), it is held that token mental events are identical with token physical events, and that the individuation conditions of token mental events need not make reference to features beyond the bodies of their subjects.

Some theorists appear to argue that the individuation conditions of token demonstrative thoughts are determined by the identity of the particular object thought of (e.g. McCulloch ibid.; Evans, ibid.). This seems not to be an option for the version of externalism canvassed in this essay. The reason why is that in a token physicalist theory of mind (specifically, that ascribed to Macdonald (1989) in ch.3 above), the individuation conditions of token mental events do not violate The Solipsism Claim (see p.3 above). So some other, motivated, way of individuating demonstrative thoughts is required.

Our discussion focuses on the question of the individuation conditions of demonstrative thoughts considered as a type of intentional state. It may be held that the type identity of demonstrative thoughts hinges on the identity of the particular object thought of. Alternatively, it may be held that the type identity of demonstrative thoughts hinges on the type identity of the object thought of. It will be seen in the next section that neither of these options is helpful. It is evident, then, that some work is required in order to determine the individuation conditions of demonstrative thoughts.

In this chapter we note the object-dependency of demonstrative thoughts; and in chs.9 and 10 we try to develop an account of the individuation conditions of such thoughts which sits happily with token physicalism. It should be said, further, that the mere object-dependency of demonstrative thought (considered as a type of intentional state) seems not to be sufficient for type externalism to be true with respect to such thoughts. According to Burge's definition, internalism is a thesis which rejects the view that there is a "necessary or deep individuative relation between the individual's being in states of those kinds and the nature of the individual's physical or social environments" (Burge, 1986a, pp.3-4). Thus it can be seen that internalism denies that features of the environment of the subject are relevant to the individuation conditions of the thoughts of the subject. Hence, in the Twin Earth case (ch.1 above) an argument which showed that the thoughts of the Twins are merely object-dependent when they desire water/water* would not be sufficient for externalism with respect to the thoughts of the Twins. Externalism seems to require the stronger claim that the thoughts of the Twins are individuation-dependent upon contextual factors - i.e. the presence of water/water* in their respective environments. Given the interpretation of internalism offered by Burge (ibid.) it would seem to follow that for type externalism to be true with respect to demonstrative thoughts such thoughts must be individuation-dependent on features of the environments of their subjects - and not simply object-dependent. So for it to be the case that type externalism is true for demonstrative thought, a means of binding the individuation conditions of such thoughts to the environment of their thinker seems to be required. Our main tasks in this chapter are to consider how the individuation conditions of demonstrative thoughts might look, and to consider the claim that such thoughts are object-dependent.

One immediate difficulty for our present task is caused by interpretation of the terms "demonstrative" and "indexical". For example, Evans (1985,p.291) appears to regard the terms as equivalent; Peacocke (1981, p.187) indicates that, in his view, demonstrative thoughts form a sub-class within the class of indexical thoughts; and Davies (1982, pp.288-289) distinguishes indexical demonstrative thoughts from perceptual demonstrative thoughts.

Another commentator, Yourgrau, proposes the following pattern of usage - which will be employed here. He suggests that demonstratives constitute a class of expressions which have in common the property of indexicality (1990, p.1; also Linsky, 1967, p.37). By "indexicality" Yourgrau means "context sensitivity" (ibid.). The reference of demonstratives is, thus, said to be affected by varying combinations of these three factors: (i) the identity of their users, (ii) the spatial locations of their users, and (iii) the temporal locations of their users. This feature of demonstratives helps to distinguish them from other referring expressions the references of which are much less sensitive to the context of their use, e.g. "Bertrand Russell", "The fourth planet in the solar system" etc.

It should be added that the pattern of usage recommended by Yourgrau is being taken here to be applicable both to demonstrative expressions, and to demonstrative thoughts. Hence demonstrative thoughts are thoughts which have in common the property of indexicality.

The distinction referred to by Davies (1982, pp.288-289) is one worth drawing attention to, but now, in the light of Yourgrau's proposed usage, the distinction can be said to be one between perceptual demonstrative thoughts and other (nonperceptual?) demonstrative thoughts. Davies does not spend time clarifying the distinction he makes, but roughly, it is between demonstratives such as "This", and "That", and other demonstratives such as "Here", "Now", and "I". The latter demonstratives always seem to succeed in referring; simply by uttering, e.g., "now" it seems that one refers to a point in time. But many utterances of "This" and "That" seem more closely bound up with perceptions of the scene in front of their utterers. An aimless, so to speak, utterance of "That" does not seem to refer to anything unless the speaker centres his attention upon a feature of his environment (e.g. a smell, a sound, or an object). In contrast, an aimless utterance of "Now" does still seem to succeed in referring to a point in time.[1]

The reason why Davies' distinction is being discussed here is due to the fact that it is perceptual demonstrative thoughts which are to be at the centre of our concerns. And it is the question of their individuation conditions which is to be addressed: are perceptual demonstrative thoughts to be individuated in a way congenial to type externalism? [2]

One further preliminary distinction is this. It is possible to draw distinctions within the class of perceptual demonstrative thoughts. E.g. the following seem to specify examples of three subclasses within the class of perceptual demonstrative thoughts: (i) That's Thatcher; (ii) That's torn; and (iii) That carpet is torn. In the first case the demonstrative

159

combines with a proper name; in the second case the demonstrative combines with a predicate; and in the third case the demonstrative combines with a sortal, or kind term, and a predicate. (It will be seen later that (ii) and (iii) do not belong to different subclasses and that in (ii) there is tacit employment, in thought, of a kind concept - a hidden sortal as one might say.) In the interests of manageability, it is perceptual demonstrative thoughts of types (ii) and (iii) which will be the main subject of our discussion. Such thoughts typically concern perceptually salient features of the subject's immediate surroundings. Evans describes such thoughts as being "information-based" in the sense that they are prompted by perceptual information from the object thought of (1982, p.145). It seems, further, that other subjects are required to be suitably related to the object demonstrated by the utterer if they are to be in a position to understand the utterance. For example, if S says "That's torn" whilst pointing to an area of carpet, it has seemed plausible to some commentators that a hearer H could not understand S's utterance unless he is aware of what is being referred to by S (e.g. Evans, 1982, p.306; McCulloch, 1989).

Another way to attempt to bring out the particular character of perceptual demonstrative thoughts is via the distinction between referring to objects and having thoughts about them. An infant might be taught to say "Albert Einstein". It might then be said that the infant succeeds in referring to Einstein via the use of his name. But this seems to be distinct from the claim that the infant can be ascribed a thought about Einstein when he uses the name.

In the case of proper names this distinction does seem to have some work to do, as the example just given suggests. But when subjects use demonstratives there seems to be what may be described as an ease of access between the thought and the object. Just by looking around my room and focusing, say, on any one object in it, I can entertain a demonstrative thought about that object. If I give voice to my demonstrative thoughts, e.g., "That's nice", "That was purchased in Woolworth's", a hearer can understand them provided, it seems, he knows which object is being demonstrated.

It could plausibly be claimed, in the light of these considerations, that the gap between referring to an object O and entertaining thoughts about O is much more conspicuously present in cases where "O" is a proper name, than where "O" is a demonstrative expression. The reason for this is that demonstratives tend to be used most in the presence of the object demonstrated whereas proper names are employed in ways other than this.

The distinction being suggested here is far from unassailable since, for example, demonstratives can be used to refer to objects not presently in view but which have been encountered in the past (e.g. "That German we met on holiday"). But it seems reasonable to claim that enough has been said to indicate strongly the intimate nature of the connection between demonstrative thoughts and immediate surroundings.

Finally, it should be made explicit that in employing the term "perceptual demonstrative thought" we are referring to a type of way of thinking. Apparent features of this type just noted include: (i) their context sensitivity; (ii) that there is an apparent relationship between perceiving the object demonstrated and understanding a demonstrative expression concerning that object; and (iii) that there is an ease of access which demonstrative thoughts possess but which other types of thought seem to lack (e.g. thoughts whose specifications include proper names). Let us turn, now, to consider how demonstrative thoughts are to be individuated.

2. The individuation conditions of demonstrative thoughts

We begin by considering that that-clauses are adequate to specify the individuation conditions of demonstrative thoughts; it will be seen that they are not. We then consider supplementing that-clauses with an additional component - an E-component; it is suggested that some such component is required in a specification of the individuation conditions of demonstrative thought considered as a type of intentional state.

Are that-clauses adequate?

In considering the nature of demonstrative thought the fact that demonstrative expressions feature in ascriptions of demonstrative thoughts might be taken as a useful indicator of their individuation conditions. For example, in ascribing to a subject S the belief that that is F it could be claimed that S's thought that that is F is composed of a demonstrative component which is the psychological equivalent of the demonstrative "That", together with S's conception of the property being ascribed to the object demonstrated. Thus a description of the individuation conditions of demonstrative thought might be this: [(Dem), (...is F)] where "Dem" stands for the psychological state undergone in thinking demonstratively of an object; and "...is F" stands for S's conception of the property whose instances are described by "...is F".

Hence it could be said that the constituents of S's belief that that is F involve S's focusing on a salient feature of his environment, and thinking of it as instancing a particular property. The expression employed in the last paragraph can be employed to characterise S's belief that that demonstrated object is F; so we get S believes that that is F, and this can be expressed schematically as [(Dem), (...is F)] - call these the demonstrative component and the predicative component respectively.

Further, it is evident that some time index is required in specifications of demonstrative thoughts since a subject's belief concerning a demonstrated object - say, a vase - must occur at a particular time, otherwise it would not be possible to explain why, e.g., S reaches out at that particular time for the vase. So in addition to the demonstrative and predicative components, some temporal index is required to be included in our description of the individuation conditions of demonstrative thought, e.g.

$$[(Dem), (...is F), [t]]$$

These components, are the demonstrative component, the predicative component, and the temporal index respectively. Is the characterisation suggested here adequate for the explanation of action on an object? That it is not can best be seen by exploiting an example provided by McCulloch (1989, pp.199-204).

A criterion apparently suggested by Frege concerning the question of the identity of sinne (senses) is this: If a subject will assent to an expression M but not to an expression N then M and N have distinct senses (see Evans, 1982, p.18); the criterion is described by Evans as "The Intuitive Criterion of Difference" (ibid.) . The criterion suggested by Frege to discriminate between senses might usefully be employed in explanations of action; specifically, where M and N are expressions employed to represent an agent, S's, conception, at a time t, of a state of affairs A, if S acts differently when he entertains M than when he entertains N, then M and N represent distinct conceptions of A. Put differently, it is not the case that M and N are identical characterisations of S's cognitive state at t, if they result in distinct actions when the states which M and N characterise are exchanged one for the other. McCulloch exploits Frege's criterion to suggest that that-clauses cannot adequately specify the contents of demonstrative thoughts.

McCulloch constructs an example in which a commuter S approaches a railway station and sees what he takes to be two trains, a train at the north end of the platform which, he believes, is bound for Manchester, and a train at the south end of the platform which, he believes, is bound for London. S interprets the situation in the way outlined due to the fact that the station is small and so too is the station platform. Unknown to him it is one train that he sees - ELT (extra-long train) - which is at the station and which is so big it protrudes at each end of the platform; ELT is actually London-bound.[3]

Suppose it is considered to be the case that that-clauses containing demonstrative expressions are adequate to represent the content of demonstrative thoughts. The problem with this claim is that S would assent to (i) "That train is bound for London" uttered whilst pointing to the south end of the platform, and dissent from (i) if it is uttered whilst pointing to the north end of the platform. By Frege's intuitive criterion of difference (providing it is agreed that S is a rational subject) the first and second utterances of (i) cannot be taken to accurately represent what it is that S believes since S both assents to (i) and dissents from (i).

Further evidence that (i) inadequately characterises S's cognitive state can be gleaned from the fact that if (i) is an adequate specification of S's cognitive state there should be no incompatibility between the acts which S performs on the basis of his belief that (i). But plainly there will be such an incompatibility since S will happily walk to the north of the platform but will refuse to go to the south of the platform.

The inadequacy of that-clauses to specify content in cases of this kind can be taken to suggest the need for an additional component to our characterisation of the individuation conditions of demonstrative thought. Commentators in this area tend to exploit Fregean "modes of presentation" to fulfil such a role (e.g. McCulloch, 1989) - i.e. to denote how S conceives of ELT. Hence as ELT is presented to S under one mode of presentation, M, he will assent to (i) That train is going to London, and as ELT is presented to S under a different mode of presentation N he will dissent from (i). So the difference in S's thoughts under his two conceptions of ELT can be represented thus,

S believes that [(Dem), (M), (...is F), [t]],

or

S believes that [(Dem), (N), (...is F), [t]]

Given the close links between demonstrative thought and perception which we have noted so far in this chapter it can be claimed that M and N refer to aspects of S's perceptual experience when he views ELT first from one perspective (e.g. when he views the end which protrudes from the northern end of the platform) and then from another perspective (e.g. when S views that end of ELT which protrudes from the south end of the platform).

The additional cognitive component shown by M and N in the above example can be said to be that component of demonstrative thought which takes up any slack left from inadequate specifications of content by that-clauses. Let us describe it as the experiential component of demonstrative thought, and denote it schematically thus "(E)".[4]

The experiential component (the E-component)

The experiential component appealed to here need not be regarded as mysterious. As S approaches the station he looks at the train from a particular viewpoint or perspective and the properties of this perceptual experience can be said to enter into the individuation conditions of S's thought. Further, it may be supposed that the perspective from which S views the train is one which other commuters may also experience, e.g. if they are similarly equipped sensorily speaking, and if they approach the station by the same route that S does; so other subjects may experience tokens of the same type of E-component as is experienced by S. This suggestion has obvious affinities with remarks such as "You must look back at the shore from the end of the pier. It's a wonderful sight."[5]

Also, it is reasonable to point to the fact that in explanations of action the explanations seek to capture how things seem to the agent - references to agents' conceptions appear to be a necessary feature of action explanation. Adequate explanations successfully capture the way things seemed from the perspective of the actor; it can easily be accepted that such explanations involve reference to the thoughts of the agent - his beliefs and desires at the time of his action. (In explanations of the actions of others one refers to the way the relevant state of affairs is conceived of by the actor). And since demonstrative thought is so closely linked with perceptual experience the claim that the properties of such experience should enter into the individuation conditions of demonstrative thoughts does not seem implausible.[6] By way of elaborating, briefly, the nature of the experiential component of demonstrative thought, the so-called "sensational properties" (Peacocke, 1983, e.g., p.5) of perceptual experiences can be appealed to. It can be said that the character of S's perceptual experience of viewing that part of ELT which is located at the south end of the platform, is different from the character of his perceptual experience when he views the part of ELT which protrudes from the north end of the platform. So the E-component can be said to include a specification of the character of the perceptual experience - i.e. the sensational properties of the experience. Further, although a blind commuter and a sighted commuter might each entertain demonstrative thoughts concerning ELT, it seems plausible that their thoughts will differ in certain respects. They may have the same representational content (e.g. as specified in a that-clause such as "That train is London-bound") but distinct sensational properties due to the differences in the sensory capacities of the blind and the sighted commuter.

Peacocke makes certain claims about sensational properties which need not be taken on here. For example he says they cannot be specified in that-clauses - such specifications account only for the representational content of perceptual experiences. As sensational properties are appealed to here, no such strong claim is required, e.g. it may be said that the thought we ascribe to S could be expanded along the following lines: ELT, as it appears from the place where S is located, given S's psychological state at t, the lighting conditions (etc.) at t, and S's actual posture at t, appears to S to be thus and so. Such a characterisation still omits something of the character of S's perceptual experience, but it goes some of the way towards providing a description of S's psychological state at t, when he perceives ELT.[7]

What needs to be asked now, is whether an argument-place needs to be left for specification of an object in the description of the individuation conditions of demonstrative thought (considered as a type of intentional state). If it is true that demonstrative thoughts are object-dependent (in a sense yet to be made clear) it would appear to be reasonable to allow an argument-place for the specification of an object in a description of the individuation conditions of demonstrative thought. Further, there seem to be at least three possible ways of construing such an argument-place: first, as a specification of some object or other; second, as a specification of the object's type; or third, as a specification of the identity of the particular object thought of. So, the individuation conditions for (perceptual) demonstrative thoughts would then look as follows:[8]

$$\{[(Dem) <O>], (E), (...is F), [t]\}$$

First, however, we need to ask whether demonstrative thoughts are object-dependent - at least in the sense that it is a necessary condition for a subject to entertain a demonstrative thought that there is an object thought of.

3. The object-dependence of demonstrative thought

Consider a Twin Earth case in which S on Earth thinks demonstratively of a vase and points to it; S* on Twin Earth, however, merely hallucinates that he is perceiving a vase (one which looks the same as that thought of by S). As noted in ch.1 above, a first, epistemic, motivation for the claim that demonstrative thought is possible in S*'s case stems from the observation that the psychological states of S and S* apparently share much in common in the example given above. This motivation may be described as the motivation from first person symmetry (cf. McCulloch, 1989, p.209); it is so-called due to the fact that it stems from reflections upon one's own psychological states which fuel the intuition that the psychological states of S and S* are of the same type even though S's thought is directed at an object whereas S*'s is not.

If the example is elaborated and it is said that our subjects each utter the words "That's red" and simultaneously point their respective fingers to the same (twin) location, then again it can seem highly plausible to say that the psychological states of the subjects are of the same type. This can be described as the motivation from third person symmetry (cf. McCulloch, ibid.), i.e. when viewed from the third person perspective the behaviour of the subjects can be described in the same way.

In addition to these two motivations there is the further point that the psychological states of the subjects could be adequately characterised by the use of the (E)-component in our demonstrative thought type and by the use of descriptivist-style content specification.

How should these points be responded to? Take the first-person symmetry question. First, from the fact that it seems to S* that he is seeing a vase it cannot be concluded that his thought is of the same type as S's. Considerations in part one above indicate that even though S and S* might take themselves to be thinking thoughts of the same type when they respectively desire water/water*, this seems not to be sufficient for it to be true that their respective thoughts really are of the same type.

Also, it is not clear that the psychological states of S and S* are in fact of the same type. It was suggested above that S*'s psychological state at t could be described thus: it seems to S* that he is seeing a vase, and it seems to S* that the vase is red. Although it might be thought that these descriptions apply also to S's psychological state at t it can be claimed that they do not. Surely a report of S's psychological state at t would state that S perceives a vase at t, not merely that it seems to S that he is seeing a vase. It is clear that there is a big difference between seeing something and merely seeming to see it. So it seems reasonable to conclude that there is sufficient reason to doubt the veracity of the first person symmetry supposed to obtain between the psychological states of S and S*. First person reflection upon the contents of one's thoughts is not necessarily veridical; and, on closer examination, the reports of the

166

contents of the psychological states of S and S* do not turn out to be of the same logical type (since S sees a vase and S* merely seems to see a vase).

The plausibility of the motivation from third person symmetry may also be queried. Both the claim that S and S* behave in the same type of way, and the claim that they make the same type of utterance are open to criticism. Concerning the first of these two claims, recall the distinctions referred to in ch.3 above between action and behaviour, and between acts narrowly and broadly construed, It can be accepted that, at t, S and S* behave in the same way in so far as their bodily movements are of the same type. But the mere fact that the bodily movements of two subjects are of the same type is not sufficient for it to be the case that their actions are of the same type. To use a hackneyed example, two subjects with the same name might each go through the bodily movements involved in signing their name, but one might be practising his signature and the other signing a will - same bodily movements, different act performed. To apply this general point to the case under discussion here, it can be claimed that S performs a broad act-type describable as pointing at a vase and a narrow act-type describable as pointing. S*, on the other hand, only performs the second of these; at best it could be said that S* attempts to point to something, it could not be said that S* does point to something. Although both acts are pointings, only S's act is of the type pointing at a vase; clearly S*'s act is not of this last type. So this aspect of third person symmetry can be seen to be dubious.

Concerning the claim that S and S* undergo the same type of psychological state due to the fact that they give voice to the same type of thought in their respective utterances of (e.g.) "That's red", the following objection may be raised. It may be claimed that the utterances of two subjects when considered from the third person perspective can be described thus: (i) S said "That's red", (ii) S* said "That's red". The fact that (i) and (ii) include the same expression is clearly what motivates the claimed third person symmetry between our subjects. But consider what is said by (i) and (ii). When S says "That's red" he is stating of the referent of "That" that it is red - he is referring to the vase. The same cannot be said of S* due to the fact that there is no referent of "That" when uttered by him. The difference between the utterances of the two subjects in cases of this kind may be put thus: S refers to the vase, whilst S* merely attempts to refer to the vase (cf. McCulloch, 1989, p.213). Since this difference between the two utterances is clearly a substantial one the claimed third person symmetry between S and S* can be said to be false.

A further reason for doubting the claim that S and S* give voice to the same type of thought in (i) and (ii) can be gleaned from consideration of the notion of understanding the thought expressed by the subjects. It is plausible to suppose that if a subject gives voice to a legitimate thought then there are certain conditions which are relevant to the understanding of the thought by another subject (cf.ch.9 sec.1 below). It can be claimed that in the case of expressions of demonstrative thought at least one of those conditions is that there is an object demonstrated. This claim is supported by the observation that if a hearer of S can perceive the same part of the room that S can when S utters "That's red" the hearer can be said to understand S by virtue of the fact that the hearer is in a position to determine to what S is referring. Contrast this uncomplicated situation with a situation in which the hearer hears S*'s remark "That's red" i.e. when there is no object demonstrated. It seems clear that the hearer will either be puzzled or will press S* for further information "What's red?" In the event of there being no object the hearer, if he is charitable, is likely to describe the incident as one in which S* took himself to make a claim about a vase but failed to do so. Again, this observation threatens the claimed symmetry between S and S* when their utterances are considered from the third person perspective.

More generally, it can be pointed out that thought ascriptions take into consideration not just what a subject does at a time t but also what he has done, or is likely to have done prior to t, and what the subject goes on to do after t. For example, having drawn attention to the red vase S might walk over to it and examine it, and perhaps even give an anecdote about the vase. If S* behaved in that fashion in the absence of there being an object demonstrated and later talked as if there was a vase in the same way that S does actually discuss the vase, then that would seem to be evidence of asymmetry, rather than symmetry, when the psychological states of S and S* are considered from the third person perspective.

In addition to the motivations from first and third person symmetry a third motivation for adopting the descriptivist account of demonstrative thought in the absence of a demonstrated object was mentioned above. This stems from the fact that a formal characterisation is available to characterise such states, and, apparently, it is one which allows there to be thoughts in the absence of a demonstrated object - i.e. due to the fact that the demonstrative is eliminated in favour of a description. There are two points to be made about this third motivation.

First, it is not clear that such characterisations are fully adequate. This is due to the fact that a thought of the form "That's F" where there is no referent for the demonstrative must, presumably, in the descriptivist account, have the truth value False since no object in the domain over which the variables range satisfies the description, e.g. "the unique x such that x is the cause of these psychological experiences...".[9] Characterisations of such thoughts in that descriptivist form do not indicate why it is that the thought is false: is it due to the fact that no object in the domain satisfies the description, or is it due to the fact that the object which does satisfy the description does not possess the property ascribed to it? This can be described as a failure in the adequacy of such characterisations.

The second point is this. Even if such characterisations are shown to be adequate the fact of their availability cannot be taken to license ontological claims concerning the nature of thought (of course the same applies to the theory of quantification outlined in ch.3 above); such a claim would be an outrageous example of the tail wagging the dog.

Also, it seemed plausible in chs.3 and 4 above that explanations which recruit narrow act-types owe their intelligibility to explanations which employ broad act-types. This has the general implication that acts prompted by hallucinatory experiences are intelligible only against a background of successful actions.

So it appears that there are strong and plausible grounds for rejecting an account of demonstrative thought which allows the possibility of there being demonstrative thought in the absence of there being an object thought of.

However, as noted at the start of this chapter, showing the object-dependency of demonstrative thoughts, seems not to be sufficient to show that externalism is true with respect to such thoughts. This is the case since externalism seems to require not just that thoughts are object-dependent, but that their individuation conditions are externalistically constrained. The individuation conditions of demonstrative thoughts must be constrained by contextual factors if they are such that externalism is true of them. By way of attempting to show how the individuation conditions of demonstrative thoughts can plausibly taken to be externalistically constrained, I turn now to consider the theory of demonstrative thought proposed by Gareth Evans (1982).

Notes to chapter eight

1. See also Shoemaker (1984, pp.8-10) and his point that "First person statements [have an] immunity to error through misidentification" which demonstratives such as "This" and "That" lack. Also,Evans, 1982, p.188.
2. To repeat, the discussion of demonstrative thoughts focuses mainly on perceptual demonstrative thoughts, and considers the

individuation conditions of these where they are construed as a type of intentional state.

3.   This is a variant on an example provided by Perry (1977, pp.58-59); see also Peacocke's "That phone is that phone" (Peacocke, 1981, p.188).

4.   Compare, also, Davies (1982, p.291) and his reference to "[An] experiential element" in demonstrative thought.

5.   See esp. Peacocke, 1981, p.189; and Russell's "perspectives" (1917, p.134). Further, it is plausible that ELT will be presented under a distinct type of E-component for a blind commuter who hears what he takes to be two trains as he approaches the station (cf. McCulloch, 1989, p.203). The blind commuter (BC) can be taken to be thinking demonstratively of a train he hears if, e.g., he thinks "That's my train". The demonstrative component of BC's thought involves his focusing his attention on a certain part of his environment, namely the train. The E-component of BC's demonstrative thought will differ in type from the E-component of a sighted commuter when he thinks demonstratively of the same train. The same may be said of a commuter who is colour blind. Both he and the commuter with normal vision can think demonstrative thoughts with the same representational content (e.g. captured in a that-clause such as "That's London-bound") but there are differences in the sensational properties of the thoughts of these two commuters. As suggested in the text, such differences stem from differences in the perceptual faculties of the two subjects.

6.   It should be said that the strategy being considered will prove enormously complex; in effect it attempts to specify the conditions necessary for the possibility of thought. Having stated this, it will be assumed henceforth that the project is at least viable, and it will be assumed also that there is no need to specify such factors as the mental state of the subject (e.g. is he alert or drowsy etc.) in the attempt given here to explicate demonstrative thought. A more thorough treatment, however, would require the working out of such details (see Peacocke, 1983, 1986).

7.   A parallel account could be given to characterise the psychological state of a blind commuter who, say, exploits his sense of hearing rather than his sense of sight in demonstrative thoughts he entertains concerning the train (cf. note 5).

8.   " <O> " represents any of three options just referred to - i.e. identity of the particular object thought of, object-type, or just, some object or other.

9.   Of course the problem of referring expressions which lack

referents is what motivated the descriptivist strategy originally, i.e. in Russell's theory of descriptions.

9 Evans' theory of demonstrative thought

Gareth Evans (1982) has produced one of the most sustained and highly regarded theories of demonstrative thought. I propose to outline the main aspects of Evans' theory with the aim of recruiting certain features of it in support of a type externalist account of (perceptual) demonstrative thought.[1]

1. Evans' "know which" requirement

Evans has proposed the view that a significant class of thoughts which concern objects are subject to the constraints of Russell's Principle; this is the principle that "...a subject cannot make a judgement about something unless he knows which object his judgement is about" (Evans, 1982, p.89; Russell, 1912, p.58). Evans claims that demonstrative thoughts are such a class of thoughts (Evans, 1982, e.g. p.173, pp.72-73).[2] According to Evans, for a subject to entertain a thought "Fa" which involves the ascription of a property F to an object a, it is necessary for the subject to have (i) an Idea of an object, and an Idea of a; and (ii) an Idea of a property and an Idea of F.[3] Concerning (i), this consists in an appreciation of the fact that there are objects and that these are distinct from one another due to their possession of an individuating property. Such an individuating property is described by Evans as the "fundamental ground of difference" (ibid., p.107) of the object. Typically, the fundamental ground of difference of an object is determined by its spatio-temporal location and the sort of object it is (cf. Evans, ibid., p.178).[4] If a subject has an idea of the fundamental ground of difference of an object, then the subject has a fundamental Idea of the object.[5]

A further requirement proposed by Evans is this. In order for a subject S to have a fundamental Idea of O, S must be able to think of O as satisfying an indefinite number of predicates, e.g. that O is F, is G, is H and so on. Evans calls this constraint the Generality Constraint (ibid. pp.100-105).

With respect to (ii), very briefly, Evans' view seems to be that S has an Idea of a property if he knows what it is for subject-predicate expressions to be true; and an Idea of a specific property if he has the discriminatory capacities that would be expected of someone who knows the difference between two properties e.g. F and G. Also, in Evans' account, S must meet the demands of the Generality Constraint with respect to F - i.e. so that he can think that a is F, that b is F, that c is F, and so on.

Application of Russell's Principle to demonstrative thoughts has the consequence that a subject cannot effect a judgement that that is F unless he knows which object is the referent of the demonstrative. The considerations of the last chapter, and the apparent close relations between demonstrative thought and perception may lead one to suppose that satisfaction of the know which requirement in the case of demonstrative thought is closely linked to perceptual acquaintance with the demonstratively presented object. But can this intuitive link be made sharper; can it be shown that acquaintance with the demonstratively presented object is necessary for satisfaction of the know which requirement?

As noted, then, for Evans, a subject S who entertains a thought "That is F" in the presence of a demonstratively presented object must know the truth conditions of the thought. The subject must know which object is being referred to, and what it is for an object to satisfy the predicate "...is F". Further, S must satisfy the demands of the Generality Constraint with respect to his thought. With these points in mind let us continue.

I will, first, provide two lengthy quotations from Evans in which he tries to summarise his proposals, and then go on to elaborate these, identifying three main aspects of his account. The three aspects are (a) the distinction between space conceived egocentrically and space conceived publicly, (b) the notion of an information-link, and (c) the distinction between conceptual and nonconceptual content. Each of these aspects of Evans' account are relevant since they indicate conditions which must be met for a subject to satisfy the know which requirement. Here are the quotes:

(I) A thought about a position in egocentric space (including the utterly non-specific here) concerns a point or region of public space in virtue of the existence of certain indissolubly connected dispositions, on the part of the subject, to direct his actions to that place, and to treat perceptions of that place as germane to the evaluation and appreciation of the consequences of the thought. This dispositional connection with a place rests upon a vastly complex network of links between perception and action which allows us to speak of the existence of a unified egocentric space, and in this context, the subject may be said to have an adequate Idea of a point in public space in virtue of his general capacity to impose a conception of public space upon egocentric space (1982, p.168).

(II) Given the subject's general knowledge of what makes propositions of the form "p = P" true, for arbitrary p, when P is an Idea of a position in his egocentric space, and given that he has located, or is able to locate, the object in his egocentric space, he can then be said to know what it is for "This = the object at p now" to be true (for arbitrary p). Hence he can be said to have an adequate Idea of the object" (ibid., pp.170-171).[6]

Concerning quote (I), here is a rough outline of what Evans seems to be saying; this outline makes use of terms which have not yet been elaborated here, but it conveys (hopefully) the general thrust of Evans' position. A subject S has an adequate Idea of a position in public space due to his possession of the capacity to unify egocentric and public space, and the fact that such places are possible locations of information which may be of relevance to S (e.g. the location of food, or books).

Concerning quote (II), the claim is that providing a subject S knows how to determine the truth conditions of expressions such as "This place = P where P stands for an Idea of a place (e.g. the place where the damp patch on my kitchen floor is), then S possesses the capacity to determine the truth conditions of "This = the object at p now".

(a) Egocentric and public space

In quote (I) the expressions "egocentric space" and "public space" feature prominently. The notion of egocentric space is characterised by Evans by reference to "here-thoughts". Evans claims that "here-thoughts" should be conceived of holistically so that for a subject to have the concept that "here it is F" he must have concepts such as "up there it is

174

F", "over there it is F", and "behind me it is F" (cf. Evans ibid., p.153). So it is being claimed that the capacity for here-thoughts is dependent upon the capacity to entertain thoughts about a range of places. These places are perceived from a perspective with the perceiving subject at its centre - i.e. references to foreground and background are perceiver-relative. (Recall Marr's references to "a viewer-centred co-ordinate frame" (1985, p.124) (ch.4, sec.2 above).)

The perspectival nature of spatial thinking, construed in this way can be taken to suggest what Evans refers to as "Egocentric spatial thinking" (1982, pp.151-170); this denotes subjects' conceptions of the locations of objects and places. Naturally, there may be a gap between a subject's conception of, say, where an object O is located, and where it is actually located. In such a case, it can be said that there is a mismatch between the egocentric and the actual placing of O.

What is required for a subject to be accredited with an adequate Idea of a point in public space? As far as I can discern, Evans gives two main requirements; each of which can be described as dispositional (cf. quote (I) above).

Concerning the first requirement, what is required for a subject to have an adequate demonstrative thought concerning an object is that the subject has the capacity to "unify egocentric and public space" (ibid., p.165) so that the subject's conception of where he is matches up with where he actually is: that is, there is a coincidence between actual and egocentric space. Evidence that a subject S has the kind of capacity referred to can be gleaned from the facts that, say, he can find his way around the area where he lives, and can direct others. If S can do this, it can be regarded as evidence that he has a cognitive map of the area (ibid. p.163; Neisser, 1976). Another way to describe the kind of ability which possession of a cognitive map of an area implies, is to say that possession of such information is hypothesis-generating (cf. Evans, 1982, p.162); that is, if S has a cognitive map of an area, say the centre of Manchester, he can think thus: if I walk from Market St., along Deansgate, past Kendal's, then John Dalton St. will be on my left.

So on Evans' account it can be seen that subjects are required to possess the capacity to map egocentric onto public space; possession of such a capacity may be manifested in the way just outlined.

The second requirement for the possession of an adequate Idea of a position in public space is that the subject has "stable dispositional connection[s]" (ibid. p.164) with places in the relevant area. The importance of this second condition can be shown by discussion of an example. Suppose a subject thinks "My bicycle is downstairs in the kitchen". It may be said of the subject that, providing he knows where

175

he is in relation to the kitchen he intends to refer to, he is able to satisfy the 'know which' requirement with respect to the place where his bicycle is located. But if, for example, the subject falls asleep whilst he is upstairs and is unknowingly moved to an identical-looking room in another house, it may be claimed that the subject does not have an adequate Idea of the place where his bicycle is since his egocentric placing of the bicycle does not match up with its actual location; worse, the system of co-ordinates which the subject would ordinarily employ to locate his bicycle is a system which does not apply to his present location. That is, the subject conceives himself to be located in his house and determines the locations of objects within the house by reference to a framework; the framework being his house. If he is unknowingly moved to another, identical-looking house, the framework - or system of co-ordinates - which S believes to be relevant to determining the truth value of the thought "My bicycle is downstairs in the kitchen" is not actually relevant to the determination of the truth value of the thought, since he is in another house. This can be taken to suggest that failure on the part of S to match up egocentric and public space - specifically, failure to employ the appropriate framework of co-ordinates - renders S unable to satisfy the know which requirement with respect to the location of his bicycle. The example provides an indication of how stable relations between subjects and locations may be a factor in their capacity to entertain certain thoughts.

Having spent some time elaborating the egocentric/public distinction, we turn now to a second element of Evans' account: the notion of an information-link between subject and demonstrated object.

(b) Information-links

After noting the close intuitive relationship between demonstrative thought and perception, Evans asserts that "...an information-link between a subject and an object is a crucial necessary condition of [perceptual demonstrative thought]" (1982, p.145). To see why this might be thought to be the case, consider an example in which a subject points to a rug and says "That's worn". If the hearer H of this remark is not in the room when the utterance is made, it seems plausible to say that H is not in a position to determine the truth conditions of the utterance because he does not know what the referent of "That" is when the utterance was made - in Evans' terms, there is no information-link between H and the rug.[7]

Another example intended to suggest the same conclusion is this. Suppose S is blindfolded, points a finger out in front of him, and utters the words "That's pretty" (cf. Evans, ibid., p.171). Coincidentally, when S makes this remark there is indeed a pretty antique in the general direction of where S is pointing. Evans points out that there is no information-link between S and the antique; this is due to the fact that S is blindfolded. In such a case, according to Evans, S does not understand his own remark; again, this is due to the fact that S is in no position to determine the truth conditions of his own utterance. (Strictly, it should be added that at the time of his utterance S has no idea of his location in relation to the vase - say, e.g., he was brought into a house he had not previously visited and knew nothing about.)

Although an information-link between subject and object is held to be a necessary condition of a perceptual demonstrative thought, it is not held to be a sufficient condition. Evans writes "...the sheer existence of an information-link between subject and object does not guarantee the possibility of demonstrative thought about the object" (ibid., 148); what is required is that "the subject can, upon the basis of that link, locate the object in space" (ibid., p.150).

The reasons why stem from the role of the know which requirement on thought which is proposed by Evans in which entertaining a thought is tied to the capacity to determine its truth conditions. In demonstrative thoughts, objects are placed for subjects by a particular cognitive faculty, specifically one which is concerned with what Evans terms "nonconceptual states" (e.g. 1982, p.227; cf. also ch.3, sec.2 above).

(c) The conceptual/nonconceptual distinction [8]

Evans suggests a distinction between two types of cognitive operation undertaken by two types of cognitive faculty. One, more primitive, cognitive faculty - call it faculty-(i) - provides information exploited by a more sophisticated cognitive faculty - call it faculty-(ii).

Evans writes that the information provided by what I am calling faculty-(i) "...serves as input to a thinking, concept-applying, and reasoning system; so that the subject's thoughts, plans and deliberations are also systematically dependent on the informational properties of the input" (1982, p.158). So faculty-(i) provides faculty-(ii) with information concerning the environment of the subject. At least some of the cognitive operations which are undertaken by faculty-(ii) (e.g. judgements) are based, systematically, on the information provided by faculty-(i). E.g. a decision to press a fire alarm may be based upon the perception that there is a fire in the room.

Further, at least part of what Evans means by "nonconceptual" is that no conscious inference is required on the part of the subject, e.g. from

177

receipt of the information to deducing where in the auditory/visual field it came from (ibid., p.157, pp.123-124). The suggestion is that when a subject's senses are stimulated, e.g. by a noise in his vicinity, the subject is able to locate the direction from which the sound has come, in relation to his own position, without the need for conscious inference (ibid.,p.123).[9] Evans is contrasting such a position with a position in which such placing of the causes of perceptual stimulii by a subject is done consciously; the latter kind of cognitive operation is said to include a conceptual component, where this indicates the presence of a conscious inference on the part of the subject.[10] So "nonconceptual" is contrasted with "conceptual" in Evans' account (1982,pp.151-170); and it seems that nonconceptual information is arrived at without inference, whilst conceptualised information does require some inferential work.

There are two positions in play here: in one, the placing of the causes of sensory stimulii experienced by subjects is carried out, unreflectively, by the perceptual system without the need for conscious inference on the part of the subject. In a second, distinct position, the placing of the source of sensory stimulii is the result of conscious inference on the part of the subject.[11]

In standard cases of perceptual encounters with objects, Evans claims that the spatial component of thoughts prompted by such encounters - specifically demonstrative thoughts about the object perceived - is nonconceptual: in such cases, subjects need not make an inference to locate the object; their perceptual experience typically places the object for them.[12]

It needs now to be shown why it is that Evans takes standard cases of demonstrative thoughts to be nonconceptual (i.e. in the sense that they are based upon information presented by the perceptual faculty). As far as I can determine, Evans gives two arguments for that claim (1982, pp.157-159). The claim is that causes of sensory stimulii are placed by subjects unreflectively. Such cases are standard by virtue of the fact that the cause of the stimulus is in the vicinity of the subject; and are nonconceptual by virtue of the fact that the subject places the cause of the stimulus unreflectively. For Evans, it is in virtue of the fact that subjects are able to do this - to place causes of sensory stimulii - that it is legitimate to ascribe to them structured spatial experiences. Evidence for such ascription lies in the ability of such subjects to judge (e.g.) that a sound is coming from the right rather than the left (cf. Evans, ibid.,p.159). Further, the fact that subjects are able to place objects in the way just indicated renders them capable of satisfying the know which requirement with respect to the object thought of. For Evans, it seems, the object is individuated by virtue of its spatio-temporal relations to

178

other objects. Faculty-(i) delivers, so to speak, such information to the subject.[13]

The first of Evans' arguments is an argument from evolutionary considerations. It is pointed out that, assuming humans evolved from less cognitively sophisticated organisms, it can be accepted that at some stage in the history of the human species, causes of sensory stimulii would be placed (located) unreflectively by such primitive organisms. So, for example, food sources, predators, light sources may each be placed by these primitive organisms without their having the capacity for reflection upon the incoming sensory information. Such reflection might usefully be described as a second-order faculty involving reflection upon first-order informational states (cf. Davidson, 1984, ch.11).[14]

Evans' claim here seems wholly acceptable. Even if there is some reflection upon their experience undertaken by cognitively primitive creatures, that cannot be usual since such creatures generally move e.g. either towards or away from light sources and so on, and do so manifestly unreflectively.

Evans' second argument recruits empirical work undertaken by Weiskrantz et. al. (1974; 1986). The research, on brain damaged patients, suggests the presence of a capacity to locate sources of light in spite of such subjects' denials that they see anything (see also Johnson-Laird, 1988, pp.358-359; Eysenck and Keane, 1990, pp.81-82). This phenomenon can be taken to suggest the kind of separation which Evans is out to establish: a separation between (i) a cognitive faculty which places sources of stimulii without conscious effort on the part of the subject (i.e. faculty-(i)), and (ii) a more sophisticated cognitive faculty which exploits the information provided by the faculty referred to in (i) (faculty-(ii)). (In Weiskrantz's subjects there is, so to speak, an obstruction between the two faculties caused by neuronal damage.) The importance of this distinction - between faculties (i) and (ii) - is that it can be asserted that the information delivered by faculty (i) is not unstructured; by this I mean it has informational properties, e.g. that the source of the stimulus is, say, roughly two feet to the left of the subject. Faculty (i), then, can be said to provide faculty (ii) with structured information concerning stimulii sources; so faculty (i) provides faculty (ii) with information about the environment of the subject.

A further example which seems to lend support to Evans's view that there are these two kinds of cognitive faculty is this. One may be involved in a discussion with another person; whilst the discussion is ongoing, there is music playing in the background. On occasion, though one seems not to be listening to the music, a particular passage strikes one as particularly catchy. The occurrence of this phenomenon indicates that information is being provided to the subject by the perceptual system, e.g. faculty-(i), whether or not the subject is consciously aware that it is; e.g. one might not be consciously aware that one is listening to the background music but still be capable of singling out passages which one finds significant in some respect.[15]

In summary of Evans' theory, it may be said that first, for S to entertain a demonstrative thought concerning an object O it is necessary that S satisfy the demands of the know which requirement with respect to O. For S to do this, (a) S must possess the capacity to process spatial information; evidence of the possession of such a capacity is manifested in the subject's movements. (b) There must also an information-link between O and S such that S can locate O without invoking the resources of faculty-(ii) (hence, it turns out that demonstrative thoughts are object-dependent on Evans view). And (c) relatedly, the information from O must be nonconceptual - simply acquired by the resources of faculty-(i). It should be stressed that though Evans employs the term nonconceptual to describe the information acquired in faculty-(i). This does not mean that the information is unstructured. If it was unstructured, that would leave faculty-(ii) with too much inferential work to do.

2. Comments on Evans' theory

The know which requirement is so central to Evans' theory that some comment and possible criticism on the requirement is necessary. Two questions which internalists seem certain to raise are these: (1) Is it really necessary, as Evans claims, for the possibility of a subject S entertaining a demonstrative thought concerning an object O, at t, that the subject satisfy the know which requirement with respect to O at t? And (2), even if the answer to (1) turns out to be "Yes", it may plausibly be asked whether acquaintance with O at t is a necessary condition for the possibility of S's entertaining a demonstrative thought concerning O at t.

Concerning the first question, a briefly stated example can be taken to suggest that the know which requirement is a necessary condition for demonstrative thought. If a subject S thinks of some salient object "That's F" he is, trivially, making a judgement about the object to the effect that it is F. Determination of the truth value and the truth conditions of the thought depends upon S's knowing of which object "...is F" is being asserted (see e.g. Evans 1982, section 9.2).

The claim that there is a close relationship between judging and truth seems unobjectionable: when a subject judges, the judgements have truth conditions. Given acceptance of this modest claim, then the know which requirement seems easy to accept since a subject will not be in a position to determine even the truth conditions of his demonstrative thought unless he knows which object is the object of his judgement. Evans (1982, p.106), points out that the know which requirement is a minimal demand on subjects' thoughts concerning objects. He points out that it is reasonable to require there be some discernible cognitive difference between two subjects, one of whom thinks that p whilst the other lacks that thought. The subject who entertains the thought is required to know its truth conditions, and to satisfy this it is necessary that he knows which object is the object he is thinking of. (But see ensuing discussion in which it is asked whether one can meet the demand that one know the truth conditions of a demonstrative thought in the absence of perceptual acquaintance with it.) [16]

Concerning the second question, as Russell's Principle appears as quoted earlier (last section), there is no obvious reference to perceptual relations which hold between subjects and objects. If it proved possible to know which object one's thought concerned without the receipt of sensory information from that object, then, evidently, one would be deemed capable of satisfying the principle.

Consider demonstrative thoughts; could a subject meet the know which requirement without being in receipt of sensory information from the object to which the demonstrative expression refers? The following example suggests not.

A subject H outside a room hears someone U inside the room give utterance to a demonstrative thought such as "That's torn". Here the hearer, outside the room, is not in receipt of sensory information from the object demonstrated. Does it thereby follow that H cannot meet the know which requirement?

One possible option would be to say that H can go into the room and ask U what he was referring to. But what is typical about perceptual demonstrative thoughts is that they are prompted by objects which are either currently perceived or which are taken to be currently perceived (e.g. as in hallucination). Subjects entertain demonstrative thoughts on the basis of sensory information they are either receiving or take themselves to be receiving from currently perceivable parts of their immediate vicinity. So although H might be ascribed a demonstrative thought concerning the object referred to by U once he (H) has entered the room, it does not appear plausible to claim that H's thought at the time of his hearing U's utterance is a demonstrative thought concerning the object (call it O) to which U is referring. These considerations suggest that H cannot meet the know which requirement with respect to O at the time of U's utterance t by virtue of the fact that H can meet that requirement with respect to O at a later time t'.

Suppose it is suggested that H is able to meet the know which requirement by virtue of his employment at t of a descriptive thought such as "The object currently being referred to by U is torn". The difficulty with this kind of descriptivist response again stems from the observation that demonstrative thoughts typically concern objects which are in the range of one's senses; so whilst it may be possible for H to demonstratively identify a sound emerging from the room, it seems less plausible to say he can demonstratively identify an object in the room since those objects are hidden from H's view. [17]

Although these two attempts to defend a construal of the know which requirement which does require perceptual contact between the object and the thinker have intuitive plausibility, they are far from decisive. What is needed is a means of clarifying the difference in the thoughts of H and U with respect to O at t. One way to bring out such an alleged difference is to point to the fact that U (assuming he is cognitively competent) is in a position to determine both the truth conditions of his demonstrative thought "That's torn", uttered at t, and the truth value of the thought. Further, U is able to do this on the basis of his present perceptions of the demonstrated object. This last feature of U's thought sits well with the intimacy, noted earlier, between demonstrative thoughts and present perceptual experiences. Whilst it appears acceptable to claim that U is able to determine the truth conditions and truth value of his thought, the same does not appear to be true for H with respect to O.

Consider first the truth value of U's thought. H hears its utterance at t but clearly cannot, at t, determine the truth value of the thought. H cannot, at t, determine the truth value of the thought due to the fact that he does not know which object is being referred to by U. This latter fact (the fact that H does not know which object is being referred to) strongly suggests that H does not know the truth conditions of U's utterance. Now, it might seem obvious to some theorists that H does not know the truth conditions of U's utterance at t, but in another, descriptivist sense there can seem a strong temptation to claim that H does indeed know the truth conditions of U's utterance. For example, it may be claimed that if H thinks "The object currently being referred to by U is torn" then H knows the truth conditions of U's thought (this is considered by Evans (1982, p.314)). There are conflicting intuitions here so it may be best to spell matters out.

First, it can be agreed that, at t, U is, whilst H is not, in a position to determine the truth value of U's thought concerning O. Second, on one set of intuitions, H is unable to determine the truth value of U's utterance due to the fact that he does not know the truth conditions of U's utterance; H does not know the truth conditions due to the fact that he does not know what the referent of "That" is. But third, by a different set of intuitions, H does know the truth conditions of U's utterance by virtue of his employment of a descriptive thought such as "The object currently being referred to by U is torn".

So far, then, the major justification for the claim that there is a difference in type between the thoughts of H and U with respect to O is that U can determine the truth value of his thought on the basis of his currently being in receipt of sensory information from O.

Are there other ways of bringing out the alleged difference in the way H and U know the truth conditions of U's thought? First, consider what is involved in the determination of the truth value of the thought. Recruiting some other aspects of Evans' theory, it can be pointed out that U's thought about O is direct; O is located for U by U's perceptual system - by faculty (i) as that was described earlier. But for H, he has to ask a question which U is not required to ask, H needs to know which object it is that U has referred to before he can determine the truth conditions of U's thought; U does not have to do this.[18]

The difference which I am attempting to bring out here might be better expressed as follows. H is required to undertake a two-stage procedure to determine what thought it is to which U is giving voice (cf. Evans, 1982, p.313). To determine the truth conditions of U's thought, H has first to arrive at the belief that some object, $a = O$ - i.e. that some object is the object to which U is referring. Then, to determine the truth value of U's thought that O is torn, H has to determine whether O is in fact torn. Whether or not U has to undertake the second stage of the process which H can be said to undertake, it seems plausible to claim that U is not required to undertake the first stage - i.e. U is not required to ask himself, of the salient objects in the room, "Is this the one I'm referring to?", and then, thinking of another object "Is this the one I'm referring to?" and so on. So it seems reasonable to claim both that U knows the truth value of his thought, and that the way he knows its truth conditions differs from the way in which H can be said to know its truth conditions - i.e. when H employs a descriptive thought to the effect that "The object, whatever it is, to which U is referring, at t, is torn". These considerations seem to lend support to the view that that H's thought concerning O involves a conceptual element which is not present in U's thought concerning O (see,esp. Evans, ibid., pp.145-151 on the distinction between standard and circuitous information links).

A further indication that H's not being in receipt of sensory information from O makes a difference in the respective thoughts of U and H is this. Suppose U says later to H "Yes, that vase was certainly something to see". H clearly has much less information about O than U here, and this could manifest itself in the later actions of U and H. E.g. If they return to the room where U initially saw the vase, and if there are a number of vases in the room, H would not know how to pick out the vase pointed to by U earlier; U would not face this difficulty. Even if the original vase has been replaced by a replica the fact that U returns to the location in the room where the original vase was, indicates that the information received from O makes a difference in the thoughts of the subject - a difference which can be manifested in what the subjects later go on to do. (Cf. Evans' claims concerning the importance of "a continuing information-link between subject and object" (1982,p.174).)

A way of attempting to cement the alleged intuitive connections between current perceptions and demonstrative thoughts may be to claim that if a subject entertains a demonstrative thought concerning an object O, then he is in a position both to determine the truth conditions and the truth value of the thought, and can do so on the basis of the sensory information presently being received from the demonstrated object. Such thoughts are described by Evans as being "identification-free [and not] identification-dependent" (1982, pp.180-181). The subject's placing (via faculty-(i)) of the object thought of does not require prior placing of other objects; e.g. as may occur in the following kind of cognitive operation undertaken by a subject who is informed that S's favourite vase is next to the vase made in China: Since that object is G, that must be F (where F stands for "...is S's favourite vase", and G stands for "...is made in China").[19]

Consideration of the type of case discussed in this section suggests that the know which requirement applies to demonstrative thought by virtue of the fact that a subject can only satisfy that requirement if he is in receipt of sensory information from the object at the time of the thought. These considerations seem to bear out the intuitive view of the intimate nature of the links between demonstrative thought and perception - they provide positive answers to our two questions. Also, the example points to an ontological dependence between demonstrative thoughts of the type entertained by U and demonstrative thoughts of the kind attempted by H. In order, finally, to entertain a demonstrative thought concerning O, H must get into a position in which there is an information-link between himself and O. In the absence of such a link it is clear that U is able, not simply to entertain thoughts concerning O at t, but to recognise O at a later time; H plainly cannot do this.

In sum, then, as a consequence of U's perceptual encounter with O, he is able to perform three kinds of cognitive act which H cannot. First, U is able to recognise O whilst H cannot. Second, U is able to understand the utterance of "That's F" without undertaking the kind of two-stage procedure which H is required to undertake; in Evans' terms, U's demonstrative thought concerning O at t is identification-free whilst H's is identification-dependent. Third, U can, whilst H cannot, give voice to a demonstrative thought concerning O at t.

Evans claims that for a subject S to possess an Adequate Idea of a place P, he must have "a stable dispositional connection with [the place concerned]" (ibid. p.161). This might be thought to open up the possibility of effecting the contextualisation of intentional types which is required for externalism. The possibility may be thought to open up due to the fact that simply moving S to a different spatial location has consequences for his intentional states; when located in his own house S's thought that his bicycle is downstairs is true, but when S is unknowingly moved, his thought is false.

In response to Evans, suppose it is argued that a descriptive identification of P is possible and that, therefore, even when moved to the identical-looking house S still has an Adequate Idea of P since this is identified descriptively as "The place where my bicycle is = P". Assuming that S's bicycle is in the original house, it might seem that S is able to identify P - i.e. via the identification of his bicycle.

However, such a response (the descriptivist strategy again) need not create problems for Evans' account. This is because S is under the impression that his bicycle is downstairs, and, in the example, it is not. So it seems underhand to suggest that S can locate a place P via the identification of an object (S's bicycle) the whereabouts of which S is unaware. The lacuna in S's knowledge would be revealed if he is asked to direct another subject T to P. It would be of no help to T if S says "P = the place where my bicycle is" (i.e. it is to be assumed that T can identify S's bicycle). Hence it seems fair to say that Evans' account is not vulnerable to the kind of descriptivist response just offered.[20]

It should be said that the construal of Evans just canvassed exploits the subject's lack of knowledge that he has failed to maintain stable dispositional relations with the place concerned. It seems to be the case that Evans allows that such dispositions remain stable whether the subject is aware of this or not.

If this latter interpretation of Evans is correct, S would be said to have an adequate Idea of P even when he has been unknowingly moved. This is because the fact that S has been moved need not affect his general capacity to map egocentric onto public space. Also, his relations to the objects and places in his environment remain "continuous" in spite of the fact of S's being moved. S traces a regular path through space and time in the example; he might later come to realise what had happened - that a trick had been played upon him - and be able to put into effect his capacity to unify egocentric and public space. This need not affect his capacity to entertain adequate Ideas concerning objects in his environment.

With specific reference to demonstrative thoughts, consider that S, when moved unknowingly into the identical looking room, thinks demonstratively of a vase e.g. "That vase is pretty". It may be thought that S's egocentric placing of both himself and the vase do not match up with S's actual placing. But clearly judgement on this matter depends upon the frame of reference which is to be appealed to. If the co-ordinate system which is to constitute S's egocentric placings of objects is just to be his immediate vicinity - say the room in which he is located - then there are no grounds for the assertion that there is any difference between S's thought "That vase is pretty" when this is thought in either S's actual room or the counterfeit room. However, it seems to be the case that for Evans at any rate, the relevant co-ordinate system is not just the subject's immediate vicinity (e.g. Evans, 1982, p.169). If that were the case, then there would be no point on insisting on the hypothesis-generating character of cognitive maps which Evans discusses (see above).

So it seems clear that in Evans' own account it would be accurate to say that when S demonstratively identifies the vase in his own room, egocentric and public placings of the vase coincide. But when S entertains what seems to be the same type of thought in the counterfeit room there is a mismatch between egocentric and public placings of the vase - i.e. providing the co-ordinate system is wider than just S's immediate vicinity. In spite of the apparent difference between S's thoughts in the two cases, Evans seems to claim that S has an adequate Idea of the demonstrated vase in both cases.

What these considerations indicate is that in Evans' account for a subject S to entertain a demonstrative thought concerning an object O it is necessary that S possess the capacity to map egocentric onto public space, and that, whether S is aware of the fact or not, S proceeds through space and time in a regular fashion - this, evidently, is how the expression "a stable dispositional connection" is intended to be understood.

It should be stressed that Evans' view appears the more plausible here. Suppose it is claimed that subjects can only entertain demonstrative thoughts when they know their locations. This would entail that when S wakes up in the counterfeit room he cannot think demonstratively of objects in it. This seems absurd. Think also of a sailor who is shipwrecked on a desert island with no idea of his location. Again, it is unmotivated to claim that he cannot entertain demonstrative thoughts with respect to, e.g. bits of driftwood and exotic fruits around him.

3. Evaluation

We turned to consider Evans' theory in the hope of clarifying the individuation conditions for demonstrative thoughts. Considerable progress has been made. It should be said that Evans' theory lends further support to the claims made in ch.8 concerning the object-dependency of demonstrative thoughts. Discussion of the saga of H and U above indicates the plausibility of the claim that subjects must meet the demands of the know which requirement with respect to demonstrative thoughts, and that satisfaction of this requires an information-link between subject and object. So this buttresses the claim that an objectual component should feature in a description of the individuation conditions of demonstrative thoughts.

In addition, the distinction between conceptual and nonconceptual content can be exploited to point to distinctions between characterisations of the individuation conditions of demonstrative thoughts which favour internalism, and those which favour externalism. This is due to the fact that the conceptual/nonconceptual distinction helps to show why descriptivist construals of the (Dem) component are less well-motivated than characterisations which employ singular referring expressions. In descriptivist construals of demonstrative thought, demonstrative expressions employed in attributions to subjects of demonstrative thoughts are replaceable by descriptions without loss of explanatory adequacy. This is taken to suggest the reducibility of demonstrative thought to descriptive thought - that demonstrative thoughts are merely a sub-class of descriptive thoughts.

But on a second construal of the (Dem)-component, demonstrative terms employed in attributions of demonstrative thoughts to subjects are not eliminable in favour of descriptions.

Recall that in descriptivist construals, demonstratives are replaced by a description (e.g. "The unique x such that..."). Consider the sort of cognitive operation undertaken by a subject thinking demonstratively. Recall also the saga of H and U discussed earlier. It was asked whether H and U could be said to satisfy the know which requirement. It was conjectured that both H and U may be said to know the truth conditions of U's utterance "That's torn". U knows the truth conditions by virtue of the fact that his perceptual experience places the referent of the demonstrative for him. Further, the information received from the object is nonconceptual. So in this account of demonstrative thought (i.e. that put forward by Evans) the ineliminability of the demonstrative employed to characterise U's thoughts concerning O, e.g., "That", has more than logico-semantic significance; it indicates the directness of the relations between the thinker and the object. Contrast that account with the account given of the way in which H was said to know the truth conditions of the thought uttered by U. It was mooted that H may deploy a description such as: "The object presently being pointed at by U is torn". This can plausibly be said to involve a two-stage cognitive operation; the first entails locating the object which satisfies the description "...is the object presently being pointed at by U", and the second stage entails predicating of the object identified by the first stage "...is torn". This latter two-stage procedure may be said to involve a conceptual element; at least in the sense that it is cognitively much more complex than U's thought. The complexity of H's thought can be indicated further by noting that it requires the Idea of an information-link (i.e. between U and the object) - no such Idea is required for U.

If the analysis of the difference between the thoughts of H and U just given is accepted, it seems unmotivated to claim that the (Dem)-component should be characterised descriptively. This is because subjects (if Evans' theory of demonstrative thought is accepted) do not satisfy the know which requirement - with respect to the objects they respectively think of - by undertaking the kind of two-stage operation undertaken by H. This suggests that the (Dem)-component should not be construed descriptively in cases of perceptual demonstrative thought.[21]

We end this chapter with two further points, each of which concerns the need for additional components in our characterisation of demonstrative thoughts. Evans' theory brings out the importance of spatial thinking in the ascription of content. Subject's actions take place within a framework of locations, and it seems plausible to hold that some representation of this framework is a necessary condition of action (cf. Evans, 1982, pp.151ff; and Peacocke, 1982, ch.3). As noted above, it is necessary for a subject to entertain a demonstrative thought that his perceptual faculties (what was described above as faculty-(i)) place objects for him - otherwise the subject cannot satisfy the demands of the know which requirement with respect to the object thought of. This suggests the need for a spatial component in our characterisation of the individuation conditions of demonstrative thoughts in addition to the components described in ch.8. Hence, the individuation conditions of such thoughts look as follows

$$\{[(Dem) <O>], (E), (...F), [spat...], [temp...]\}$$

where "[spat...]" indicates the spatial context in which the subject's actions occur, and, as before, the temporal index indicates the time the thought occurs.[22]

The second point concerns the absence of a component which stands for what may be termed a sortal concept, and discussion of the possibility of inclusion of a sortal in the individuation conditions of demonstrative thoughts will take place in ch.10.

Notes to chapter nine

1. It should be said that Evans' theory owes much to Strawson's work (Strawson, 1959).
2. Russell's Principle, in this context, has also come to be known as the know which requirement on thought. I will use these two terms interchangeably.
3. Evans employs the term "Idea" as a rough analogue of the term "concept" (Evans, ibid., p.104, fn.23, fn.24); I will follow his usage in this chapter.
4. Spatio-temporal properties alone are not considered fundamental in Evans' sense due to the possibility of a single object being a member of two distinct kinds, e.g. a statue may also be a piece of clay (Evans, 1982, p.107,p.178).
5. It should be stressed that Evans takes subjects to possess such knowledge tacitly rather than explicitly - it is manifested by the way subjects behave and the judgements they make.
6. I have made some notational changes to quote (II) which do not affect its content. As I understand Evans, an adequate Idea of an object, or place, consists in a capacity to determine the truth conditions of a proposition which refers to the object, or place (see e.g., Evans, ibid., p.115). So an adequate Idea of the referent of "This" in "This is F" would consist in the subject's capacity to know what it would be for that proposition to be true or false. It seems that, providing I know my location (in a sense to be made clear shortly) I would be said to have adequate Ideas of any object in my immediate vicinity since I could determine the truth conditions of propositions such as "That's pretty", "That's red" and so on (e.g. "That's red" is true iff the object demonstrated is red). With reference to the relationship between adequate and fundamental Ideas. Evans writes "I have allowed (4.3) that a fundamental Idea of an object will involve... a sortal, but a demonstrative identification need not itself constitute a fundamental

189

Idea. It will be adequate but not fundamental..." (1982, p.178). So, for Evans, an Idea may be adequate but not fundamental. The kind of case Evans seems to have in mind here is when, say, S points to a cow and thinks "That's ready to be milked". S will have an adequate Idea of the cow since he is in a position to determine the truth conditions of his thought. Further the spatio-temporal location of the cow serves to individuate it for the purposes of a demonstrative thought about it. But such an adequate Idea falls short of being a fundamental Idea of the cow; perhaps only the cow's owner has such an Idea, it would be constituted by some individuating property e.g. "...the best milk producer in the herd".

7.   But see next section for the view that H's predicament can be characterised harshly or sympathetically (and note 18 below).

8.   This has been referred to previously (ch.3). If the distinction is accepted it should be pointed out, with Burge (1986a), that the internalism/externalism debate can thus be seen to have at least two battlegrounds. One of which centres on nonconceptual content (the information dealt with by what will be termed faculty-(i)), and the other on conceptual content. Burge's arguments concerning perceptual content centre on nonconceptual content, and Macdonald's centre on conceptual content.

9.   This seems to be what is meant by the rather obscure expression "...a subject's perceptual experience places an object for him" (McDowell, 1990, p.257; also Peacocke, 1991).

10.   E.g. suppose S is unable to remember which room he slept in last night. He later concludes "This is the room I slept in last night" but not on the basis of memories of how the room looks but on the presence of certain evidence, e.g. his false teeth and spectacles. Here S thinks demonstratively about the room but the thought that the room is the one he slept in last night stems from inferential work done by faculty-(ii). Plausibly, Evans claims that demonstrative thoughts are not of this nature; they do not require inferential work.

11.   An exchange between McDowell (1990) and Peacocke (1991) focuses on the question of whether the information-link between an object and a perceiver has to be veridical for a subject to have a demonstrative thought about the object. McDowell says it does, but Peacocke says all that is required is that the subject exploits the information-link to locate the object. (Both are discussing a case in which the actual object lies within the perceptual field of the subject.) Evans does seem to express the view ascribed to him by

Peacocke (see, e.g. Evans, 1982, p.172); but textual evidence can also be found for McDowell's interpretation (see, e.g., Evans, ibid., p.146, fn.8 "...we cannot speak of an information-link when there is any process of inference on the part of the subject"). Peacocke's interpretation seems to allow a conceptual element into demonstrative thought which McDowell following Evans, is concerned to exclude.

12. Standard cases are contrasted with circuitous cases in which such an inference is typically required (see Evans, ibid., p.150). Put another way, standard cases are less cognitively demanding than circuitous cases; the latter take up more information-processing time, it may be said, than the former.

13. I referred earlier (note 9) to the expression "...a subject's perceptual experience correctly places an object for him" (McDowell, 1990, p.257). By saying that an experience places an object, McDowell appears to be attempting to make Evans' point that the subject need not do this himself reflectively.

14. Relatedly, Burge points out that in Marr's theory of vision "It is assumed that visual systems have evolved to solve certain problems forced on them by the environment" (1986a, p.28).

15. This is the phenomenon of subliminal perception (Eysenck and Keane, 1990, ch.3).

16. It may be objected that this section began by addressing the question of the relationship between thoughts and objects, and has transformed this into a question about the relations between judgements and objects. However this does not seem to be objectionable in the present context due to the fact that demonstrative thoughts typically have the logical form of expressions for which the question of their truth arises - i.e. whether they are construed descriptively or not (e.g. "The unique x such that x is the cause of these experiences, is F", or "That's F".

17. Even memory demonstratives, e.g. "That German we met" appear to stem from actual acquaintance with the object.

18. H's predicament can be characterised harshly or sympathetically. Harsh characterisations will say he knows neither the truth conditions nor the truth value of U's utterance. Sympathetic characterisations will say H knows the truth conditions but not the truth value.

19. See also Peacocke's account of thoughts which are "identificationally basic" (1983, p.140).

20. S's attempted descriptive identification of P suggests a parallel with

a subject who has a map of the area in front of him with P marked on it but who remains unable to locate P because he does not know his own location in relation to where P is marked on the map (cf. Peacocke, 1983, p.76).

21.   In support of the point being made here the so-called "minimax" principle may be appealed to according to which "Human cognitive processes...are geared to achieving the greatest possible cognitive effect for the smallest possible processing effort" (Sperber and Wilson, 1986, p.vii).

22.   That is, "That demonstratively thought of object O, instances the property F". The thought occurs at time t, in spatial framework S, and the thought itself has certain properties - those signified by the E-component.

10 An externalist theory of demonstrative thought

1. The need for a sortal

It was suggested in chapter eight that there seem to be three discernible subclasses within the class of (perceptual) demonstrative thoughts. It was stipulated that our attention will focus (mainly) on subclasses (ii) and (iii). Specifications of the contents of the members of (ii) were claimed to include a demonstrative, and a predicate expression (e.g. "That's F"); specifications of the contents of the members of (iii) were claimed to include a demonstrative, a kind term or sortal, and a predicate expression e.g. "That F is G", where "F" is a variable for the members of a kind K, e.g. carpets.[1]

With respect to the term "sortal", I (roughly) follow Wiggins' use (1980, e.g.,pp.7-8): Within the class of predicates, a distinction can be made between sortal predicates and other kinds of predicates. The former refer to kinds such as carpets, donkeys, bowls, humans. Other predicates may be employed to ascribe properties to members of the kinds referred to by sortal predicates. E.g. "Socrates is drunk", "Socrates is tall", "That carpet is torn", and so on - these are predicates of qualification (to use Aristotle's term *Categories*, ch.4).

In addition to "sortal predicate", Wiggins also uses the term "Sortal concept" (op.cit., pp.8-9); for him, that is what "a particular sortal predicate stands for" (ibid.). In Wiggins' usage the concept of F is distinguished from subject's conceptions of instances of F. But in what follows, the term "sortal concept" will be employed to denote a certain type of concept employed by a subject in demonstrative thought. Thus, consider an example in which a subject S gives voice to a demonstrative thought by uttering, e.g. "That cow needs milking" (so, a that-clause employed to characterise S's thought can be said to be of the form "That

F is G" - as above). It may be claimed that corresponding to "F" in the that-clause employed to describe S's thought, there is a concept F which S employs in thought when he judges that that F is G.[2]

If it is the case that it is a necessary condition for a subject to entertain a demonstrative thought that he employ a sortal concept in such a thought, it may be claimed further that an argument-place for a sortal concept should feature in the individuation conditions of demonstrative thought. If accepted, it seems to follow either that subclass (ii) thoughts are not demonstrative thoughts, or that they are more properly regarded as members of subclass (iii). Since it is implausible to deny that subclass (ii) thoughts are demonstrative thoughts, it would appear that they should, more properly, be regarded as subclass (iii) thoughts - i.e. if it is accepted that sortal concepts are necessary constituents of demonstrative thoughts.

Consideration of Evans' theory, in addition to the considerations of ch.8, strongly suggest that demonstrative thoughts are object-dependent. But as noted earlier (ch.8 sec.1), the mere object-dependency of demonstrative thoughts seems not to be sufficient for externalism with respect to such thoughts.[3] One way to argue for type externalism with respect to demonstrative thought is to argue that their individuation conditions must include an argument-place for a sortal concept, and further that externalism is true for these constituents of such, demonstrative, thoughts. In this section I try to provide an argument to show that sortal concepts must figure in the individuation conditions of demonstrative thought.

Evans' theory has been endorsed in the last chapter. According to him it is a necessary condition for a subject S to have a fundamental Idea of an object that the subject employ a sortal in that Idea (e.g., 1982, p.178). But Evans holds that entertaining a demonstrative thought concerning an object O does not require the employment in thought of a sortal. Provided the subject meets the demands of the know which requirement with respect to O, then S can be said to entertain an adequate (but not fundamental) demonstrative Idea of O.[4] Evidently, then, for Evans, a subject can meet the demands of the know which requirement with respect to O, without employing a sortal concept in his demonstrative thought concerning O.

I propose, now, to put forward four arguments against Evans and in support of the claim that demonstrative thinking requires employment of a sortal concept. The first argument recruits certain claims made by Davies (1982, p.291; cf.also Peacocke,1981). Davies points out, in relation to visual perception, that when a subject entertains a demonstrative thought concerning, say, an object in front of him, there are an indefinite number of ways in which the object may be conceptualised. For example, consider that S entertains a demonstrative thought concerning a man d who is standing in front of S at t - e.g. "That man is F". It can be pointed out that S's thought could concern "[A] temporal slice of a man, a front surface of a man, a mereological union of parts of a man, an aggregate of molecules constituting a man and doubtless various other objects...which are not identical with the man d" (1982, p.291). It seems plausible to suggest that given the indefinite number of sortals under which the man could be subsumed some conceptualisation of the man must be employed by S when S thinks demonstratively about him. From the perspective of satisfaction of the know which requirement it seems to matter that perceived objects are subsumed under concepts. As Evans argues, it seems that satisfaction of the know which requirement demands that a subject's perceptual system place the perceived object - the object of the demonstrative thought. For example, in thinking a demonstrative thought concerning one man in a crowd of men (say, "That man is bald"), it seems necessary to the placing of the object thought of that it is distinguished from other members of the crowd, and, from other possible objects of thought (e.g. empty spaces in the crowd, loud ties and so on). So it seems that some conceptualisation of what is perceived is involved in satisfaction of the know which requirement as this applies to objects thought of demonstratively.[5]

A second argument in support of the need for a sortal in the individuation conditions of demonstrative thoughts is this. In consideration of the extent to which a subject can be in error with respect to the type of object O he is thinking of whilst still being accredited with a demonstrative thought about O, it said, by Evans, that "There would be a question about how seriously mistaken [with regard to O's type] one has to be for this to be the consequence" (1982, pp.196-197); the consequence referred to is that such a mistake "deprives the attempted thought of content" (ibid., p.196).

The suggestion here seems to be that there are, in effect, limits to error in the entertaining of demonstrative thoughts. For example, consider a demonstrative thought of the form "That's F" in which "F" stands for a predicate of qualification (see above; henceforth I will call what are referred to by such predicates properties - at the cost of some accuracy but with the benefit of brevity) and not a sortal predicate. It seems plausible to suggest that in order to entertain a demonstrative thought concerning an object O the property one ascribes to O must at least be one which O could intelligibly instantiate. If accepted, it follows that there are, indeed, limits to error in subjects' thinking about objects. Put another way, it can be proposed that there is a relation of appropriateness between the demonstrative aspect of the thought and the predicative aspect; this is such that the property ascribed to the object referred to by the demonstrative component of the thought must be one which it, intelligibly, could instantiate.

For examples of the kind of inappropriateness being appealed to here, consideration of the perceptual modalities might prove instructive. The following demonstrative expressions each seem coherent in that the property ascribed to the sensory experience is appropriate to the sensory modality through which the experience occurs. (a) "That looks purple" (e.g. said of a visually perceived vase). (b) "That smells sweet" (e.g. said of an olfactorily perceived flower). (c) "That sounds loud" (e.g. said of an aurally perceived noise, say, a lawn mower). (d) "That tastes spicy" (e.g. said of a gustatorily perceived mouthful of curry).

But consider now the following demonstrative expressions.(e) "That touch is loud". (f) "That smells purple". (g) "That sounds acidic". (h) "That sounds purple". (i) "That tastes purple". (j) "That light is black".

In the case of expressions (a)-(d) the properties ascribed to the experiences are appropriate to the sensory modality. But this is not the case in expressions (e)-(i). It is reasonable to suppose that one would have, at least, grounds to doubt whether their utterer has given voice to a demonstrative thought since they indicate a mismatch between the property ascribed to the experience, and the sensory modality supposed to have been employed. These examples motivate the claim that there are limits to the extent to which subjects can be in error with respect to their thoughts. Examples which do not make reference to sensations include the following: (k) "That's the Prime Minister" (said of a stone). (l) "That's a pool of acid" (said of a cupboard).

It is of course possible to construct numerous other such examples - i.e. of category mistakes (Ryle, 1949). What they indicate is that there do appear to be constraints of intelligibility concerning which properties can be ascribed to which particulars.

Given acceptance of the point that there are such constraints - such limits to error - it can be claimed that in a demonstrative thought when, say, a subject judges "That's F", some conceptualisation of the object thought of must take place. It appears that the subject must at least take it to be the case that the referent of "That" is, at least, something which could be F. Of course, mere logical possibility is too weak here. So the possibilities are implicitly constrained by physical laws and by normative considerations operant in the relevant linguistic community.[6]

Acceptance of this proposal would require that Evans weakens the demands of the Generality Constraint (see ch.9 above). As it stands, it seems that Evans requires that subjects be able to conceive of the object thought of as satisfying an indefinite number of predicates. But if the present proposal is accepted it would entail that subjects are required to be able to think of O as satisfying predicates which O could intelligibly satisfy. It seems to me that, if anything, such a modification of the Generality Constraint strengthens Evans' position. For Evans

> [If] a subject can be credited with the thought that a is F, then he must have the conceptual resources for entertaining the thought that a is G, for every property of being G of which he has a conception (Evans, 1982, p.104)

Hence, according to Evans, if S has a conception of what it is to weigh 10 kilos and to think of an object O, then S must be able to think of O as satisfying the predicate "...weighs 10 kilos". But as indicated by the earlier examples concerning thoughts which exploit subjects' sensory modalities there do seem to be restrictions upon which predicates objects can intelligibly be claimed to satisfy. E.g. if S sees an ant or a feather and thinks "That ant/feather weighs 10,000 kilos" it would not be clear that S has given voice to a genuine thought. So perhaps Evans's Generality Constraint requires modification to the effect that subjects must be able to think of the object thought of as satisfying predicates - within the conceptual repertoire of S - which O could intelligibly satisfy.

A third argument runs as follows. Suppose that a parrot is asked a question, e.g. "What are you looking at Polly?" Suppose further that the parrot utters the word "That" in apparent reply to the question. It is clear that the parrot would not be taken to have given voice to a demonstrative thought. What seems to be occurring in such a case is that the parrot's ability to make sounds is not related to conceptual resources which relate those sounds to features of the parrot's environment. It is clear that the parrot is in receipt of sensory information since he can perceive features of his immediate environment. So it might reasonably be claimed that the parrot's perceptual faculties (faculty-(i)) place the relevant stimulii for it. Yet, one would reasonably want to deny that the parrot has given voice to a demonstrative thought concerning the referent of "That" (even if there is one). This intuition, it seems, is motivated by the view that the parrot's conceptual resources are not sufficiently adequate to enable the parrot to entertain demonstrative thoughts concerning features of his environment - i.e. when the parrot utters the word "That".

A fourth and final argument that demonstrative thoughts necessarily include a sortal concept is this. Consider a situation in which S gives voice to a demonstrative thought by uttering the words "That's good".

Suppose that the utterance takes place in a room, a lounge. There is a book on the carpet between S and another subject H, in view of each of them. S and H are discussing books they have read recently. It seems clear that in order to understand S's utterance, H needs to supply it with a sortal. Presumably, H would not take S to be referring to the carpet - given the context. And, the predicate "...is good" is one which intelligibly applies to books. If the account suggested here is correct, the sortal book will be employed by S when he entertains the demonstrative thought concerning the book but is not expressed in his utterance of it. This example indicates that in both the communication and the understanding of demonstrative thoughts, the speaker appears to employ a sortal in thought, and the hearer supplies the utterance with a sortal if none is employed by the speaker.

Of these four arguments, perhaps the third is the weakest. But they seclaim that sortal concepts figure in demonstrative thoughts. Their employment can be explicit, as in thoughts of the form "That F is G", or they can be implicit, as in the example given in the last argument.

One possible objection to the claim may stem from the view that subjects can entertain demonstrative thoughts concerning objects without knowing which sortal applies to the object; if an elephant is charging towards S and if S has never heard of elephants (if he lacks the concept elephant), it seems S can still think "That's out to kill me"; and in so doing express a genuine thought with truth conditions.

However, the claim is not being made that subjects necessarily employ the correct sortal in their demonstrative thoughts - i.e. one which the object must satisfy. Rather, a much weaker claim is being made; this is that subjects must employ some sortal concept when they entertain demonstrative thoughts. In the elephant example the fact that the subject ascribes the property of being dangerous to the elephant indicates that some concept is being applied which conceptualises the object thought of, e.g., animal.

2. Externalist individuation of demonstrative thought: the problem of the objectual component

We are now in a position to set out the individuation conditions of (perceptual) demonstrative thought. Recall that we are considering how to individuate the intentional type (perceptual) demonstrative thought. Recall further that token externalism is ruled out due to its apparent incompatibility with a token physicalist theory of mind. Our considerations so far suggest that the individuation conditions of the intential type demonstrative thought should include the following the components, all of which would be instanced in a particular token demonstrative thought.

$$\{[(Dem),\ <O>,\ (S)],\ (E),\ (...\phi),\ [t\ (...)],\ [s\ (...)]\}$$

These are the dem-component, the objectual component, the sortal component, the E-component, the predicative component, the temporal index, and the spatial component.

The (Dem)-component, specifies a type of psychological state in which subjects make judgements concerning features of their environment. Consideration of Evans' theory of demonstrative thought indicates that specification of the Dem-component should employ a singular referring expression, a demonstrative, and not a description. Further, the considerations of ch.8 (sec.2) and ch.9 indicate that token demonstrative thoughts require an object thought of; specifically, one within the perceptual field of the subject. Thus, in specifications of the individuation conditions of demonstrative thought an objectual component is required to complete or saturate the dem-component.[7] The objectual component must be filled for a subject to entertain a demonstrative thought; token demonstrative thoughts require an object thought of. Hence, specifications of demonstrative thought in terms of the individuation conditions of this type of thought must include an objectual component.[8] Given that the object thought of in token demonstrative thoughts, must be an object perceived by the subject, externalism with respect to demonstrative thought might be thought to follow (but see what follows for a rejection of this view).

However, the need for inclusion of an objectual component in the individuation conditions of demonstrative thoughts generates a particular problem for the version of externalism canvassed in this essay: type externalism constrained by a token physicalist theory of mind. For example, in ch.8 above three possible options for construal of the objectual component were mooted: that it is an argument-place (a) for some object or other, (b) for the type of object thought of, or, (c) the particular object thought of.

As it stands, (a) seems too weak to bring externalism since it amounts to mere object-dependency. As we saw in ch.8 (sec.1) above, externalism seems to require that thoughts are not merely object-dependent but are individuation-dependent upon features of the environment of the subject. However, given that demonstrative thoughts require an object perceived, and that such an object will be one which occurs in the environment of the subject, it may be thought that the construal of the objectual

199

component suggested in (a) is sufficient for externalism with respect to demonstrative thoughts. This seems to follow since demonstrative thoughts will be existence-dependent upon objects occurring in the environment of the subject.

It seems to me, though, that such a dependence relation falls short of what is required for externalism. This is because externalism asserts the individuation-dependence of certain psychological states on certain environmental features. So the identities of the objects thought of seems to matters in externalism; i.e. not simply that they happen to be located in the environment of the subject. Externalism seems to require that certain thoughts are individuation-dependent upon objects thought of, not simply due to the locations of those objects, but due to the identities of those objects.

I will return to discuss option (b), but for now a point needs to be made regarding (c). It should be clear that acceptance of (c) is problematic for the type externalist who rejects token externalism. This is the case since if (c) is taken on, then demonstrative thoughts which concern numerically distinct objects will count as different in type. For, within the class of (perceptual) demonstrative thoughts it is possible to distinguish types of thoughts, e.g., a belief that that is red, is distinct from a belief that that is green. Consider that the individuation conditions of such types hinge on the identity of the particular object thought of. It then follows that if S entertains a demonstrative thought concerning a vase V, and counterfactually V is replaced by an identical-looking vase V', then S's demonstrative thoughts are held to differ in type. Such a view seems profligate in its positing of explanatory types: a different explanatory type for each numerically distinct particular demonstratively thought of.

If (c) is rejected on these grounds, we are left with option (b). In this, the type identity of the thought - i.e. within the class of demonstrative thoughts - turns on the type identity of the object thought of. This is certainly congenial to type externalism, and is, of course, incompatible with internalism.

It should be said that acceptance of option (b) has the consequence that, in a Twin Earth case, if S and S* think demonstratively of identical-looking vases in their respective worlds, then their demonstrative thoughts count as thoughts of the same demonstrative type. But this consequence is still compatible with externalism with respect to such thoughts since the individuation conditions of the thoughts are determined, in part, by the type identity of the objects they respectively think of.

A more serious problem with option (b) is that it conflicts with the intuition that what matters to the individuation conditions of demonstrative thoughts is the identity of the particular object thought of. It seems to matter that it is this particular vase, say, that one is thinking of rather than some other identical-looking vase (cf. ch.8, sec.3). For example, suppose S thinks of vase V1 at t1, (1) "That vase is mine". Suppose further that S leaves the room and V1 is replaced by a replica V2; S then returns to the room and thinks again (2) "That vase is mine" at t2. By option (b) it has to be accepted that S's demonstrative thoughts at t1 and t2 are of the same type since they concern particulars of the same type. Yet, the thoughts of S at t1 and t2 clearly have different truth conditions. This matters since it is the vase referred to in (1) that S thinks he owns; and that S would claim to recognise at t2; and that an utterance of S's, at t1, such as "That is my favourite vase" would be taken to refer to. So the difficulty for type externalism in taking option (b) lies in the fact that its adoption implies that two token demonstrative thoughts such as those given voice to by S in (1) and (2) are held to be of the same type, yet they differ in truth conditions.[9]

It seems then that although a persuasive case can be made to show that demonstrative thoughts require an object thought of, it is problematic to explain how this object-dependence should be characterised. There seem to be difficulties with all three options - (a), (b) and (c). Option (a) is evidently not sufficient for externalism. Option (b) binds demonstrative thoughts to the environments of their subjects in so far as the type identities of token demonstrative thoughts are determined by the type identity of the object thought of. But in doing so, option (b) seems to provide motivation for token externalism - i.e. in which token demonstrative thoughts are individuation-dependent upon the particular object thought of. And, as seen, option (c) seems too profligate in its positing of explanatory types. According to option (c), the objectual component of the intentional type demonstrative thought should include a specification of the identity of the particular object thought of. This has the undesirable consequence that within the class of demonstrative thoughts, token demonstrative thoughts which concern numerically distinct objects will count as different in type - i.e. within the class of demonstrative thoughts. So, to repeat our earlier example, suppose a subject S thinks demonstratively of a vase V at t. Suppose further that, counterfactually, S had thought demonstratively of an identical-looking vase V'. By option (c) since S's thoughts concern numerically distinct objects, they count as different in type. In support of individuating types of demonstrative thoughts in this way it may be pointed out, again, that in the case of demonstrative thoughts, the identity of the object seems essential to the identity of the thought since it is that particular object which is thought of, may be recognised, and about which information

201

may be communicated. But even given this point in favour of option (c) it seems to involve positing far too many types of thoughts.

Let us move on to consider the remaining components of demonstrative thought. Thus far, the (S)-component merely points to the need for a sortal concept in demonstrative thinking. A way to exploit this for externalist purposes may be to argue that externalism is true for the relevant sortal concept employed in thought.

Two examples which lend support to the claim are these. The first concerns a shipwrecked sailor S. Suppose S ends up on a remote island. He is looking around for food. He sees something which looks exactly like an apple. Naturally he goes to collect it. It turns out, however, to be a stone - apple-shaped, and with a covering of light moss which causes it to look like an apple. As in the cases of misperception discussed in chs. 3 and 4 above, it seems clear that S's actions are explicable due to his thinking that the stone is an apple. We can imagine that he entertains demonstrative thoughts concerning the stone as he approaches it e.g. "That looks juicy" etc.

A second example is this. It was argued in the last section that bare utterances of 'That' do not seem to count as demonstrative thoughts unless some sortal is presumed. So consider a case in which an infant is learning to speak. The infant might point to a toy and utter "That". In such a case it seems that the hearer, if he is sympathetic, will take the child to be giving voice to a thought with, roughly, the content "I want that toy". The point, for our purposes, of this example is that the hearer supplies the utterance of "That" with a missing or tacitly employed sortal. The sortal selected, it seems plausible to presume, will hinge upon contextual factors relating to which particular kinds of objects are present in the environment of the subject or are usually present in that environment.

Hence, there does seem to be a plausible way of recruiting the sortal component of demonstrative thought for externalist purposes. Such a component binds the individuation conditions of such thoughts to contexts inhabited by the subject in such a way that the identities of the objects encountered by the subject are relevant to the individuation conditions of demonstrative thought.

It is evident, though, that the sortal component cannot bear the main burden in relation to the typing of token demonstrative thoughts, and that this is for the same reasons that option (b) above proved open to objection. If it is claimed that two token demonstrative thoughts are thoughts of the same type due to their employing the same sortal component, e.g. vase, it will transpire that distinct token thoughts concerning distinct vases will turn out to be thoughts of the same type.

And as noted in the discussion of option (b) above, it seems to be the case in demonstrative thought that the identity of the particular object thought of is crucial to the identity conditions of the thought. So thoughts concerning different objects should differ in type (again, assuming token externalism is not an option).

With regard to the (E)-component, this was described above in ch.8. It does not seem to be a constituent of demonstrative thoughts which could be exploited by externalists since it captures aspects of the subject's experience and, if anything, seems more congenial to internalism than to externalism (i.e. if it is allowed that a subject could have an experience identical in quality whether or not there is a stimulus beyond the body of the subject which provokes the experience).

With respect to the predicative component (that which ascribes a property to the object thought of), it needs to be said that any internalist account of demonstrative thought will inevitably employ such a component. The descriptivist strategy involves eliminating singular referring expressions in place of descriptions which objects in the relevant domain either satisfy or fail to satisfy. Since internalist accounts of demonstrative thoughts must feature a predicative component it can be taken that inclusion of such a component will not be objected to on internalist grounds. However, it needs to be said that there do appear to be uses of demonstratives in which no (quality) predicate features. E.g. a bare utterance of "That" (perhaps said whilst pointing to a large spider), in response to a question "What are you staring at?"

Such usages do seem to involve a sortal concept, but they certainly cause a difficulty for the claim that the predicative component is a necessary constituent of demonstrative thoughts. Perhaps this suggests that a more modest claim should be made for the present enterprise; specifically, that we are characterising only (perceptual) demonstrative thoughts in which predications are made of the object thought of. An argument that externalism is true for such thoughts is still a substantial claim.

The need for a temporal index on demonstrative thoughts stems from the fact that the time of the thought matters from the perspective of explaining the subject's actions. E.g. if S moves to pick up a vase at t it is due to his entertaining a thought concerning the vase at t. I cannot think of a plausible way in which externalists might recruit this component for externalist purposes.

Finally, with regard to the spatial component, Evans's theory brings out the importance for thinking subjects, that they possess the capacity to locate stimulii in their environments - e,g, such a capacity seems to be a necessary condition for the possibility of action. One way in which this

203

feature of Evans' theory might be recruited by externalists is to claim that demonstrative thoughts are typed by reference to a spatial framework, specifically that in which the subject is located and has a cognitive map of. But as seen previously (ch.9), this option has the unacceptable consequence that, e.g., persons who do not know their locations cannot entertain demonstrative thoughts concerning objects they perceive; that simply cannot be right.

To summarise: A description of the individuation conditions of demonstrative thought should include a demonstrative component, an objectual component and a sortal component. The objectual component completes the demonstrative component by supplying it with an object thought of. And the sortal component indicates that the object thought of demonstratively must be subsumed under a sortal concept. Further components include an E-component, a predicative component (though perhaps only when predications are made of the object thought of), and temporal and spatial components. With the possible exception of the predicative component, the remaining components are individually necessary and jointly sufficient for the possibility of a subject's entertaining a token demonstrative thought. But the problem of how to specify the objectual component remains. Token externalism seems a plausible option since it seems that demonstrative thoughts are individuation-dependent upon the object thought of. Yet, token externalism has been rejected in this essay due to its apparent incompatibility with token physicalism. But the only alternative view apparently available to the type externalist is to make the type identity of token demonstrative thoughts dependent upon the identity of the particular object thought of. This has the undesirable consequence of profligating explanatory types: one type for every particular object thought of. It also seems problematic to characterise the tokens of such types; it is not at all clear how that could be done.

Hence, it is evident that demonstrative thoughts seem to create a particular problem for type externalists who oppose token externalism. I propose now to try to outline a possible solution to the problem. This will involve a little backtracking.

3. A way out?

According to a token physicalist theory of mind, token mental events are identical with token physical events. According to token externalism, token mental events are individuation-dependent upon features beyond the bodies of their subjects. One way to characterise this feature of token mental events is to say that their individuation conditions are essentially relational. But it seems plausible that token neurophysiological events are not essentially relational - their individuation conditions do not make reference to features beyond the bodies of their subjects. So there is this problem for token externalism: it seems plausible that if two things are identical then "any essential property of one must be an essential property of the other" (Kripke, 1972, p.148). But clearly, if it is accepted that token neurophysiological events are not essentially relational and that token mental events are essentially relational - by token externalism - then token externalism cannot be 'coherent (assuming the truth of a token physicalist theory of mind).

This problem with token externalism can be illustrated in another way. Token externalism conjoined with token physicalism seems to imply that it is necessary that a token mental event m and a token neurophysiological event p are identical; hence, if p occurs, then, necessarily, so must m; and also, of course, the occurrence of p is sufficient for the occurrence of m. But this consequence of token externalism conjoined with token physicalism seems implausible for at least two reasons. First, it seems possible that p could occur in the absence of any mental event, for example in a world in which there are no mental properties (cf. McLaughlin, 1985, p.365). And second, it seems possible that p could occur and not be identical with m but with some other mental event m'. For example, consider that token demonstrative thoughts are individuation-dependent upon the object thought of. Thus suppose a token mental event d is a demonstrative thought which is individuation-dependent upon the object thought of, O. Further, suppose d is identical with a neurophysiological event p. It seems plausible that, counterfactually, if a subject S had thought demonstratively of a different object O', then, by token externalism d is individuation-dependent upon O' and not O. Yet, the neurophysiological event which is identical with S's demonstrative thought about O' may still have been p. In effect, this is an application of Macdonald's point that "[No] physical event is essentially an exemplification of an intentional (or any other) mental property" (1990, p.402).

Each of these two considerations, especially the second, seem to cast considerable doubt on the plausibility of token externalism. Further, the examples suggest that the relationship between token mental and physical events is a contingent one and that, therefore, token externalism is ruled out.

However, it seems to me that this case against token externalism can be exploited to aid the type externalist attempt to provide an account of the individuation conditions of demonstrative thoughts. For example, suppose the following claims are allowed: (1) that token physicalism is true; (2) that "[No] physical event is essentially an exemplification of an intentional (or any other) mental property" (1990, p.402); (3) that a token demonstrative thought d is individuation-dependent upon the object thought of.

It might then be suggested that adoption of claims (1), (2) and (3) need not amount to token externalism since token externalism seems not to be compatible with (2). So it can be allowed that a token demonstrative thought d is individuation-dependent upon the object thought of O. And further, that d is identical with a neurophysiological event n (by token physicalism). And still further that d need not figure in the individuation conditions of n due to the fact that the occurrence of n is neither necessary nor sufficient for the occurrence of d. This position exploits an apparent contingency in the nature of the relationship between token mental and physical events. The contingency is indicated in the example given above concerning demonstrative thoughts about objects O and O'.

The position just described falls short of token externalism, since token externalism seems incompatible with (2) above. Yet the position allows the type externalist to hold that token demonstrative thoughts are individuation-dependent upon the object thought of. Hence, it can be allowed that the objectual component in the individuation conditions of the intentional type demonstrative thought should specify the particular object thought of. And this is sufficient to bind such thoughts to the environments of their subjects, and hence for type externalism with respect to such thoughts. Such a position seems to lie in uncharted territory between token externalism and token internalism. The token demonstrative thought d is essentially the event it is, yet it is only contingently identical with neurophysiological event n.

There are two general points that remain to be made in this chapter. The first concerns a possible consequence of the view that demonstrative thoughts are object-dependent. And the second concerns what may be termed "hybrid thoughts" - i.e. demonstrative thoughts which concern natural kinds.

In chapter one above it was noted that epistemic motivations for internalism can be gleaned from consideration of three kinds of case. In the first it is supposed that a subject thinks demonstratively of an object he presently perceives. In the second it is supposed that the subject has a demonstrative thought concerning a qualitatively identical, but distinct type of object. In the third case, the subject merely takes himself to entertain a demonstrative thought, e.g., due to an hallucinatory experience. Blackburn, who constructs this example, suggests that if demonstrative thoughts are said to be object-dependent, then in the third kind of case the externalist has to assert that the hallucinating subject has no thought (1984, pp.312-328). Recall that since it seems clear that the subject is entertaining a thought, such considerations comprise epistemic motivations for internalism.

But it seems clear that one need not be committed to the view that when subjects hallucinate they do not undergo psychological states. What can be claimed is that the subject has a psychological experience which instances a particular type of E-component but in which there is no object perceived. The considerations of ch.8 provide plausible reasons for resisting the claim that subjects who hallucinate do entertain demonstrative thoughts. But this claim is perfectly compatible with the claim that such subjects do undergo some kind of psychological state when they have hallucinatory experiences (as Evans indicates (1982, p.45)).

A second concluding point concerns the relationship between demonstrative thoughts and thoughts about natural kinds. It is clear that subjects can entertain demonstrative thoughts approximately characterised in that-clauses such as "That's water", "That's gold", or "That's a duck". The question arises of how such thoughts are to be categorised. It seems simplest to describe these as hybrid thoughts. They contain both demonstrative and natural kind components. Their individuation conditions will depend upon there being an object thought of (otherwise there will be no demonstrative thought) and on the natural kinds present in the environment of the subject. Hence, if it is accepted that externalism is true for natural kind thoughts, it follows that externalism is true for demonstrative thoughts which concern instances of natural kinds.

Let us turn, now, to consider natural kind thoughts at greater length, and, finally, to lay aside Loar's argument for narrow content which was described in ch.1 above.

Notes to chapter ten

1. Examples of the type "That's an F" where, e.g. "F" stands for a kind term (e.g. "That's a duck") can be assimilated to subclass (iii). This is due to the view that such thoughts seem to involve application of a concept to the object perceived, e.g. "That animal is a duck",or perhaps "That bird is a duck". See below concerning the need for such a component in demonstrative thoughts.

2. Standardly a sortal is employed, but occasionally more general terms are employed e.g., animal rather than elephant, fruit rather

than apple. In spite of ambiguity here I will persist with the use of the term "sortal concept" to indicate a constituent of demonstrative thoughts which involves some conceptualisation of the object thought of by the subject.

3.   I.e., at least, object-dependency is not sufficient for strong externalism - cf. note 1, ch.1.

4.   On this question, Peacocke (1983, pp.110-111) seems to insist on the need for a sortal, but he backtracks in a footnote and requires only an individuating property of the object (ibid., fn.4); as in Evans' account, spatio-temporal properties apparently perform such a role in the case of demonstrative thought.

5.   The last argument simply exploits the point made by Evans that the information accessed by (what was described above as) faculty-(ii) from (what was described as) faculty-(i) is structured information. Further, it may be added that Evans himself emphasises the importance of subjects' employing "[A] controlling conception" (1982, p.145) of the objects of demonstrative thought.

6.   For instance, example (g) in the list above might be understood in the context of a discussion concerning musical styles. In discussion of so-called "Acid Jazz" it might be said that a certain sound is "acidic". These considerations also indicate that subclass (ii) thoughts are really disguised members of subclass (iii) thoughts.

7.   Of course the saturation metaphor is borrowed from Frege ("Function and Concept",p.24; in Geach and Black (1952)).

8.   If correct, this claim may be thought to show that strong externalism is true for demonstrative thought since the individuation conditions of that type of thought must make reference to objects which occur in the environment of the subject - given that demonstrative thoughts require an object perceived. But see what follows for a rejection of this claim.

9.   It might be said that this consequence is what one would expect in an account demonstrative thought, and that the tokens of such thoughts are individuation-dependent upon the particular object thought of - i.e. option (c). If one eschews a token physicalist theory of mind this option is certainly the most elegant. But recall that such a position amounts to token externalism, and that seems not to be compatible with token physicalism.

11 Thoughts which concern natural kinds

In this chapter we consider the claim that type externalism is true for thoughts about natural kinds. Since natural kind thoughts have been discussed throughout the essay, our discussion here will be brief. The discussion attempts to clarify the individuation conditions of natural kind thoughts and to take up Loar's challenge to externalism (outlined in ch.1 above) as it can be taken to apply to natural kind thoughts.

1. Individuation conditions of natural kind thoughts

As in the case of demonstrative thought, the formulation of individuation conditions for thoughts about natural kinds (henceforth, natural kind thoughts) promotes clarification of the distinct claims made by the rival theses we have been considering. Recall the individuation conditions of demonstrative thought proposed above (ch.10):

$$\{[(Dem), \ <O>, \ (S)], \ (E), \ (...is \ \phi), \ [t \ (...)], \ [s \ (...)]\}$$

(e.g. S   believes that that (demonstratively presented object) is F). Generally, it can be noted that logico-semantic motivations for either externalism or internalism centre on the Dem-component (and will centre on the NK (natural kind) component); explanatory motivations focus on the objectual or sortal components; and epistemic motivations focus on the E-component. As we saw earlier, the Dem-component requires completion with an objectual component if it is accepted that demonstrative thoughts are object-dependent; likewise, an objectual component attaches to the NK-component if it is accepted that such thoughts are both object- and kind-dependent.

It can be proposed that the (Dem)-component will need to be replaced in favour of a natural kind component, call it the NK-component. It will be argued shortly that an E-component is still required - though in modified form due to the fact that natural kind thoughts are not so bound up with present perceptual experiences as demonstrative thoughts seemed to be. The objectual component will be required to be kind-specific for type externalism to be true.[1]

It may be pointed out, though, that not all ascriptions of natural kind thoughts involve a predicative component, e.g. S desires a gold ring. However there are two responses which might be made to this point. First, it could be argued that S's desire is prompted by the belief that gold is valuable and so a complete specification of the beliefs and desires which lead to some action of S's (say, buying a gold ring) will be seen to include natural kind thoughts which do include a predicative component. Second, the predicative component need not be regarded as of central importance in relation to the question of the individuation conditions of natural kind thoughts due to the fact that truth of internalism or externalism can be decided independently of the question of whether there is a need for a predicative component in natural kind thoughts.

The temporal and spatial components can still be included for the same reasons as they occur in our individuation conditions of demonstrative thought. And, it would seem, no sortal component need feature since the NK-component will be specified by a kind term. Thus, most attention is to be directed at the NK-component, the E-component, and the objectual component.

2. The NK-Component

Just as specifications of demonstrative thought involve the employment of a demonstrative which signals the need for a Dem-component in the individuation conditions of such thought, so, it can be claimed, specifications of natural kind thoughts require a component which performs a parallel role. Such a component can be termed the "NK-component" and its presence in thought is signalled by the employment of a natural kind term in attributions of intentional content (e.g. S desires a gold ring).

Suppose a subject does not employ a natural kind term when, say, he is invited to give voice to his thought concerning the relevant stuff, e.g., he might employ a demonstrative. Providing the subject satisfies the appropriate conditions for entertaining a demonstrative thought, he can be said to be thinking demonstratively about a natural kind. In the last chapter it was suggested that such thoughts be termed "hybrid thoughts".

A typical manifestation of the dispute between internalists and externalists is the question of the eliminability or otherwise of singular terms in favour of descriptions (cf. ch.3 sec.1, ch.4 sec.1 above). The ontological issue which is supposed to rest on the question is this. If singular terms are replaceable by descriptions, then the relevant thoughts are descriptive thoughts and not singular thoughts; the implication being, here, that descriptive thoughts are thoughts for which internalism is true and for which externalism cannot be true. To see why, recall that the Fregean theory of thought outlined in ch.3 above, is centrally related to the claim that the semantic power of referring expressions is dependent upon their having a referent. When applied to the theory of thought, this meaning-theoretic claim has the consequence that thoughts whose specifications require singular terms are not available in the event of there not being a referent for the relevant term. (This was described earlier (ch.3) as a logico-semantic motivation for externalism.) In the opposing descriptivist theory, thoughts are available whether or not the apparent referring expressions employed in their specifications have referents.

Given this outline of the nature of the dispute, then, it should be clear that type externalists will argue for an NK-component which is specified by a natural kind term - one which is not eliminable in favour of a description. On the other hand, internalists will argue that natural kind terms are eliminable in favour of descriptions (the descriptivist claim), and that this indicates that natural kind thoughts are more properly described as descriptive thoughts.

In relation to the descriptivist claim as it applies to natural kind terms, recall the discussion of that issue in chs.3 and 4 above. The conclusion reached was that descriptive characterisations of thoughts involving natural kinds are insufficiently fine-grained to explain actions involving natural kinds, e.g. purchasing them. (See below also for further support for that conclusion.)

Does this mean, then, that we can accept unproblematically the claim for an NK-component in natural kind thoughts? An immediate difficulty may be this. In the Fregean logico-semantic motivations for externalism described above (ch.3) we saw that singular terms complete or saturate first-level functors to determine a truth value for the relevant functor. This account appears relatively unproblematic for referring expressions such as proper names and demonstratives. But surely natural kind terms are referring expressions which are of a distinct logical level than, e.g., proper names and demonstratives. This difference can be illustrated by

211

the fact that on the occasion of their employment, e.g., demonstratives refer to one object only; the same applies to correct employment of proper names. But that is not true of natural kind terms; if it is agreed that they do refer, then they refer either to an abstract object - the natural kind itself considered apart from its instances - or to the sum total of its instances. Put another way, natural kind terms are general terms and not singular terms and the Fregean logico-semantic motivation for externalism seems not to account for this fact.[2]

It could be argued that the Fregean treatment of referring expressions (as described in ch.3 above) does seem capable of dealing with natural kind terms thus: consider any first-level functor, "...is F" into which we enter a natural kind term e.g. "Gold is F". This determines the value True/False just in case gold is F or otherwise. Recall that the procedure, so to speak, for determining the truth values of first-level functors begins when a referring expression is entered into the functor; the object referred to by the referring expression is presented to the function (to which the functor refers) and a truth value is determined. Consider how this procedure might work in the case of natural kind terms. It would require the presentation to the relevant function either of every instance of the natural kind or the presentation to the function of the natural kind itself. These remarks indicate that the Fregean semantic theory as construed in this essay is able to cope with natural kind terms along similar lines as it copes with other referring expressions. However, what I hope to have indicated here is that natural kind terms are terms of a different logical level than the terms which were employed to explicate the theory earlier (ch.3).

So the conclusions of this section are two-fold (i) that natural kind terms are not eliminable in favour of descriptions in specifications of natural kind thoughts; and (ii) that there is a minor anomaly in treating natural kind terms as referring expressions of the same logical level as demonstratives and proper names - though not one which bears on the internalism/externalism debate.[3]

3. The E-component (again)

Earlier in this essay (ch.1) two problems concerning the philosophical explication of the nature of the relationship between thoughts and objects were referred to; the first involves cases in which two subjects conceive of distinct objects in the same way (our Twin Earth cases), and the second involves cases in which a subject conceives of the same object in different ways (cf. Loar and Pierre (ch.1 above), and our discussion of

S and ELT (ch.8)). It is this latter kind of case which we will be discussing in this section.

Hence, the example to be discussed in this section is one in which a single subject conceives of a single object in two distinct ways. The challenge presented to type externalists by such a case is to say why factors beyond the body of the subject have an explanatory role to play in accounting for the behaviour of the subject.

Loar's challenge to externalist individuation of psychological states has not yet specifically been addressed (but see the account of Macdonald's treatment of such cases in chs.3 and 4 above). I propose to re-work Loar's example so that it involves thoughts which concern natural kinds rather than thoughts concerning London.

It can be supposed that whilst in France S acquires beliefs about tigers (without ever having seen one) such that they are wild, run free, have black and orange stripes, but are never found in zoos. Thus S will assent to the French equivalent of "Tigers are never found in zoos".

As before, S moves to London. He then acquires a job at London Zoo but S fails to realise that the animals which are called "tigers" at London Zoo are the same type of animals of which he heard about whilst in France.

Suppose p stands for "Tigers are found in zoos"; and that p' represents the French equivalent ("Les tigres se trouvent dans le zoo"). Suppose further that p' is a fair translation of p - that a competent bilingual speaker will assent to both p and p'. S, however, will assent to p and will dissent from p' even though p and p' express the same proposition - by normal criteria.

Further, so that failures of inference and behavioural evidence can be seen to be present in this reworking of Loar's example, it can be supposed that S has promised his Mother a photograph of a tiger taken by him and that even though S encounters tigers on a daily basis he has not taken the photograph he has promised to his mother. Thus our statement of Loar's example now includes inferential failure on the part of the subject which is manifested by his failure to behave in ways one would expect of him - i.e. given that we know the nature of his promise to his mother.

So in the example discussed here (same object or object-type, but different conceptions) the E-component of the subject's thought are apparently of distinct types; one prompted by perceptual encounters with instances of the kind, the other prompted by descriptions of properties of the kind. Alternatively, it may be said that only those thoughts of Pierre's which stem from perceptions of tigers involve an E-Component. In our example, the subject conceives of the same natural kind in distinct ways;

he has failed to realise that the things of which he has knowledge by description, so to speak, are of the same type as the things of which he has knowledge by acquaintance.

In Twin Earth cases, although the E-components of the respective thoughts of the subjects are of the same type, Type externalists claim that the thoughts of the subjects are type-distinct. The type of case we have discussed in this section presents a different kind of challenge to the externalist. In this kind of case the externalist has to show why the thoughts of the subject whilst in London and in France should be regarded as being of the same type in spite of the differences in the E-components of the thoughts.

Let us now turn to consider the objectual component.

4. The objectual component

Earlier discussion of the Twin Earth case seemed to show the thoughts of the Twins to be of distinct types. But in relation to Pierre-type cases it needs to be shown why the subject's thought should be typed by reference to factors beyond the body of the subject as opposed to by reference to the (distinct) types of E-component involved.[4]

As seen above (chs. 3 and 4), in Pierre cases what stands in need of explanation is what S fails to do rather than what S actually does. Second, explication of the mismatch between S's intentions and his actions will involve appeal to S's conceptions of the relevant states of affairs. And, thirdly, and most crucially, it can be claimed that the fact that S's conceptions are conceptions of the same natural kind which explains his failure to act, and which thereby makes it the case that S's thoughts are not independent of environmental features.

There should be nothing objectionable in the first two of these claims; the interest of the kind of example we are discussing centres on the failure of subjects to act in accordance with their apparent intentions. Also, it has been found necessary to refer to agents conceptions of states of affairs in explanations of their actions. So the main point of contention is the third point.

Loar's claim, when applied to natural kind thoughts, appears to be that S's belief about what he (S) calls "Tigres" and his belief about what he calls "Tigers" have distinct contents. This is the case, Loar contends, due to the fact that the beliefs have distinct conceptual roles (ch.1 above). The assumption here is that S's belief that p (Tigers are found in zoos) taken in conjunction with his desire to fulfil his promise to his mother, makes it highly probable that if S does believe that p then he will photograph a tiger; since S does not do so - in spite of his having ample opportunity - it can be inferred that S does not believe that p.

It might be added, in support of Loar's view, that if S will assent to p and dissent from p' then, by the Intuitive Criterion of Difference (Evans, 1982, p.18; ch.8 sec.2 above), it is not the case that S's belief that p and his belief that p' are intentional states with the same content.

Of the London/Londres case, Loar claims "Clearly there are two beliefs, and they are as distinct as my beliefs that Paris is pretty and that Rio is pretty" (1985, p.103). If, not unreasonably, we extend this claim to thoughts about natural kinds, Loar's position would be one in which S's beliefs about what he calls "Tigres" and what he calls "Tigers" could be said to be as distinct as his beliefs about tigers and mercury.

Such a claim seems highly implausible. First, it does not appear possible to construct a situation which is appropriately analogous to that under discussion here in which the kind of mistake which Loar conceives to be possible is in fact feasible. The reason why is that as these types of examples are constructed it is required that a subject assent to and dissent from two propositions which most competent bilinguals would consider adequately close translates of each other; in our case the propositions were p ("Tigers are found in zoos") and p' ("Les Tigres se trouvent dans le zoo").

By Loar's reasoning it should prove possible to construct a case in which the majority of competent bilinguals will assent to e.g. q ("Gold is yellow") and q' ("L'eau est jaune"). But this does not seem to me to be plausible. If the majority of French-English bilinguals judged q and q' to express distinct propositions then it would not be the case that q and q' were translates of each other.

Additionally, of course, it may be pointed out that q and q' have distinct truth conditions, but p and p' share the same truth conditions; and it seemed to be the case that what is puzzling about Kripke's cases is that the propositions the subject believes have the same truth conditions - unbeknownst to the subject, but otherwise a well-established fact.

In effect Loar's claim carries the consequence that in expressions of the form "A is F" (where "A" stands for any French or English natural kind term, and "F" for any French or English predicate) it is possible to construct cases in which the majority of competent French-English bilinguals will regard two sentences as adequate translates of each other. This seems implausible for the reason stated in the last paragraph; and seems not to be a feature of the type of situation which we are concerned to explicate.

Continuing this line of criticism, it was noted earlier that what needs explaining in Kripke's puzzle is the mismatch between the subject's intentions and his actions. The mismatch is discernible due to the fact that the referring expressions in p and p' are co-referential. (Loar seems just to ignore this.) Thus it is important, in setting up the puzzle, that the beliefs of the subject are about the same thing or in our case, natural kind.

In spite of the above criticism of Loar's handling of Kripke's puzzle it does seem that Loar has a solid motivation for the claim that S's beliefs about tigers which he develops whilst in France are distinct from the beliefs about tigers which he develops whilst in London; the motivation stems from the inferential failure on the part of S to which we have referred above. Further, as we have seen, it must be agreed that S's conceptions of tigers differ when he is in France and London.

Note that, strictly speaking, all that is required for externalism is that intentional types with an objectual component are recruited in explanation of S's action or inaction. This is a weaker position than one according to which externalists are required to specify the content of S's thoughts at a particular time.

An externalist position could allow for the difference in S's conceptions of tigers. This could be done by acknowledging what we have already seen - i.e. that the E-components of S's beliefs about tigers are of a distinct type. Loar takes that difference in type to indicate that S's beliefs are distinct in type. But against him it can be argued it is the fact that the intentional states of S concern the same natural kind that is most relevant to the typing of those states. This warrants the claim that S's conceptions of Tigers only serve to explain his failure to photograph one when it is accepted that his conceptions are of one kind of object. This indicates that explanation of S's failure to act involves tacit reference to tigers.

If internalism is true no reference to tigers is required in explanation of the explanandum event (S's not taking the photo); but if (type) externalism is true referential components of S's psychological states do perform explanatory work.

Internalists may invoke the descriptivist strategy, and suggest that whilst in France S believes that a tiger is any object which satisfies (e.g.) the predicates "...is wild" and "...has black and orange stripes". But in London S can be said to believe that an object cannot be a tiger if it does not satisfy the predicate '...is wild'. So two distinct intentional types may be recruited, one which specifies predicates such as "...is wild" and another specification of the identity conditions of which would not include the predicate "...is wild". On this internalist strategy explanation of S's failure to act in ways one may expect of him can proceed by pointing to the difference in type between the thoughts entertained by S in France and in London. Further, no referential component is recruited, only predicates, quantifiers etc.

But externalists can claim that it is the fact that S fails to realise that "Tigers" and "Tigres" name instances of the same natural kind that explains his failure to act in the ways one would expect of him (qua rational subject). Hence, explanation of S's failure to act will invoke intentional states which include an objectual component - namely, one which specifies the kind tiger. Support for that view derives from the observation that it is the fact that S's conceptions are conceptions of the same type of object, and his failure to realise this, which explains why S does not (e.g.) take a photo of a tiger - i.e. does not behave in ways which may reasonably be expected of him. In effect, the externalist proposal here seems simply to follow from the fact that the descriptivistic characterisations of S's intentional states posited in the last paragraph will be inadequate to explain S's inaction until is pointed out that the conceptions attributed to S are conceptions of the same type of object - i.e. that the predicates cited in the descriptivist characterisation of S's thoughts are satisfied by instances of the same natural kind. It is this point which seems to resolve the issue in favour of externalism (cf. our discussion of Macdonald's position (ch.3, sec.3 above).

The view that the thoughts of S in the situation described above are of distinct types stems from the view that they have distinct conceptual roles as manifested by S's failure to photograph a tiger.

But the crucial issue which Loar appears not to notice, is that the salient factor in this case is that S's conceptions are conceptions of instances of the same natural kind. The fact that Loar does not see this as important is evident in his claim, quoted above, which implies that S's thoughts are as distinct as two thoughts about distinct natural kinds (Loar, 1985, p.103). In support of the claim that it is this aspect of the case which is crucial it can be appreciated that what makes these cases puzzling is that the subject's thoughts concern the same object without his realising it.

Consider again the conditions under which content attributions occur. As before, subjects are ascribed thoughts about the objects with which they commonly interact. In the case of S, however, such ascriptions cannot be made unproblematically. This is due to the fact that, if we first encounter S in London - at the zoo, say - and we proceed in the manner of the radical interpreter, we should most likely ascribe to S a host of thoughts about tigers.

Perhaps, if we got to know S a little better, learned of his history, and of the beliefs he has about animals he calls "Tigres" it would become evident to the interpreter that S has failed to infer that "Tigres" and

"Tigers" name the same animals. This would especially be so if S informed the interpreter of his desire to fulfil his promise to his mother to photograph a tiger. It would strike the interpreter as odd that S had not done this. This indicates again the point that the source of the puzzle is that the subject's conceptions are conceptions of instances of the same natural kind.

If these claims are accepted, it can be agreed that an objectual component will feature in natural kind thoughts. It features by virtue of the fact that reference to features beyond the body of S is required to rationalise S's inaction. In spite of the fact that S does not have perfect knowledge of all the properties of tigers, his day to day contact with tigers and his obvious knowledge of many of the properties of tigers justify the attribution to S thoughts typed by reference to the kind tiger. Explanatory considerations support this claim since, as we have seen, an interpreter of S's actions - say, during the course of his work at the zoo - appears to be justified in attributing thoughts about tigers to S.

We might attempt to characterise S's thoughts about tigers in France and London respectively thus:

(F) France: {["Tigres", <Tiger>]), (E), (...is F), [t (...)], [s (...)]}

(L) London: {["Tiger", <Tiger>], (E'), (...is F), [t (...)], [s (...)]}

The main difference in the two thoughts lies with the E-component. In this case, the E-component in (F) is of a different type to the E-component in (L) due to the fact that the conception of tigers which S acquires in France stems from verbal descriptions of these, and the conception of tigers which S acquires in London stems from actual acquaintance with tigers. Only if one is an internalist will one argue that that thereby renders (F) and (L) thoughts of distinct types. The argument raised against Loar above can be taken to cast doubt on the claim that S's beliefs are of distinct types merely due to the fact that the states have distinct properties (e.g. different inferential relations, different types of E-component).

With respect to the Intuitive Criterion of Difference, the characterisations offered above of (F) and (L) render explicable the fact that S may dissent from (F) (e.g. "Les tigres se trouvent dans le zoo") and assent to (L) ("Tigers are found in zoos"). The differing E-components in (F) and (L) account for S's not realising that "Tigres" and "Tigers" name the same animals. But the fact that S types his thoughts differently, as we have seen, need not be taken to indicate that his thoughts are of distinct types.

For externalists, the question of the typing of S's thoughts centres on the objectual component "$<...>$". This is intended to represent a component of thought which is kind-dependent: that is, its ascription to S stems from his dealings with tigers. Put this way, it is not clear that externalism requires that for a subject to entertain a thought of type O, then he must necessarily be acquainted with an instance of O. In the example we have discussed, it seems only that if the subject is in regular interaction with instances of Os, and meets other criteria (e.g. being rational), then S's thoughts concerning Os can be typed as O-thoughts. This way of construing externalism makes acquaintance with Os together with satisfaction of certain other criteria sufficient for a subject's being ascribed thoughts about Os (e.g. for those necessary for content attribution cf. Evans, 1982). However, it should be stressed that satisfaction of these sufficient criteria does not show their satisfaction to be necessary for entertaining thoughts about Os - that issue has not been addressed in this chapter.

So, in (F) and (L), we have an NK-component with an attached objectual component (one which taxonomises the thought within the class of natural kind thoughts), an E-component, a predicative component, and temporal and spatial components. The NK-component has an objectual component attached and this signifies that the inclusion of such a component is necessary for the explanatory efficacy of these intentional types. It is possible to explain S's failure to realise that "Tigres" and "Tiger" name the same kind of animal by appeal to the differing types of E-component in (F) and (L). It is possible, further, to maintain externalism by arguing that both (F) and (L) should be typed by reference to the relevant NK component. Explanatory considerations suggest that this should be the case.

This concludes our discussion of natural kind and demonstrative thoughts. I propose to end the essay now with a brief conclusion.

5. Conclusion

Part one of the essay concerned the motivations for internalism and externalism respectively. Ontological and explanatory motivations for internalism seemed open to significant objections. But whilst logico-semantic motivations for externalism seemed weak, explanatory motivations seemed persuasive and to outweigh the ontological and explanatory motivations for internalism.

Epistemic motivations for internalism stem from a broadly Cartesian view of the mind; and a fundamental feature of this view is the intuition that subjects occupy a position of epistemic authority with respect to the contents of their thoughts. Externalism seems to conflict with this intuition, and part two of the essay involved attempts to resolve the conflict. Burge seemed able to show how externalism is compatible with the view that subjects know what they think, but, it was argued, he is unable to show how subjects possess such knowledge authoritatively. Davidson's proposals attempted to eschew the Cartesian introspectionist model of first person authority, and, apparently, all other such relational models. It was suggested that, contra Davidson, subjects' authority with respect to thoughts concerning presently undergone sensation states may best be explained within a relational model of first person thinking. But this could not be carried over to apply to other kinds of intentional states and it was suggested that, with respect to such states, we endorse Davidson's proposal that a presumption of first person authority is a necessary condition of interpreting the speech of other subjects. No epistemic basis for the presumption could be identified. Perhaps the legacy of Cartesianism casts a long shadow over this part of the essay, and a more satisfactory account of first person authority will emerge only when the Cartesian model of mind is less pervasive.

The third part of the essay focused mostly on demonstrative thoughts, with a final chapter on thoughts concerning natural kinds. It is fair to say that demonstrative thoughts have been considered by many theorists to be the most likely candidates for externalist exploitation. But the attempt to constrain an account of demonstrative thoughts with a token physicalist theory of mind led to significant problems in specifying the individuation conditions of such thoughts. The manoeuvre set out in chapter 10 (sec.3) appears to resolve the problem. Chapter 11 involved further consideration of natural kind thoughts. Loar's challenge to externalism was addressed, recruiting, in effect, Macdonald's strategy described previously in ch.3 (sec.3).

Finally, it might be useful to point out that this essay is intended to contribute to the further elaboration of the externalist paradigm. It displays some of the problems which beset that paradigm (e.g. in part two), but, hopefully, it also displays some of its strengths (e.g. in parts one and three).

Notes to chapter eleven

1.   It may be the case that natural kind thoughts exhibit an ontological

220

dependence upon demonstrative thoughts - i.e. if it can be shown to be the case that demonstrative thoughts are necessary for the possibility of natural kind thoughts.

2. Kripke claims that "[T]erms for natural kinds are much closer to proper names than is ordinarily supposed" (1972, p.127) - though Putnam disagrees (1975).

3. Kripke's claim (Kripke, 1972) that natural kind terms are rigid designators has prompted much philosophical debate and it might be wise to add a note to make clear how some of the issues spawned by Kripke's claim bear on the issues of this chapter. The major point of contact between Kripke's claim and the matters under consideration here lies with the view that natural kind terms, being rigid designators, do not have sense, only reference (sense is construed narrowly by Kripke as what is expressed by a description which an object satisfies or fails to satisfy (cf. Kripke, 1972, p.27)). Independently of the correctness or otherwise of such a view it can still be claimed that subjects have conceptions of natural kinds. So independently of the question of whether natural kind terms have sense it can be asserted that a subject conceives of a natural kind in a particular way - i.e. that Kripke's claim about natural kind terms need not necessarily apply to natural kind thoughts.

4. Although he expresses the point differently, Loar (1988a) exploits the claim that that-clauses are inadequate to individuate psychological content to show internalism rather than externalism.

Bibliography

Alston, W. (1971), Varieties of Privileged Access, *American Philosophical Quarterly*, Vol.8, pp.223-241.

Armstrong, D.M. (1968), *A Materialist Theory of Mind*, Routledge & Kegan Paul, London.

Armstrong, D.M. (1973), *Belief, Truth and Knowledge*, Cambridge University Press, Cambridge.

Asimov, I. (1984), *Asimov's Guide to Science*, Penguin, Harmondsworth.

Ayer, A.J. (1956), *The Problem of Knowledge*, Pelican, Harmondsworth.

Berkeley, G. (1734), *A New Theory of Vision*, Everyman, London.

Bilgrami, A. (1987), An Externalist Account of Psychological Content, *Philosophical Topics*, Vol.XV, No.1, pp.191-226.

Bilgrami, A. (1988), Reply to Loar, in Grimm and Merrill (eds), 1988, pp.110-120.

Blackburn, S. (1979), Thought and Things, *Aristotelean Society Proceedings*, supplementary vol. 53, pp.23-41.

Blackburn, S. (1984), *Spreading the Word*, Clarendon Press, Oxford.

Boghossian, P. (1989), Content and Self-knowledge, *Philosophical Topics*, Vol.17, pp.5-26.

Borst, C.V. (1970) (ed), *Mind/Brain Identity Theory*, MacMillan, London.

Brueckner, A. (1992), What an Anti-Individualist Knows Apriori, *Analysis*, Vol.52 pp.111-118.

Burge, T. (1977), Belief de re, *Journal of philosophy*, Vol.74, pp.338-363.

Burge, T. (1979a), Individualism and the Mental, *Midwest studies in philosophy*, vol.4, pp.73-121, (eds) French, P.A., Uehling, T.E.,

Wettstein, H.K., University of Minnesota Press, Minneapolis.

Burge, T. (1979b), Sinning against Frege, *Philosophical review*, Vol.88, pp.398-432.

Burge, T. (1982a), Other Bodies, in *Thought and Object*, (ed) Woodfield, A., pp.97-120, Oxford University Press, Oxford.

Burge, T. (1982b), Two Thought Experiments Reviewed, *Notre Dame Journal of Formal Logic*, Vol.23, pp.284-293.

Burge, T. (1986a), Individualism and Psychology, *Philosophical Review*, Vol.95, pp.3-45.

Burge, T. (1986b), Intellectual Norms and Foundations of Mind, *Journal of Philosophy* Vol.83, pp.697-720.

Burge, T. (1988a), Cartesian Error and the Objectivity of Perception, in (eds) Grimm, R.H., Merrill, D.D., University of Arizona Press, Tuscon, pp.62-76.

Burge, T. (1988b), Reply to Matthews, in (eds) Grimm, R.H., Merrill, D.D., University of Arizona Press, Tuscon, pp.86-98.

Burge, T. (1988c), Individualism and Self-knowledge, *Journal of Philosophy*, Vol. 85, pp.649-665.

Burge, T. (1989), Individuation and Causation in Psychology, *Pacific Philosophical Quarterly*, Vol.70, pp.303-322.

Campbell, K. (1980), *Body and Mind*, University of Notre Dame Press, Notre Dame.

Churchland, P.M. (1979), *Scientific Realism and the Plasticity of Mind*, Cambridge University Press, Cambridge.

Churchland, P.M. (1989), *Matter and Consciousness*, MIT Press, Cambridge (Mass.).

Clare, A. (1976), *Psychiatry in Dissent*, Tavistock publications, London.

Clarke, A. (1990), *Microcognition*, MIT press, Cambridge. MIT.

Davidson, D. (1980), *Essays on Actions and Events*, Oxford University Press, Oxford.

Davidson, D. (1984a), *Inquiries into Truth and Interpretation*, Oxford University Press, Oxford.

Davidson, D. (1984b), First Person Authority, *Dialectica*, Vol.38, pp.101-111.

Davidson, D. (1987), Knowing One's Own Mind, *Proceedings of the American Philosophical Association*, Vol.60, pp.441-458.

Davidson, D. (1988), Reply to Burge, *Journal of Philosophy*, pp.664-665.

Davies, M. (1982), Individuation and the Semantics of Demonstratives, *Journal of Philosophical Logic*, vol.11, pp.287-310.

Davies, M. (1986), Individualism and Supervenience, *Proceedings of The Aristotelean Society* suppl., Vol.60, pp.263-283.

223

Davies, M., (1991), Individualism and Perceptual Content, *Mind* Vol.C, no.4, pp.461-484.

Davies, M., (1992), Perceptual Content and Local Supervenience, *Proceedings of the Aristotelean Society*, pp.21-45.

Dennett, D. (1982), Beyond Belief in (ed) Woodfield, A., 1982, pp.1-95.

Dennett, D. (1981), *Brainstorms*, Harvester Press, Sussex.

Descartes R. (1970) *Philosophical Writings*, (eds) Geach P.T., Anscombe E., Open University Press, Hong Kong.

Dummett, M. (1981), *The Interpretation of Frege's Philosophy*, Duckworth, London.

Durkheim, E. (1895), *The Rules of Sociological Method*, (ed) Lukes S., (1982), MacMillan, London.

Edwards, S.D. (1990), *Relativism, Conceptual Schemes and Categorial Frameworks*, Avebury, Aldershot.

Edwards, S.D. (1993), Formulating a Plausible Relativism, *Philosophia* vol.22, pp.63-74.

Evans, G. (1982), *The Varieties of Reference*, (ed) McDowell, J., Oxford University Press, Oxford.

Evans, G. (1985), *Collected Papers*, Oxford University Press, Oxford.

Evnine, S. (1991), *Donald Davidson*, Polity Press, Cambridge.

Eysenck, M.W., Keane M.T. (1990), *Cognitive Psychology*, Laurence Earlbaum Associates, London.

Field, H. (1978), Mental Representation, *Erkenntnis*, Vol.13.

Flew, A. (1964) (ed), *Body, Mind and Death*, MacMillan, London.

Fodor, J. (1975), *Language of Thought*, Harvester, Sussex.

Fodor, J. (1981), Cognitive Science and the Twin Earth Problem *Notre Dame Journal of Formal Logic*, Vol.23, pp.98-118.

Fodor, J. (1987), *Psychosemantics*, MIT Press, Cambridge (Mass.).

Fodor, J. (1991), A Modal Argument for Narrow Content, *Journal of Philosophy*, vol.88, pp.5-26.

Forbes, G. (1987), A Dichotomy Sustained, *Philosophical Studies*, Vol.51, pp.187-211.

Forbes, G. (1990), The Indispensability of Sinn, *The Philosophical Review*, vol.99, pp.535-563.

Frege, G. (1892), On Sense and Meaning in Geach, P. and Black, M. (eds) 1980, pp.56-78.

Frege, G. (1892) The Thought, in Salmon and Soames (eds) 1988, pp.33-55.

Geach, P., Black, M. (1980) (eds) (3rd edition), *Translations from the Philosophical Writings of Gottlob Frege*, Blackwell, Oxford.

Geach, P. (1957), *Mental Acts*, Routledge & Kegan Paul, London.

Georgalis, N. (1990), No Access for the Externalist, *Mind*, Vol.99, pp.101-108.

Grimm R.H., Merrill D.D., (1988) (eds), *Contents of Thoughts*, University of Arizona Press, Tuscon.

Haack, S. (1978), *Philosophy of Logics*, Cambridge University Press, Cambridge.

Heil, J. (1988a), Privileged Access, *Mind*, Vol.97, pp.238-251.

Heil, J. (1988b), The Epistemic Route to Anti-Realism, *Australasian Journal of Philosophy*, Vol.66, pp.161-173.

Hume, D. (1739), *A Treatise of Human Nature*, (ed) Selby-Bigge L.A., Oxford University Press, Oxford.

Humphreys, G.W., Bruce V. (1989), *Visual Cognition*, Lawrence Earlbaum Associates, London.

Johnson-Laird, P.N. (1988), *The Computer and the Mind*, Fontana, London.

Kant, I., (1929) *Critique of Pure Reason*, (ed. and tr.) Kemp-Smith N., MacMillan, London.

Kaplan, D. (1990), Thoughts on Demonstratives, in Yourgrau, P.(ed) (1990), pp.34-49.

Kim, J. (1976), Events as Property Exemplifications, in Brand M., Walton, D. (1976) (eds) *Action Theory*, Dordrecht: Reidel, pp.158-177.

Kim J., 1985, Psychophysical Laws, in LePore and McLaughlin (eds), 1985, pp.39-386.

Kim, J. (1990), Supervenience as a Philosophical Concept, *Metaphilosophy*, vol.12, pp.1-27.

Kripke, S. (1972), *Naming and Necessity*, Blackwell, Oxford.

Kripke, S. (1979), A Puzzle About Belief, in (eds) Salmon S., Soames, S. (1988), pp.102-148.

LePore, E., McLaughlin, B. (1985) (eds) *Actions and Events: Perspectives on the Philosophy of Donald Davidson*, Blackwell, Oxford.

LePore, E. (1986) (ed), *Truth and Interpretation: Perspectives on the Philosophy of Donald Davidson*, Blackwell, Oxford.

Lennon, K. (1990), *Explaining Human Action*, Duckworth, London.

Lewis, H. (1985), Is the Mental Supervenient on the Physical? in *Essays on Davidson, Actions and Events* (ed) Vermazen, B, Hintikka M.B., (1980), pp.159-172, Oxford University Press, Oxford.

Linsky, L. (1967), *Referring*, Humanities Press, New Jersey.

Loar, B. (1981), *Mind and Meaning*, Cambridge University Press, Cambridge.

Loar, B. (1982), Conceptual Role and Truth Conditions, *Notre Dame Journal of Formal Logic*, Vol. 23, pp.272-283.

Loar, B. (1988a), Social Content and Psychological Content, in (eds) Grimm, R.H., Merrill, D.D. (1988), pp.99-110.

Loar, B. (1988b), A New Kind of Content in Grimm R.H., Merrill D.D. (eds), 1988, pp.121-139.

Locke, J. (1690), *Essay Concerning Human Understanding*, Everyman: London.

Macdonald, C. (1989), *Mind-Body Identity Theories*, Routledge, London.

Macdonald, C. (1990), Weak Externalism and Mind-body Identity, *Mind* Vol.99, pp.387-405.

Macdonald, C. (1991a), Weak Externalism and First Person Authority (unpublished manuscript).

Macdonald, C. (1991b), Anti-Individualism and First Person Authority (unpublished manuscript).

Macdonald, C. (1992), Weak Externalism and Psychological Reduction, in Charles D., Lennon K. (eds) (1992), *Reduction, Explanation and Realism*, Oxford University Press, Oxford, pp.133-154.

Macdonald G., Pettit, P. (1981), *Semantics and Social Science*, Routledge and Kegan Paul, London.

Marr, D. (1982), *Vision*, Freeman, New York.

Marr, D. (1985), Vision: the philosophy and the approach, in (eds) Aitkenhead A.M., Slack J.M., 1985, *Issues in Cognitive Modelling*, London: Earlbaum Publishers.

Matthews, R.J. (1988), Comment on Burge, in (eds) Grimm, R.H., Merrill, D.D., 1988, pp.77-86.

McCulloch, G. (1989), *The Game of the Name*, Clarendon Press, Oxford.

McCulloch, G. (1986), Scientism, Mind and Meaning,in Pettit P., and McDowell, J. (1986), pp.59-94.

McDowell, J. (1977), On the Sense and Reference of a Proper Name, in *Reference, Truth and Reality*, Platts, M., (ed) (1980), Routledge & Kegan Paul, London, pp.141-166.

McDowell, J. (1985), Functionalism and Anomalous Monism, in LePore E. and McLaughlin J., (eds) (1985), pp.387-398.

McDowell, J. (1984), De Re Senses, in *Frege: Tradition and Influence* (ed) Wright C. (1984), Blackwell, Oxford, pp.98-109.

McDowell, J. (1986), Singular Thought and the Extent of Inner Space, in Pettit and Mcdowell (1986), pp.137-168.

McDowell, J. (1990), Peacocke and Evans on Demonstrative Thought, *Mind*, Vol. 99, pp.255-266.

McGinn, C. (1977), Anomalous Monism and Kripke's Cartesian Intuitions, *Analysis* Vol.37, pp.78-80.

McGinn, C. (1982a), The Structure of Content, in (ed) Woodfield, A. (1982), pp.207-258.

McGinn, C. (1982b), *The Subjective View*, Oxford University Press, Oxford.

McGinn, C. (1982c), *The Character of Mind*, Oxford University Press, Oxford.

McGinn, C. (1989), *Mental Content*, Blackwell, Oxford.

McKinsey, M. (1991), Anti-Individualism and Privileged Access, *Analysis*, vol.51, pp.9-16.

McLaughlin, B. (1985), Anomalous Monism and the Irreducibility of the Mental, in Lepore and McLaughlin (eds) 1985, pp.331-368.

Neisser, U. (1976), *Cognition and Reality*, W.H.Freeman, San Francisco.

Newton-Smith, W. (1981), *The Rationality of Science*, Routledge & Kegan Paul, London.

Newton-Smith, W. (1985), *Logic: an Introductory course*, Routledge & Kegan Paul, London.

Parfit, D. (1986), *Reasons and Persons*, Oxford University Press, Oxford.

Peacocke, C. (1981), Demonstrative Thought and Psychological Explanation, *Synthese* Vol.49, pp.187-217.

Peacocke, C. (1983), *Sense and Content*, Clarendon Press, Oxford.

Peacocke, C. (1986), *Thoughts: An Essay on Content*, Blackwell, Oxford.

Peacocke, C. (1991), Demonstrative Thought, *Mind*, Vol.100, pp.1-11.

Perry, J. (1977), Frege on Demonstratives, in Yourgrau, P. (ed) (1990), pp.50-70.

Perry J., (1979), The Problem of the Essential Indexical, in Salmon, N. and Soames, S. (1988), pp.83-101.

Pettit, P., McDowell, J. (1986) (eds), *Subject, Thought and Context*, Clarendon Press, Oxford.

Pettit, P., Jackson, F. (1988), Functionalism and Broad Content, *Mind*, Vol., 97, pp.381-400.

Place, U.T. (1956), Is Consciousness a Brain Process?, in Borst (ed) (1970), pp.42-51.

Plato (1954), *Phaedo*, tr. Tredennick, H. (1954), Penguin, Harmondsworth.

Platts, M. (1979), *Ways of Meaning*, Routledge, London.

Putnam, H. (1960), Minds and Machines in Flew (ed) (1964), pp.288-294.

Putnam, H. (1975), The Meaning of "Meaning", in *Language, Mind and Knowledge:Minnesota Studies in the Philosophy of Science*, vol.7, (ed) Gunderson K., pp.131-193.

Putnam, H. (1981), *Reason, Truth and History*, Cambridge University Press, Cambridge.

Quine, W.V.O. (1960), *Word and Object*, MIT Press, Mass.

Quine, W.V.O. (1969), *Ontological Relativity*, Columbia University Press, New York.

Quine, W.V.O., Ullian, J.S. (1978), *The Web of Belief*, Random House, New York.

Ramberg, B.T. (1989), *Donald Davidson's Philosophy of Language*, Blackwell, Oxford.

Root, M. (1986), Davidson and Social Science, in LePore, E. (ed) (1986), pp.272-304.

Rudder-Baker, L. (1988), Cognitive Suicide, in Grimm, R.H., Merrill, D.D. (eds) (1988), pp.1-18.

Russell, B. (1912), *The Problems of Philosophy*, Oxford University Press, Oxford.

Russell, B. (1917), *Mysticism and Logic*, Unwin, London.

Russell, B. (1950), *An Inquiry into Meaning and Truth*, Unwin, London.

Russell, B. (1956), *Logic and Knowledge*, Marsh, R.,C. (ed), Unwin, London.

Ryle, G. (1949), *The Concept of Mind*, Hutchinson, London.

Sainsbury, R.M. (1979), *Russell*, Routledge and Kegan Paul, London.

Sainsbury, R.M. (1985), Critical Notice: The Varieties of Reference by Gareth Evans, *Mind*, Vol.94, pp.120-142.

Sainsbury, R.M. (1986), Russell on Acquaintance, in Vesey, G. (ed) (1986), pp.219-244.

Salmon, N., Soames, S. (1988) (eds), *Propositions and Attitudes*, Oxford University Press, Oxford.

Schiffer, S. (1980), Truth and the Theory of Content, in Meaning and Understanding Parret, H., Bouveresse, J. (eds) (1980).

Searle, J.R. (1983), *Intentionality*, Cambridge University Press, Cambridge.

Searle, J.R. (1992), *The Rediscovery of The Mind*, MIT Press, Mass.

Segal, G. (1989a), The Return of the Individual, *Mind*, Vol.98, pp.39-57.

Segal, G. (1989b), Seeing What Is Not There, *Philosophical Review*, Vol.98, pp.189-214.

Segal, G, (1991), Defence of a Reasonable Individualism, *Mind* Vol. 100, no.4, pp.485-494.

Shoemaker, S. (1984), *Identity, Cause and Mind*, Cambridge University Press, Cambridge.

Skinner, B.F. (1953), *Science and Human Behaviour*, MacMillan, New

228

York.

Smart, J.J.C. (1959), Sensations and Brain Processes, in Borst, C.V. (ed) (1970), pp.52-66.

Sperber, D., Wilson, D. (1986), *Relevance*, Blackwell, Oxford.

Stich, S. (1978), Autonomous Psychology and the Belief-Desire Thesis, *The Monist*, vol.61, pp.573-591.

Stich, S. (1983), *From Folk Psychology to Cognitive Science*, MIT Press, Cambridge.

Strawson, P.F. (1959), *Individuals*, Methuen, London.

Strawson, P.F. (1950), On Referring, in *Logico-Linguistic Papers*, Strawson P.F.(1971) (ed), Methuen, London, pp.1-27.

Tarski, A. (1956), The Concept of Truth in Formalised Languages, in his *Logic, Semantics, Metamathematics*, Clarendon Press, Oxford, pp.152-278.

Tollison, C.D. (1982), *Managing Chronic Pain: A Patients Guide*, Sterling, New York..

Urmson, J.O. (1986), Russell on Universals, in Vesey, G. (1986) (ed), pp.245-248.

Vesey, G. (1986) (ed), *Philosophers Ancient and Modern*, Cambridge University Press, Cambridge.

Weiskrantz, L. (et.al.) (1974), Visual Capacity in the Hemianopic Field following a Restricted Occipital Oblation, *Brain*, vol.157, pp.709-728.

Weiskrantz, L. (1986), *Blindsight: A Case Study and its Implications*, Oxford University Press, Oxford.

Wiggins, D. (1980), *Sameness and Substance*, Blackwell, Oxford.

Wiggins, D. (1984), The Sense and Reference of Predicates, in Wright, C. (ed) (1984), pp.126-143.

Williams, B. (1978), *Descartes: The project of Pure Enquiry*, Pelican, Harmondsworth.

Williams, M. (1990), Externalism and the Philosophy of Mind, *Philosophical Quarterly*, Vol.40, pp.353-380.

Wilson, E. (1979), *The Mental as Physical*, Routledge, London.

Wilson, M.D. (1969) (ed), *The Essential Descartes*, Signet, New York.

Wittgenstein, L. (1958), *Philosophical Investigations*, Blackwell, Oxford.

Woodfield, A. (1982) (ed), *Thought and Object*, Clarendon Press, Oxford.

Wright, C. (1984) (ed), *Frege: Tradition and Influence*, Blackwell, Oxford.